BRUCE LEE
FIGHTING SPIRIT

BRUCE THOMAS was born in the north-east of England and moved to London as a teenager to become a professional musician. He is known principally as the bass player with Elvis Costello and the Attractions, having recorded and toured internationally with the band since 1977. He is also a sought-after session musician, having played on records by Paul McCartney, Tasmin Archer and Suzanne Vega. *The Big Wheel*, his critically acclaimed first novel, was shortlisted for the Ralph J. Gleason prize for music writing. He trained with the late *kung fu* master Derek Jones at his school in West London.

BRUCE LEE

FIGHTING SPIRIT

BRUCE THOMAS

SIDGWICK & JACKSON

First published in this corrected edition by Sidgwick & Jackson

This updated edition published 2002 by Sidgwick & Jackson
an imprint of Pan Macmillan Ltd
Pan Macmillan, 20 New Wharf Road, London N1 9RR
Basingstoke and Oxford
Associated companies throughout the world
www.panmacmillan.com

ISBN 0 283 07357 8

1 3 5 7 9 8 6 4 2

A CIP catalogue record for this book is available from
the British Library.

Typeset by SetSystems Ltd, Saffron Walden, Essex
Printed and bound in Great Britain by
Mackays of Chatham plc, Chatham, Kent

CONTENTS

CONTENTS

LIST OF ILLUSTRATIONS

The author and publishers have made every effort to trace the copyright holders of illustrations used in this book. In the event that any have been inadvertently overlooked, please contact the publishers so that the situation can be rectified in future editions.

ACKNOWLEDGEMENTS

I gratefully acknowledge the invaluable help of the following people in the preparation of this book: Tsuyoshi Abe, Julian Alexander, Don Atyeo, Alex Ben Block, Dave Cater, Russell Cawthorne, Hawkins Cheung, Ruby Chow, Paul Clifton, Catherine Campaigne, Felix Dennis, Marianne Dresser, David Duguid, Pat Eldred, Craig Frischkorn, Marshall Gooch, Lindy Hough, Richard Grossinger, Dan Inosanto, Paula Inosanto, Derek Jones, Steve Jones, Maggie Kayley, Taky Kimura, Tom Kuhn, Dr 'Don' Langford, Brandon Lee, Dan Lee, Bey Logan, Larry McCallister, Paula Morrison, Doug Palmer, Audrey Pasternak, Owen Potts, Shannon Robins, Bill Ryusaki, Michael Scording, Bob Wall, Fred Weintraub, Curtis Wong and Dr Peter Wu.

Foreword

In the early 1970s, Bruce Lee's swift and sudden emergence as the world's greatest action star was followed by an explosion of interest in the martial arts. While I was aware of the Bruce Lee phenomenon, my own ambitions at that time lay in musical directions.

After many years as a touring musician, I began to concentrate more on studio work and also began writing. Finally, I was in one place long enough to practise seriously the martial arts taught by Derek Jones at his school in West London.

One day, Derek came over to my house and left me his video tapes of Bruce Lee fight scenes. Derek himself had trained with two of Bruce's contemporaries and considered that, if anything, he had been most enlightened about the fighting arts from watching Bruce Lee in action.

Suddenly, my own efforts in the martial arts were followed by an explosion of interest in Bruce Lee as I realized what I had overlooked previously. Only on rare occasions had I experienced that same elation, even awe, at witnessing somebody who was supreme in his particular form of expression.

Not long after this, when someone asked me what my next book was to be, I was only mildly surprised to hear myself saying, 'the Bruce Lee biography'.

Bruce Lee was a multifaceted individual. He was an innovative martial artist, both in the training hall and on film, as well as introducing *kung fu* to the West and being the major influence behind the growth of martial arts as a competition sport. As a film actor, he broke international boundaries and racial stereotypes. He was intensely ambitious and possessed a natural charisma that made him stand out even in a crowd of hundreds. He was also a family man who valued his privacy.

Yet behind all this is the *essential* Bruce Lee – a man whose art and philosophy was at the heart of everything he did. Beyond entertainment and excitement, it was Bruce Lee's avowed intention to educate his audience. I wanted to write about Bruce Lee, not in order to teach, but so that I might learn.

AUTHOR'S NOTE

If you always put limits on yourself and what you can do, physical or anything, you might as well be dead. It will spread into your work, your morality, your entire being. There are not limits, only plateaux. But you must not stay there, you must go beyond them. If it kills you, it kills you.

Bruce Lee

Bruce Lee was an extraordinary man – he bridged cultures, revolutionized the martial arts, taught a fierce philosophy of individualism, became a film icon and remade the image of the Asian man in the West. Few lives have been as worthy of careful study and reflection, yet few lives have been so syste matically obscured by exotic fantasies and B-movie-grade mystery.

In this new biography, I give a full account of the extra-ordinary events and unique energies of Bruce Lee's life. Rather than identifying one simple theme, I have chosen to follow the many conflicting paths of that life. We learn about the hyperactive child, the dancer, the philosopher, the teacher, the mystic, the athlete, the star, the self-conscious symbol, the lover, the prophet of *kung fu* – not as variations on a theme, but as contradictory roles that Lee was forced by his own sense of destiny to carry simultaneously. At its most extreme, this destiny saw intense unique disciplines being worked out on a world stage for the entertainment of millions. I outline both the excitement and the ultimate impossibility of this unique combination of energies. If, in the end, it was this impossibility that killed him, then Bruce Lee died the death that his whole life was preparing for him – a death fighting the limits of identity.

'If it kills you, it kills you.' While we may not all be prepared to make such a sacrifice in the name of becoming who we really are, it wouldn't hurt any of us to listen to Bruce Lee's insistence that self-mastery should be the goal of all human endeavour. The heroic power of Bruce Lee's words has been diluted many times over by those who would simply follow him or market him. This book is not concerned with rehashing the same old tawdry melodramas, and it is in keeping with the purpose of this book that the fierce Hollywood and Hong Kong poses are absent. It is my intent to show that Bruce Lee, the martial artist, is not a mere footnote to Bruce Lee, the star. Although Bruce Lee was not without personal ambition, conflicting goals or ulterior motives he attained the mythic heights he did only because he was grounded in the lineage of an ancient art, which he was attempting to popularize as a means of its continued transmission. The fact that, as an Englishman, I was able to begin learning a Chinese martial art from a Welshman shows that Bruce Lee was successful in that particular aim.

Bruce Lee's cult hero status is only a by-product of his actual attainment. The real value of his life is in the depth of understanding that he touched, and which he fervently wished each of us to work for in his or her own way. This is a book in the fighting spirit of Bruce Lee himself – because it tells us something *new*.

Bruce Lee has certainly taught me well, by asking me to dig deeper into myself and come closer to him in spirit, rather than rely on those who were closer to him in person, or let me fall back on the familiar images. I believe that the resulting book is the truest rendition of his life that has so far been presented.

Bruce Thomas
Los Angeles, 1995

Introduction
Bruce Lee:
A Brief Life

SHORTLY AFTER BRUCE LEE'S untimely death at
the age of thirty-two, his young widow, Linda, gave an interview for Hong Kong radio:

> It seems we were always beginning on a new life – beginning in
> films was a new life for us. Becoming famous and breaking records
> – everything was new all the time and he kept saying, 'This is just
> the beginning.' He had a long way to go, so many more things he
> wanted to do. And he also thought of it as a beginning for the
> Chinese people – what they have to show to the rest of the world.
> He was very proud of being Chinese and he wanted to show the
> world part of the Chinese culture through films. Not just the
> fighting – he wanted to add in a little bit of philosophy. He studied
> all the traditional philosophies, but then he began to form his own
> philosophy and he came to the realization that you just can't borrow
> another person's philosophy. You have to learn about yourself and
> create your own philosophy, your own way of life. Bruce believed
> that the most important thing in the world is the individual, and
> that each individual must have knowledge of himself before he can
> relate to other people. He managed to cross the barriers in com-
> munication with people. He could communicate with different

people on different levels – people who were not perhaps as intelligent as he was; or people who considered themselves as intellectuals and thought that fighting was somehow not intelligent.

Bruce Lee fought. Throughout his entire life, he fought the circumstances of his childhood – an innate physical weakness and lack of paternal guidance – then, while absorbing the art of *kung fu*, he fought in the streets. When he took up dancing, partly as a diversion to chase girls, he and his partner went on to win the Hong Kong cha-cha championships. Bruce Lee was unable to come second at anything.

On emigrating to the United States at the age of nineteen, he began to make up for lost school time, studying so intently that he learned to speak and write English better than many natives as he fought to raise himself above the thousands of other immigrants that arrived in America every year. After he opened his own *kung fu* school, he even battled his own countrymen for the right to teach the art to Westerners.

When one of Bruce's students got in a lucky punch during an informal training session, Bruce's temper flared and he beat the unfortunate student to the ground. Bruce's ambitions demanded not only that he be the best, but that he become unbeatable.

Later, as he struggled to establish an acting career, he motivated himself almost by creating conflict with his actor friends – first vowing to become a bigger star than Steve McQueen, then promising the same to Jim Coburn. On the set of his films he constantly rose to the challenges of the streetwise kids who were employed as extras. To any punk with nothing to lose who was looking for a brief moment of glory, Bruce Lee was the man to beat. Yet Bruce Lee had everything to lose: now he *had* to remain unbeatable, otherwise what did all those who streamed to see him at the theatres have to believe in? Like a gunslinger in the old West, Lee wasn't just fighting for his reputation and his livelihood: he was fighting for his life.

Yet Bruce Lee's biggest fight was always with himself. There were several currents running through him and occasionally these surfaced in tense contradictions or sudden mood shifts.

Shortly after arriving in America, in the middle of one night, he felt as if he were fighting a dark shadow. Bruce experienced a psychological crisis in which he confronted what Jung calls the 'shadow' side of the personality. Bruce Lee faced all the fears, doubts and aggressive insecurities of his life. In doing so, he began to free and integrate powerful energies which he then directed (or which directed him) into becoming a highly motivated and determined young man. After this experience, Bruce was totally committed to personal growth by means of self-help, along with a clear set of aims and ambitions. In 1969, even while fighting disappointment and rejection over an acting part that he had set his heart on, he had enough strength of spirit to write down this affirmation: within a year he would achieve fame as the highest-paid Oriental film actor in the world.

But before this bold affirmation could be fulfilled, Bruce sustained a crippling back injury and was left unable to earn a living, let alone pursue his ambitions. He later admitted about this time that he'd been truly frightened. Yet by sheer force of intent and still in great pain, he acted as if he had recovered from his injury and continued to blast ahead.

In mid 1973, the year of his sudden death, Bruce Lee was again at a critical crossroads, facing many urgent decisions about his future. In a sense, his real battle was still with himself. Perhaps the way forward was not to do as he usually did: to dig deeper into his reserves of will or push the boundaries even further, faster or higher; but simply to slow down and rest long enough to restore some balance. But Bruce had convinced himself that he relaxed by working, and that he could achieve a sense of stillness by keeping up with the frantic rate of the changes into which he had been drawn.

If there was ever an autonomous individual who justified his life by his own efforts, it was Bruce Lee. And while he never openly acknowledged the help and support that he received from his close friends, there was no need to. Bruce always gave more than thanks: he gave *himself* – even perhaps acting as a source of energy for others, which resulted in his giving away his own life force.

In his graveside speech at Bruce Lee's funeral in Seattle, James Coburn said that Bruce had helped him to bring his physical and psychological selves together. James Yimm Lee, one of Bruce's partners, had also found that his work with Bruce brought him a similar feeling both of integration and integrity – in particular, a sense of honesty and moral uplift. Another friend, Taky Kimura, said that he had only managed to survive the most emotionally devastating period of his life thanks to his training with Bruce. But his colleague Stirling Silliphant acknowledged that while Bruce was the greatest teacher he'd ever had, in any walk of life, he also believed that instead of gaining calmness and balance from the martial arts, Bruce had found only conflict and antagonism.

It is true that Bruce Lee sometimes found it hard to discipline himself. His one main character flaw was that he was a victim of impulse. Although he had prodigious will power, he couldn't always say no to certain things. There is no doubt that Bruce overcame tremendous limitations, but there is still a question of how much he was able to live out the philosophy he taught. He was plagued by impatience and a bad, even violent, temper. Sometimes he was so driven by ambition that he saw people either as a stepping stone to success or as someone to be moved out of the way.

It is not my intention to indulge in aimless criticism. But I believe that Bruce Lee would now want to be taken off the pedestal he has been put on and, at last, allowed his humanity.

For most people, Bruce Lee was gone almost as soon as he had arrived. He died before we ever came to know him, with the art and philosophy that he pursued still holding a lot of potential for Bruce himself.

He was both brashly self-confident and insecure. He remained optimistic even while under tremendous pressures, some of which were self-made. He was both a show-off and a dedicated artist, an extrovert who didn't like socializing and a philosopher with a fearful temper. Bruce Lee was as ambitious and opinionated as he was honest and sincere. Yet, despite all the contradictions and the abrasiveness, everyone who knew Bruce Lee well was by far the richer for it.

Bruce Lee *inspired* people: for all those who knew him, he somehow had a way of becoming the most significant person in their lives.

As a result of the sincere efforts he made throughout his life, Bruce Lee gained in perception and wisdom. Behind all the events and details, the gaining of perception and wisdom is the true story of Bruce Lee's life. And because this is the true purpose of all our lives, there is much to interest us in Bruce Lee's story.

There are many for whom the events and details of his life are already well known – in some cases too well known. There are fans who know that his favourite meal was beef with oyster sauce, but understand little of what he actually wished to communicate. Unfortunately, a new generation drawn to Bruce Lee gains much of its 'information' from recent releases like the Universal Pictures biopic *Dragon: A Life of Bruce Lee*. This faintly ridiculous picture bears scant relation to the truth.

It wasn't until more than two decades after her death that Marilyn Monroe's life was treated with the depth and perception it deserved. Bruce Lee has long been overdue for the same consideration. There are many people who have wished to receive more insight into this remarkable man's life than they have so far been offered.

I never met, much less came to know, Bruce Lee in life. Those who did have told their own stories. Even so, many have only been able to reiterate his concepts without illuminating them further. Others have an axe to grind or a reputation to enhance or destroy. Some, with the benefit of hindsight, have reined back on former excesses, while some of Bruce's colleagues and his doctors have openly challenged the accepted version of events. What many people have yet to realize is that the reality is far more potent and involving than anything dreamed up in imagination. The truth about Bruce Lee's life and death, the fulfilment of his great ambitions and the mastery of his chosen art are all far more remarkable than any myth or legend. *Fighting Spirit* addresses itself to this.

In his life and work, Bruce Lee was trying to reconcile perhaps the two most divergent streams of human endeavour that exist – the preoccupations of Hollywood and the inner disciplines that may be found in a Zen monastery. A career in entertainment and the pursuit of a spiritual fighting art do not often go hand in hand. While I have never suffered the kind of celebrity that Bruce Lee did, my years in an internationally successful rock group have given me enough of a taste (for my liking) of the rigours and demands that he must have faced. At the same time, I have also spent several years training with *kung fu* master Derek Jones, a direct pupil of Bruce's first practical teacher, William Cheung. Many of Bruce Lee's followers – and even many of his prominent students – make the mistake of trying to understand his methods by seeing where he finished, without *experiencing* how he *began*. They have touched only the tip of the iceberg.

Part One of this book re-examines the events of Bruce Lee's

life and explores the inner forces that drove him. In Part Two, while celebrating his uniqueness, I also offer a more complete understanding of his enigmatic death. And I further expose the disparity between how Bruce Lee is most often perceived and what he truly wished to convey – the gulf between the legend and the reality. Part Three is for those who wish to genuinely understand Bruce Lee – the essential meaning of his art, his philosophy and his true teaching. In Part Four, which is new for this edition, I speculate how Bruce Lee would have fared had he lived and consider how his unrealized potential will always be the footnote to 'Bruce Lee the icon'.

*

Bruce Lee was no ordinary man – and I hope that I have written no ordinary biography but the one by which he will be remembered in years to come. Bruce Lee's story is both an enigma and an open book, waiting to be explored.

PART ONE

THE LIFE AND WORK OF BRUCE LEE

1

CHILDHOOD

'I SMOKE OPIUM because it helps sweeten my singing voice,' said Li Hoi Cheun. Hoi Cheun* was also partial to gambling – and so it was his friends, as much as his family, who enjoyed his company and generosity. He was a comic actor with Hong Kong's Cantonese Opera, which was more a music hall than a classical company like the Peking Opera. Although Hoi Cheun wasn't a great celebrity, he had an enthusiastic following who enjoyed his dramatic flourishes, and he had done well enough to become the owner and landlord of several apartments.

Li Hoi Cheun's attractive wife, Grace, was the daughter of a Chinese mother and German father. Raised a Catholic, she had come from Shanghai to Hong Kong at the age of nineteen. While accompanying her father on his regular visits to the opera she had become taken with its comic singer and would make sure she always had a seat near the orchestra, where he would be able to see her. Her efforts to gain his attention were not in vain. Hoi Cheun and Grace were soon married and took

* In China the family name comes first.

up residence at 218 Nathan Road in the Kowloon district of Hong Kong.

The Lis' first child, a boy, died soon after birth. Not only was this a sad loss, it was also taken as a bad omen – the loss of a boy was considered much worse than that of a girl. Grace Li and her husband feared that the spirits were looking on them unkindly. Since Chinese superstition has it that the second child should be a girl, the Lis adopted a daughter named Phoebe in order to confuse the spirits. A few months later in Hong Kong, Grace gave birth to a healthy son, Peter.

Not long after, while the children were lodged with relatives in Hong Kong, Grace was accompanying her husband on the Cantonese Opera Company's tour of the United States when she discovered that she was pregnant again. While her husband continued on to New York, Grace stayed in San Francisco.

On 27 November 1940 (according to the Chinese zodiac, the Year of the Dragon) between 6 and 8 a.m. (the Hour of the Dragon) at the Jackson Street Hospital in San Francisco's Chinatown, Grace Li gave birth to another son, the third of her five children. To confuse potentially unfriendly spirits, the child was given a girl's name, Sai Fon (Small Phoenix), and one of his ears was pierced. Grace Li soon renamed her new son Jun Fan (Return Again) because she felt that he would one day return to his birthplace. The supervising physician, Mary Glover, nicknamed the boy 'Bruce' – and the name stuck. He later anglicized his family name to Lee.

The flight path into Hong Kong's Kai Tak airport is one of the trickiest in the world; planes approach between steep hills and over the rooftops of Kowloon City to swoop on to a strip of land that juts out into the harbour. Like all harbour cities, Hong Kong is most impressive when seen from the water. In the harbour, ferries, jetfoils, and junks criss-cross each other's trails; tiny sampans piloted by straw-hatted women lurch over the churning wake of the larger vessels. On the limited area of the mainland the city has nowhere to go but up. Stretching along the water's edge in a dramatic vista of steel, glass and reflected light, the buildings cling to the rising slopes of steep green hills. Where it is too steep to build, the city gives way to the mountains that form the city's backdrop.

Politically, socially and economically diverse, Hong Kong is the Asian equivalent of Manhattan. Everywhere there is a feeling of crowds, and of being swept along on a surging wave of human activity. Modern Hong Kong is an opulent and vulgar parade of flawless skyscrapers. Enclosed within the shadows of the buildings that loom overhead, Porsches, Mercedes and Ferraris sit in the tangled lines of traffic. The streets reverberate with the din of car horns, shouted conversation and the racket of construction work. For the tourist, Hong Kong is a consumer's paradise, from the silky seduction of shops selling gold, jewellery and furs to the booming electronic supermarket in Nathan Road. All hotel rooms have fax machines for the convenience of businessmen. The affluent in Hong Kong live like sultans and maharajahs. The one thing that is in greatest abundance here is cheap labour.

Behind the corporate skyscrapers and luxury hotels there is plenty of human misery to be found in the overcrowded refugee camps and dismal shanty towns that sprawl along the island creeks, in the tenement slums of the Walled City, or in the desperate groups of boat people being bundled on to flights back to Vietnam. Hastily built high-rise housing projects line the road to the New Territories.

Between the modern façade and the grinding poverty is Hong Kong as it must have been when Bruce Lee lived there as a boy. This Hong Kong is a seething maze of lanes threading between ramshackle apartment buildings, crowded shops and restaurants where garish neon signs project from every available surface. The lanes are choked with lorries, taxis and handcarts. Nowadays Chanel-suited women and young entrepreneurs with mobile phones pressed to their ears exude eager ambition as they dash along the street, jostling with locals in the traditional long shirts or black pyjama suits. Vendors shaded by canopied stalls display fruit, fish and rows of shiny hanging ducks. The atmosphere here – a complex blend of exotic food and equally exotic garbage in various stages of rot, a thick stew of smells and an oppressive muggy heat – has not changed much over the years. Though Hong Kong is invigorating, it can also be exhausting. You might find anything you want in Hong Kong, except peace and stillness.

Early in 1941, a few months after Bruce's birth, the Lee family returned to Hong Kong where the humid conditions soon made him ill. Bruce was to remain a sickly and skinny child throughout his early years.

The Lees' apartment was on Nathan Road, on the second floor of an old building above some shops. The narrow stairway had no door at street level, and street people frequently set up home in the entrance. But two sets of strong doors guarded the apartment entrance on the first-floor landing, the outer doors reinforced with thick steel bars and the inner doors containing a peephole.

Inside, the rooms were sparsely furnished. The large main room had a refrigerator at one end and a large table, and was the focus of household activity: eating, talking, reading and playing. At night, this room and all the others were used for sleeping. Most of the beds were simple iron frames with hard mattresses on them. Beyond the main room were two smaller rooms. One held two bunks; the other, overlooking Nathan Road, had a veranda with numerous potted plants and, at one time, a caged chicken.

No bedclothes were needed at night with the unrelenting humidity and heat. In the mornings there was a constant queue for the single bathroom, not that bathing did much good – one would be covered in sweat again in minutes. During times of drought, when the water supply was sporadic, the bath was kept filled and the chicken had to share the veranda with a makeshift bathing area set up behind some curtains.

When Hoi Cheun's brother died, his widow and her five children were taken in by the Lee family, as is the Chinese custom. Together with a couple of servants and Wu Ngan, an unofficially adopted child, there were sometimes as many as twenty people crammed into the apartment, along with assorted dogs, birds and fish. An Alsatian named Bobby, who slept under his bed, was Bruce's favourite dog.

It would be misleading to think that Bruce Lee came from an underprivileged background. The rent from his father's properties along with his income from the opera meant that the Lees could always afford to hire servants. But despite the fact that his father made good money, Bruce claimed that he never saw any of it. He complained about his 'miserly' father and on occasions stole money to take friends to restaurants. Yet Bruce's father was not a mean man; he was known to have paid medical bills for acquaintances who could not afford them.

Bruce's father sometimes took him to the opera. It was there that he met Siu Kee Lun, better known to his friends as Unicorn, whose father was also an actor in the Chinese Opera. Although Unicorn was three years older than Bruce, the two boys became friends. They would fight and fence with bamboo swords, with Bruce imitating Robin Hood, the hero of a popular film. Although Unicorn was older and stronger, Bruce would never admit defeat and would keep on fighting until Unicorn gave up.

Many years later Unicorn recalled that Bruce was always in

trouble with his father for fighting. Mr Lee would usually set an example by whacking his son across the head.

There is commonly a gulf between a Chinese father and his children. More important than his children's love is the demand for their respect. To help maintain his position, the father rarely loosens up. Distancing himself is the price that he pays for authority.

Bruce spent much of his early life amusing himself on the streets of Hong Kong. In a busy household he was not always missed and Bruce's mother generally had to deal with most of the trouble he caused. She paid his school fees every month, then she would get calls asking why Bruce hadn't been attending. In the end, she told Bruce that it didn't matter so much if he didn't like school, but he had to tell her where he was going to play so that she knew where he was. After that, Bruce still continued to miss school but made sure to tell his mother where she could find him.

'Bruce's character never changed,' his mother said. 'He repeated the same mistakes each time. I was disappointed with him again and again. Once I asked how he expected to earn a living if he kept on like that. He said, "I'll become a famous film star one day." I scolded him and told him that the life of a famous film star was not so comfortable as he imagined and that their lives were abnormal. I told Bruce, "You can't even behave like a normal person. How do you expect to become a famous film star?"'

But Grace Lee also has fond memories of her son. She recalls how she once saw him looking intently from the window of the house at something down the street. Suddenly Bruce jumped up and ran out of the door. When she went to the window she saw Bruce helping a blind man across the road. He told her that he just had to go and help the man who looked so sad and frustrated as everyone walked by, ignoring him.

It was Bruce's sister, Agnes, who gave him the name that stuck with him for life: Little Dragon. She recalls that even from an early age Bruce knew that he was special and was going to make something of his life. She also recalls him having nightmares and sleepwalking.

The rest of the family affectionately knew him as Mo Si Tung, or Never Sits Still. It was a perfect description of him. If Bruce was still even for a moment, they thought he was sick. The only time he stopped running, jumping and talking was when he disappeared to a quiet corner and became completely absorbed in a book. He often stayed up half the night reading. His mother believes that this caused him to become short sighted; from the age of six, Bruce began wearing spectacles.

Young Bruce took great delight in playing practical jokes, although he could barely suppress his laughter as he waited for his victim to get it. After starting out with simple gags, like packets of itching powder and electric shock tricks, his practical jokes soon became far more sophisticated. On one occasion he rearranged all the furniture in a room to confuse the cleaning-maid. Bruce once told his brother Robert to imagine he was a submarine and look up the sleeve of his jacket as if it were the periscope. As he did so, Bruce fired his depth charge and poured a jug of water down the sleeve, soaking him.

Other jokes had an edge to them that was not so funny. Once, after Bruce had pushed his sister Phoebe into a swimming pool, she caught him and held his head under the water. After that, Bruce never again entered a swimming pool.

Bruce Lee began his acting career at the age of three months. In a film called *Golden Gate Girl*, made before his parents left San Francisco, Bruce played the role of a female baby, carried by his father more as a stage prop than anything else.

His first professional role was at the age of six in the Hong Kong-made film *The Birth of Mankind*. Bruce played a street kid who fights with a shoeshine boy, played by his friend Unicorn. Also when he was six, Bruce played his first role under the name Lee Siu Lung (Lee Little Dragon, the name by which he became known in Asia), appearing with his father in *My Son, Ah Cheun*. Bruce had the more important role, being cast as the cute co-star to the top Cantonese film comic, Chow Shui. He played a streetwise kid trying to survive in the world of Hong Kong sweatshops.

Both in tragedies, and comedies such as *It's Father's Fault*, Bruce's early roles were those of street urchins and orphans. Later he played juvenile delinquents and teenage rebels in films imitating those being made in the United States. There were occasional fight scenes and already Bruce was using some of the gestures which would later become his trademarks: the admonishing finger, the thumb wiped across the nose, the brushing down of the jacket sleeves and the slow burning gaze.

Altogether Bruce appeared as a child actor in twenty pictures. The best known was *The Orphan*, a film about Hong Kong street gangs made when he was eighteen, in which he played his only leading role. Besides these early films, an equally great influence came from the films he enjoyed watching.

Between 1920 and 1949, Chinese film-making centred around the Westernized areas of Hong Kong and Shanghai, the populations of which were more cosmopolitan than most Chinese. Even so, this was highly stylized cinema still strongly based on theatrical tradition.

In 1949, director Hu Peng decided to make a film about a martial arts master, Wong Fei Hung, who lived between 1847 and 1924. The director went on to make eighty-five films featuring this character.

Up until this time most martial arts films were savage tales of revenge with ludicrously exaggerated action in which fighters could leap a hundred feet or fly through the air for a hundred yards doing endless somersaults. But both the director and the leading actor of the Wong Fei Hung movies insisted on realistic action scenes and, for the first time, the martial arts element was at the heart of the film. Apart from being a master of the *hung gar* style of *kung fu*, Wong had also practised herbal medicine. The actor who played him had an uncannily similar background.

Kwan Tak Hing was, like Bruce Lee's father, in the Cantonese Opera. He was a *wen wu* player, which meant that he had to be a martial artist as well as an actor. Like the character he now played, Kwan excelled in *hung gar*. In addition he knew the Shaolin fighting systems based on the movements of various animals. A master of the 'white crane' style, Master Kwan, as he became popularly known, was also a herbal physician and healer.

The Wong Fei Hung movies were centred around a philosophy of *wu de*, 'martial virtue'. As this epic series of films progressed, Master Kwan became as skilled as the master whose legend he honoured, as he choreographed superb battles with his main opponent, played by Shih Kien.

The young Bruce Lee could hardly have avoided being deeply influenced by these films. During the 1950s and '60s, this series of movies virtually monopolized the market. In 1956, all but four of the year's twenty-nine *kung fu* pictures featured Wong Fei Hung. Bruce could recite whole scenes of dialogue from these films.

When he was twelve years old, Bruce Lee began attending La Salle College where most of the students were Chinese

Catholics. Although he was in trouble from the start, he was fortunate enough to attract the attention of one of the better teachers, the round-faced and bespectacled Brother Henry Pang. While many of the teachers found Bruce stubborn, wild or lazy, Brother Henry was aware that although Bruce was a difficult pupil, he was also very bright, full of potential, and needed to be approached differently.

Brother Henry channelled Bruce's hyperactivity into running errands, cleaning the blackboards and opening the windows – chores Bruce willingly did. Even so, he found it impossible to sit still in class and was continually in trouble for causing disturbances. Although he showed some interest in art and history but none in biology, his brother Peter recalls that Bruce already had ambitions to become a doctor. At home Bruce spent many hours reading in bed. But while he was very interested in learning, Bruce was not much interested in schooling.

Although Bruce enjoyed some success as a child actor, he became the leader of a school gang that formed around a core of anti-British sentiment. The Chinese hated the British almost as much as they hated the Japanese. There was a long history of subjugation under British colonial rule and such bad feelings were long-standing.

At the end of a long and tedious school day frustrations would be directed against the British pupils of the nearby King George V School. Bruce's gang would gather near the school and heap insults on the British schoolboys walking up the road or gathered behind the fence in the playing field until a fight was under way. Although the British boys were bigger than the Chinese and won their share of fights, Bruce would never acknowledge defeat or admit that his gang had been beaten fairly. The fights would continue until one side was beaten or until the police arrived.

Phone calls and visits from the police began to be a regular event at the Lee household. When Bruce's father came home late from the theatre, Bruce would pretend to be asleep and hide under the blankets to avoid punishment. More often than not his mother would simply 'forget' to tell his father. To keep out of the way of the police, fights were staged on the roofs of apartment buildings, the largest areas of open space to be found anywhere in Hong Kong. When a black eye or some other injury made it impossible for Grace Lee to protect Bruce, his father, realizing what was going on, became angry and placed all kinds of restrictions on Bruce's movements. But he was not home often enough to enforce any of his rulings.

The effects on a boy of a father's remoteness have been revealingly discussed by writer and poet Robert Bly. The boy generally responds in one of two ways: he either becomes depressed and withdrawn, or he becomes a high-flyer, determined to achieve far more in his own life than his father has achieved. Although he was only a casual student of *t'ai chi*, Bruce's father was both a martial artist and a popular actor. Early in Bruce's life, something very definite about his future had been determined.

All the other early family memories confirm that aspects of Bruce's character were already formed – his impulsiveness, kindness, ambition and humour. These aspects were to reappear throughout his life.

After continuing trouble led to Bruce's expulsion from La Salle, he swept his parents through the headmasters' offices of a number of schools before finally settling, a little, at the exclusive St Francis Xavier College.

2
KUNG FU

HONG KONG IN the 1950s was a place suffering from high unemployment, a depressed economy, overcrowding, homelessness and from people simply taking advantage of one another. Thousands upon thousands of Chinese streamed into the city, escaping the communist regime on the mainland. With nowhere to go, most of them took to living in parks, on the street, in doorways or in shanties that were little more than sheets of cardboard propped up and lashed together. Some squatted on roofs; some camped in apartment building stairwells. Survival was a fierce struggle. Anyone with a job worked long hard hours every day of the year, simply to be able to eat and carry on working.

The British government of Hong Kong provided state education through elementary school. Only those who passed the entry exam for secondary school went further. Those who failed – the majority – were let loose to roam with few opportunities except bad ones. Restless youths wandered the streets – junior gangsters looking for some excitement and a little cash. They organized themselves into gangs and jealously defended their territory by every means, from single street fights to all out gang warfare. Since the British police were not armed themselves and had successfully restricted the use of firearms, most fights were either hand-to-hand or bloody affairs involving knives and machetes. Many neighbourhood gangs were loosely affiliated with a local *kung fu* school. Although Bruce was from a well-to-do family and attended an exclusive private school, he still felt himself drawn to the streets. He formed his own small gang, the Tigers of Junction Street.

William Cheung first met Bruce Lee when an uncle who had friends in the Chinese Opera invited him to attend Bruce's birthday party. Bruce later heard of Cheung's growing reputation as a street fighter who practised a formidable style of *kung fu* known as *wing chun* and sought him out to learn the style. But Cheung didn't take Bruce seriously. He later told *Inside Kung Fu* magazine, 'The Tigers were just eight people who got together, they weren't all that tough – they got their fur singed a lot. I told Bruce that because he was a film actor, he shouldn't fight but look after his appearance.'

When Bruce came off worse in a gang-related fight he stormed home and demanded to be trained in an effective martial art in order to defend himself against bullies. Although he had been shown some *t'ai chi* by his father, the slow flowing movements had little appeal for him. *T'ai chi* has more therapeutic value than anything else and needs decades of practice before it can be used as an efficient fighting art. More to the point, neither Bruce nor his father wanted to spend any more time than necessary with each other.

When Grace Lee agreed to give Bruce money for lessons, he hunted down William Cheung and asked if he could train at the same school. Only when Bruce persisted did Cheung finally take him to the Restaurant Workers Union Hall where the classes were held and introduce him to Yip Man, his master. As Bruce was a celebrity, Yip Man was pleased to take him on, and began teaching him on the spot.

Now thirteen years old, Bruce Lee took to *wing chun* with

the kind of obsessive enthusiasm that was to characterize everything to which he applied himself. Yip Man's son, Yip Chun, called Bruce 'fighting crazy'. At first Bruce was interested in *wing chun* only for street fighting, but under the instruction of Yip Man he also absorbed some of the finer points of the art. There is no doubt that this period was of supreme importance in sowing the seeds of the fighting method and philosophical art that Bruce Lee was eventually to develop. In order to understand later events, it deserves some study. What follows is the most widely accepted version of the origins of the *wing chun* style of *kung fu* that the young Bruce Lee was about to embrace to devastating effect.

Originally, *kung fu** was not the name or description of any style of martial art but a general term meaning 'the accomplishment of a difficult task' or, more simply, 'hard work and time spent'. In modern usage, *kung fu* has become accepted as an umbrella term for many of the Chinese martial arts.

According to martial arts lore, the father of *kung fu* was the Indian monk Bodhidharma who left his monastery in India to spread the teachings of the Buddha throughout China at the beginning of the sixth century. While wandering in the mountains of northern China, he stopped at a monastery called Shaolin (in Mandarin; Sil Lum in Cantonese). Shaolin literally means 'young tree' – that is, a tree that can survive strong winds and storms because it is flexible and can bend and sway.

This particular monastery was renowned for its scholarly translations of Buddhist scriptures into Chinese. But Bodhidharma had a reputation for being a pragmatic man with no

---

* Bruce preferred the Cantonese spelling, *gung fu*.

time for those who thought they were acquiring spiritual merit or wisdom simply by building temples or translating texts.

When he was not welcomed at the Shaolin monastery, Bodhidharma took refuge in a nearby cave where he lived for the next nine years, spending prolonged periods in meditation. When the seventy-year-old hermit eventually returned to Shaolin he had a presence and an authority that now went unquestioned and unresisted.

Bodhidharma found that the Shaolin monks constantly fell asleep during meditation, and realized that this was the result of disciplines that stressed the mental faculties to such a degree that their bodies became weak and feeble. So he devised a series of exercises, explaining, 'Although the way of the Buddha is preached for the soul, the body and the soul are inseparable. For this reason, I shall give you a method by which you can develop your energy enough to attain to the essence of the Buddha.'

These exercises were a series of fighting movements that served as a form of moving meditation, and also allowed the monks to defend themselves from bandits when travelling between monasteries. These movements formed the basis of Shaolin boxing and continue to this day as the root of many *kung fu* styles. Even so, Bodhidharma's primary concern was not simply with developing physical strength or practising fighting techniques, but with the cultivation of the intrinsic energy of *ch'i* – variously translated as 'breath', 'spirit' or 'life force'.

Ch'i is energy that permeates the universe and includes the vital energy of every living being. In terms of the human body, it is best understood as the flow of energy governing muscular movement, the process of breathing, the regulation of the heartbeat and the functioning of the nervous system – all physical, mental and emotional activity. What Western medicine attributes to separate circulatory, endocrine, digestive, muscular and nervous systems, the Chinese view as interrelated and having an overall effect. The development of *ch'i* is the basis of all the Taoist arts, including martial arts, philosophy and healing.

Even today, the traditional *kung fu* greeting is to place an open hand over a clenched fist, symbolizing sun and moon, whose characters in Chinese mean 'Ming'. This is a mark of respect for the Ming dynasty which was conquered by the Manchu dynasty culminating with the destruction of the Shaolin temple in 1768. Only five people, known as the Venerable Five, escaped the destruction of Shaolin. Ng Mui was the only female member of the monastery to survive; she went into hiding and continued to practise *kung fu*.

Yim Wing Chun (Everlasting Springtime) was an elegant young woman engaged to a man who lived in a distant province. Wing Chun's beauty had also attracted a local gangster's attentions and he was attempting to coerce her into breaking off her engagement in order to marry him instead. Ng Mui came to hear about these threats and devised a plan. She suggested that Wing Chun's father write a letter to her fiancé breaking off the engagement, while suggesting to the gangster that because of the great distance that the letter would have to travel, the new wedding plans should be postponed for a year. The gangster accepted the father's proposal and Ng Mui's delaying tactic succeeded.

Immediately, Ng Mui began to train Wing Chun to fight, but as the weeks sped by Wing Chun realized that a year would not be long enough to absorb all of Ng Mui's teaching. And so she began ruthlessly to strip down the techniques to their most effective minimum. Where Shaolin *kung fu* had thirty-eight 'forms' (practice routines), Wing Chun distilled them to three: the *sil lum tao* ('little idea'), *chum kil* ('searching for the opening') and the deadly *bil jee* ('stabbing fingers'). When the year had passed, Wing Chun's father informed the local gangster that his daughter would only marry someone who could defeat her in hand-to-hand combat. The would-be bridegroom, who prided himself as something of a fighter, found that his classic blocking and punching style was no use against the simple and direct fighting method of Wing Chun.

This style passed through six generations down to Yip Man,* who had begun to learn the art at the age of thirteen but did not begin teaching it until he was fifty-six. Two years later, the young Bruce Lee began training under Yip Man. Although he was a mild-mannered and slightly built man standing only five and a half feet tall, Yip Man was an imposing figure and he held definite opinions. He shunned Western clothing, would not pose for publicity photographs and felt strongly that only the Chinese should be taught *wing chun*.

Bruce Lee was attracted to the style because of its economy and directness and its emphasis on developing energy – and because it gave the 'maximum of anguish with the minimum of movement'.

Wing chun is based on the principle that the shortest distance between two points is a straight line. It has none of the big circular movements of *t'ai chi*. Although there are kicks in *wing chun*, none is landed higher than the opponent's waist; the emphasis is on gaining position for close-to fighting. All attacks are directed straight at the central axis of the opponent's body, just as it is one's own axis which is defended.

Crucial to the effectiveness of *wing chun* is the unique

* See Appendix II.

training practice of *chi sao* or 'sticking hands'. *Chi sao* is not so much an actual fighting technique as a practice designed to help one to develop sensitivity to the shifting balance of physical forces in a fight.

When two people make physical contact there exists a 'point of contact'. With sufficient practice, it is at this point that any move or intended move can be felt – a response which is called the 'contact reflex'. (This is similar to the experience of a fisherman who doesn't have to actually see the fish nibbling the bait at the end of his line to know that he has a bite.) A developed contact reflex allows one to interrupt any attack or intended attack and counter instantly and automatically.

There are three stages of *chi sao* training. At each stage, one must progress from predetermined moves to random moves and, even, at the advanced stage, to being able to practise while blindfolded. It is important to understand that while the practice routines of *chi sao* may not apply to actual combat situations, the awareness and coordination they develop are essential. *Chi sao* gave Bruce Lee his first practical experience of the interplay of the energies of *yin* and *yang* – the yielding and active forces.

All phenomena in the world can be explained, according to Chinese thought, by the interaction of two forces, *yin* and *yang*. *Yang* represents the 'masculine' creative force: heat, light, sound, activity, heaven, infinity and so on. *Yin* represents the 'feminine' receptive force: coldness, darkness, stillness, earth and the finite. *Yin* and *yang* are not concrete reality but represent the idea of changes of state and the flow and interaction of energy that lie behind every process in existence. These are relative forces. For example: an iron ball is *yang*

compared to a rubber ball, which would be *yin*; a rubber ball would be *yang* compared to a ball of butter; and a ball of butter would be *yang* compared to a raindrop. In martial arts, the moment of stillness before the arm punches is *yin*; as the arm shoots out to strike it becomes *yang*.

This concept is used to explain the way in which nature creates a third force – the sustaining energy of all existence – known as the breath of life, or *ch'i*. This process can be better understood if one imagines combining fire (*yang*) and water (*yin*) to produce steam. The resulting vapour is almost invisible, yet if contained and channelled it has great force. The Chinese pictographic symbol for *ch'i* is an iron pot of hot rice with steam lifting up the heavy lid.

The interaction of two energies to create a third force is seen in the way a bicycle is powered. Both pedals cannot be pushed at the same time: one has to be pushed while the other is released, and vice versa. The movement of pedalling requires both pressure and release, both force and relaxation, resulting in a third force: in this case, forward motion.

In the *wing chun* training exercise of *chi sao*, the student has to apply the same principles of pressure and release while attempting to 'feel' the force and intention of his opponent's moves so as to neutralize or counter them. My own teacher, Derek Jones, compared this process to the children's game of scissors, paper, stone. Scissors can cut paper, a stone can break scissors, paper can envelop a stone, and so on. With the hands and arms in a constant flowing movement between precise positions, the student has to be alert and responsive to the shifting balance of forces. His arms must be soft and sensitive enough to register small changes but without being limp. But they must also be firm and resilient enough to withstand pressure without being rigid. As the attacks and counters flow, only the one who continues to change and adapt spontaneously and without effort will prevail.

In effect, this means that the student learns to find gaps in his opponent's defence and flows into the appropriate moves as quickly and naturally as the reflex of removing your hand from a hot stove, or as automatically as the way we sign our own name.

Later, the development of skill and sensitivity allows the student to be able to feel moves and spontaneously trap his opponent's hands, literally tying him in a knot – all at the speed of reflex action. At a certain point in training this sensitivity may move beyond a purely physical skill to become a psychic faculty in which one may also become sensitive to the opponent's emotions and thoughts to such a degree that one may experience his intention to attack at the same time as he does, or even before he does.

Wing chun has one further unique training method in which a wooden dummy representing the opponent is used to simulate almost all conceivable combat situations in 108 practice moves. The wooden dummy also has the effect of toughening and conditioning the hands; the student is able to 'lock out' when striking it, using the kind of power that might injure a sparring partner or cause injury to his or her own joints when working alone.

Every day after school Bruce Lee headed straight to Yip Man's class, anticipating training by practising his kicks on the trees that he passed on the way. Even after training, Bruce would thump the chair next to him as he sat at the dinner table at home.

Before long, William Cheung began to hear complaints

from some of the older students who were coming off worse in their training encounters with Bruce. 'They were upset because he was progressing so fast. I noticed that, even when he was talking, he was always doing some kind of arm or leg movement. That's when I realized that he was actually serious about *kung fu*.'

3
FIGHTING CRAZY

A YEAR AFTER BEGINNING *kung fu* Bruce Lee also took up dancing the cha-cha, probably because of his interest in his partner, Pearl Cho, although it also served to develop his balance and footwork. Unable to do anything by halves, Bruce kept a list of over a hundred different dance steps on a card in his wallet. Along with fellow *wing chun* student Victor Kan, Bruce spent many evenings at the Champagne nightclub at Tsimshatsui, where they went to dance and admire the talents of the resident singer Miss Fong Yat Wah.

A sharp dresser, Bruce insisted on ironing his own clothes. As he left the apartment each evening, he paused for a moment in front of the mirror to check for a hair out of place and to flash the confident smile that charmed the girls.

His first serious girlfriend was Amy Chan, who later became famous in the East as film actress Pak Yan. Whenever Bruce had any money he would take Amy dancing. On their dates, Bruce would cause her in turn to laugh hysterically with him or to scream at him. In private, she found him a good-hearted person who was always willing to help his friends, but when the couple was joined by anyone else, Bruce turned into a show-off and a chauvinist.

Hawkins Cheung had also begun training with Yip Man in 1953 and he and Bruce soon struck up a friendship. Speaking to *Inside Kung Fu* magazine, Cheung said:

> We started learning *wing chun* because of its reputation against other systems. But while learning the first form we felt frustrated. We said, 'Why do you have to learn this? How can you fight like this?' Everyone wanted to learn it quickly so that they could move on to the sticking hands exercise. The single sticking hands exercise was no fun, and the younger students wanted to get through that even quicker. When we finally got to the double sticking hands exercise, we thought, 'I can fight now!' If you could land a punch on an opponent you felt proud and excited. 'I can beat him now,' was the first thought. That was our character – everyone wanted to beat his partner first and be top dog. Egos ran wild and everyone wanted to be the best.
>
> The Old Man always told us, 'Relax! Relax! Don't get excited!' But whenever I practiced *chi sao* with someone, it was hard to relax: I became angry when struck and wanted to kill my opponent. When I saw Yip Man stick hands with others, he was very relaxed and even talked to his partner. Sometimes he threw his partner out without having to hit him. When I did sticking hands with Yip Man, I felt my balance being controlled by him when I attempted to strike. I was always off balance, with my toes or my heels off the ground. I felt my hands rebound when I tried to strike him, as if he used my force to hit me, yet his movement was so slight, he didn't seem to do anything, it was not a violent movement. When I asked him how he did it, he said, 'Like this,' and he demonstrated the movement which was the same as the practice form.

Bruce Lee was also going through the same experience, common to anyone who begins serious *chi sao* practice, of not simply mastering a physical technique but also confronting the interference of emotions like fear and anger, mental attitudes, and the resolve of his spirit to persevere. He'd wanted to learn how to *fight* and found it hard to follow Yip Man's advice to practise the form more often and to do it more slowly. As Yip Man tried to convey that good or bad techniques are based on good or bad body mechanics – good form – he even suggested that Bruce stop doing sticking hands for a while.

While Bruce often carried a concealed blade or a steel toilet chain as a weapon, he didn't often use them. Most of his street fights involved ripped clothes and bloody noses from blows landed by hands and feet.

Leung Pak Chun, one of the Tigers, says, 'One day one of us was beaten up by a gang from Kowloon. Bruce and the others went off to get revenge. At first, Bruce approached them as if to talk it over, but when he got close enough to the two biggest ones, he hit them without warning.'

These two turned out to be from the family of a local Triad, and William Cheung's father, a high-ranking policeman, had to step in and mediate to prevent any further escalation of the conflict.

Bruce's sister Agnes says, 'He began to get into more and more fights for no reason at all. And if he didn't win, he was furious. Losing, even once in a while, was unbearable for him.'

Part of the responsibility for this also lay with Yip Man who, besides teaching relaxation and calmness, also advised his students not to take everything on trust and to go out and test the system.

Despite a lot of aimless aggression, the seeds of real under-standing were already beginning to take root in Bruce Lee, and there was a depth of questioning that went far beyond the brashness of his youth. Bruce even surprised himself by taking

Yip Man's advice to stop training for a while and spend some time in contemplation. Why was form so important? And what did that have to do with flowing with what was happening around him? These were the ideas that Yip Man was trying to instill in him.

As he would do throughout his life, whenever Bruce wanted to calm his fiery nature and have space to reflect, he would walk by the water or through the rain. Now he spent time walking beside the harbour, as far away from the city bustle as he could get. Thinking about it over and over again was no use. Suppose he could grow an extra head, would that increase his capacity to understand? No, it was a matter of using the form he already had more efficiently, instead of trying to force things. Would he be a better fighter if he had four arms and four legs? If there were humans like that, he thought, then perhaps there might be another way of fighting!

As he stood at the water's edge, Bruce's thoughts turned more lazily, like strange fish swimming in the deep. There was no way of telling how slowly the time was passing, except by the measure of his own breathing and heartbeat. Space and time, both, were a little more hazy as gradually the possibility of a new way of approaching things began to surface. Just as the reflections of clouds passed across the surface of the water, so he was able to see his own thoughts and feelings pass across his mind. He wasn't without feelings or thoughts but somehow, here, now, he wasn't so bound up in them. The real challenge was whether he could find the same sense of himself when fighting, when much stronger emotions were involved.

Bruce leaned down over the water and punched his fist at his own reflected image. For a second, the water parted and splashed away. As the image took shape again, his face was smiling gently. Nature had taught him something, not only about nature itself, but about his own nature. And right at that moment, there was no separation between the two.

But Bruce was soon to experience a new kind of conflict. When jealous juniors found out that he had German ancestry, they put pressure on Yip Man to stop teaching Bruce, knowing that Yip was a staunch traditionalist who believed that the art should never be taught to Westerners. Yip Man's respect for Bruce's efforts and the fact that he actually liked Bruce caused him to refuse. Soon people threatened to leave the school and no one would train with Bruce, so he left of his own accord. At first he trained with one of Yip Man's senior students, Wong Sheun Leung, who had his own group of students. Sometimes Bruce would intercept Wong's students and tell them that their teacher was sick, there was no class that day, and they should go home. With this ruse, Bruce gained extra personal instruction. Eventually, he began training every weekend with William Cheung.

At St Francis Xavier, some of Bruce's restless energy was again channelled by a teacher, this time Brother Edward, who encouraged him to enter the 1958 boxing championships held between twelve Hong Kong schools. Brother Edward, an ex-boxer himself, says of Bruce, 'He was tough, but he wasn't a bully, as some people think.'

During his weekend sessions with William Cheung, Bruce trained hard for the approaching contest. By sheer aggression and determination, Bruce blasted his way through the preliminaries, leaving three opponents knocked out in the first round. He reached the final, facing an English boy, Gary Elms, from the rival King George V School. Elms had held the title for the past three years.

In the ring, Elms began boxing in classic style. Almost

immediately Bruce was in trouble, under some pressure in the corner and swinging wildly. But despite the fact that boxing gloves are not the best aid to the subtler skills of *wing chun*, Bruce began to use some of the blocks he'd learned and then countered with the continuous punching and two-level hitting he'd been working on. He was pleased enough with his third-round knockout to note it in the diary he kept of all his fights.

Meanwhile, the street fights continued along with 'contests' against different schools, and Bruce's mother had to make frequent visits to the police station. In one such fight, the *wing chun* students fought the *choy li fut* students on the roof of an apartment building on Union Road in Kowloon. According to Wong Sheun Leung, it was Bruce who offered the challenge. Wong recalls him as a hothead who often caused trouble and showed no respect for seniors of other styles though, again, not as the delinquent that some have portrayed him to be.

Bruce's fight was set to last two rounds of two minutes each, with Wong as the referee. The fighters took up their positions and almost immediately Bruce's opponent, a boy named Chung, attacked with a punch that Bruce palmed away. The next punch caught Bruce in the eye and shook him; he reacted with a flurry of punches that fell short. He closed the distance but his blows were too wild and he was again hit on the nose and cheek. At the end of the first round, Bruce sat in his corner somewhat discouraged; his eye was swelling, his nose was bleeding and he hadn't managed to land any effective strikes of his own. Bruce told Wong that he wanted to quit, worried that he wouldn't be able to hide his injuries from his father. Wong persuaded him to go on.

As the second round opened, Bruce steadied himself and took a more determined stance, then feinted a couple of times and scored with a straight punch to Chung's face. As Chung gave ground, Bruce pursued him, hitting him repeatedly until he went down and the others intervened. Bruce was elated and held his arms aloft. The victim's parents went straight to the police and Mrs Lee was obliged to sign a paper promising to take responsibility for Bruce's good conduct.

Bruce had managed to stay in school largely by coercing other pupils to do his homework for him. Realizing that he stood more of a chance of going to jail than college, Grace Lee suggested that Bruce claim his right to American citizenship before the option lapsed on his eighteenth birthday. At first Bruce wasn't keen on the idea of emigrating, but his father rapidly warmed to it.

Bruce told Hawkins Cheung that he was going to the United States to become a dentist, but then said he would earn money by teaching *kung fu*. Cheung reminded him that he only knew *wing chun* up to the second form, along with forty of the movements on the wooden dummy. Even so, Bruce now considered himself to be the sixth-best exponent of the style, but he took note of Cheung's comments and felt that it might be a good idea to have a few showy moves under his belt before he left. He went to see a man known as Uncle Siu (Siu Hon Sang) who taught northern styles of *kung fu*. Bruce took Siu to a local coffee shop and struck a deal with him: over the following month Siu would teach him some of his moves and in return Bruce would give Siu dancing lessons. They began at seven one morning, with Siu leading Bruce through two northern-style *kung fu* forms, a praying mantis form and one called *jeet kune*, 'quick fist'. But Siu got the worst of the deal. He expected Bruce to take three or four weeks to learn the forms when Bruce actually learned them in just three days – before Siu even got going with the basic cha-cha steps.

*

Bruce had retained his friendship with Unicorn throughout their youth. Just as their fathers had similar careers, Unicorn, like Bruce, had also become a child actor. Run Run Shaw, the head of the Shaw Brothers studio that employed Unicorn, now asked Bruce to sign a contract with them. Bruce told his mother that he wanted to accept the offer, but Grace Lee managed to persuade him that his best chance of making something of his life would come from finishing his education in the United States.

Prior to leaving Hong Kong, Bruce had to apply to the local police station for a certificate that would clear him for emigration. There he found that both Bruce Lee and Hawkins Cheung were on a blacklist of local troublemakers. Over-dramatizing matters, Bruce phoned his friend: 'We're on a known gangster list! I've got to clear my name, and while I'm there, I'll clear yours too.'

A few days later a policeman called at the Cheung house-hold to ask questions about 'gang relations'. Whatever efforts Bruce had made had caused more trouble rather than clearing their names. In the end, Mr Cheung Sr had to pay to have his son's name wiped from the record so that he could go to Australia to attend college. Bruce stayed in Hong Kong just long enough to become the Crown Colony cha-cha champion of 1958. The day before he left for America, he went to say goodbye to Unicorn. Bruce told his friend that he felt his father didn't love him, nor did the rest of the family respect him. He felt that he now had to achieve something in his life, conceding that his mother was right – that if he didn't take this chance, he might well end up in real trouble.

As he was leaving, Bruce's mother slipped a hundred dollars into his pocket; his father gave him fifteen. Bruce picked up his bags but just as he left the room his father called him back. As Bruce returned, his father suddenly waved him away again. Lee Hoi Cheun had simply been enacting a Chinese tradition:

because he had made this gesture, even though his son was going far away, he would be compelled to return to attend the father's funeral. Silent and a little disappointed, Bruce picked up his bags and continued on his way.

In April 1959, Bruce made the three-week Pacific crossing to San Francisco. Although he was booked on board ship as a third-class passenger, he managed to spend most of his time in first class by giving dancing lessons there. Neat and bespectacled, he looked more like a young Clark Kent than a hot-headed troublemaker. Back in his cabin he considered what might happen once his 115 dollars disappeared.

4

RUBY CHOW'S

LEE JUN FAN fulfilled his mother's expectations and returned to San Francisco, the city of his birth. There he stayed with a friend of his father's and started a new life the best way he knew how: earning a little money by giving dancing lessons. During a break at a dance, Bruce gave an impromptu *kung fu* display witnessed by Bob Lee, the younger brother of a local *kung fu* instructor, James Yimm Lee. Bob Lee gave his brother an impressive account but James didn't follow it up.

During his first months in San Francisco, several local karate practitioners Bruce met tried to persuade him to start teaching, but he resisted the temptation saying that he first wanted to finish his own education. Bruce was seriously considering studying to become a doctor, and he was actually getting down to learning maths and improving his English.

Bruce was joined in San Francisco by his brother Peter, who stayed only briefly on his way to the University of Wisconsin from where he eventually graduated, going on to help run the Royal Observatory in Hong Kong. Peter recalls how Bruce would yell in his sleep, punching and kicking out, hurling the covers from the bed.

The insecurity of this period kept Bruce in what seemed a

perpetual state of inner conflict and defiance. Bruce's temper was triggered by even the mildest affront. But his stay in San Francisco was short and Grace Lee called on the Chows, family friends in Seattle, to take Bruce in.

Like Bruce's father, Chow Ping had been a member of Hong Kong's Cantonese Opera Company, but due to an illness had found himself stranded in New York following the United States' declaration of war in 1941. There he met his future wife Ruby, who nursed him back to health. The couple moved to Seattle where they opened a restaurant.

Ruby Chow was a tough independent woman. Not only had she flown in the face of tradition by divorcing her first husband in order to marry Ping, but she had gone against the advice of all her friends and opened the first Chinese restaurant outside Seattle's Chinatown. There she established herself as one of the most influential people in the local community. Ruby acted as a go-between for the Chinese, sorting out problems with the police or immigration authorities and advising them on personal or money matters. She would take new arrivals from Hong Kong into the household and provide temporary lodging and food in return for casual work while they found their feet in a new country. As far as Ruby Chow was concerned, Bruce Lee was no different from any of the others who passed through.

Life in Seattle came as a rude awakening for the young Bruce Lee. He'd never seen his name on a work schedule before; Bruce thought he was going to be a guest while attending school. He was given a tiny bedroom 'no bigger than a closet' on the third floor of the house and put to work as a waiter, a job that made him miserable and for which he could hardly have been less suited. Bruce Lee was not exactly a natural at taking orders and there were daily complaints from customers about his attitude. His treatment of the other waiters and kitchen staff was not much better and his relationship with Ruby Chow was one of open hostility. Ruby expected to be shown the respect she was used to getting, not to be shouted at by one of her waiters who told her she was taking advantage of him. Ruby and Bruce were both forceful personalities and neither would give way to the other.

Ruby Chow does not remember Bruce Lee fondly. When I asked her about Bruce, she didn't want to talk about him:

> If I can't say anything good about anyone, I'd rather not talk about it . . . I took care of him for four years. I raised five children and I treated him like a second son. He was just not the sort of person you want your children to grow up like; he was wild and undisciplined, he had no respect. Lots of martial arts people are insecure. Martial arts are supposed to be to defend people, but he used them to be aggressive. Did he get any better as he got older? I don't think so.

Grace Lee sent Bruce money to subsidize his small income, and occasionally he would earn a bit extra with odd jobs like stuffing leaflets in newspapers. He worked in the restaurant at night and spent his days on the studies he had neglected in Hong Kong. Bruce then enrolled at Edison Technical High School.

In a letter dated 16 May 1960, Bruce Lee wrote to Hawkins Cheung telling him that he was still practising his *kung fu* and that he was having a *wing chun* wooden dummy shipped from Hong Kong. He continued:

> At present, I'm still going to the Edison High School and will be graduated this summer. I plan to go to the University next year, that is in 1961. Well! I still don't know what I'm going to major in, but when I find out I'll write to you again. Now I find out that all

those stuff like cha-cha are just for killing time and have little fun out of it and that study always comes first. Yes, that's right, your own future depends on how well you have studied. Now I am really on my own, since the day I stepped into this country. I didn't spend any money from my father. Now I am working as a waiter for a part-time job after school. I am telling you, it's tough, boy! I always have a heck of a time!

When Seattle held an Asian Culture Day at one of its annual fairs, Edison School asked Bruce Lee to put on a *kung fu* demonstration. One man who saw a notice about the coming event was James DeMile. A former heavyweight boxing champion for the US Air Force and now a street fighter who led the Capitol Hill gang, DeMile was intrigued enough to turn up for the display.

In his neat dark suit and thick round glasses Bruce hardly looked like a fighter as he began to tell the small crowd that they were about to see something that had always been kept secret in China. The effect was heightened by Bruce's Chinese accent which made his 'r's sound like 'w's. As he ran through various *kung fu* animal styles, it looked like anything but fighting and the audience grew restless. Bruce became still and his gaze focused on James DeMile. 'You look like you can fight,' said Bruce. 'How about coming up here?'

DeMile looked every inch and every pound the fighter he was. He couldn't have been too worried as the young man beside him, who weighed 140 pounds and stood at 5 foot 7 inches, explained that he was about to demonstrate a simple fighting system devised by a tiny Buddhist nun. Bruce turned to DeMile and invited him to attack. DeMile fired out a straight right, intending to send the upstart's head sailing over the crowd.

Bruce blocked the punch easily as he countered simultaneously with his own punch that stopped a whisker away from DeMile's nose. From then on no matter what DeMile tried, Bruce was able to counter everything. The contact reflex he'd honed from years of sticking hands practice worked for him. DeMile was used to street fights in which he usually began by breaking someone's leg. He wasn't used to losing a fight, let alone being made to look helpless. The demonstration continued without mercy, ending when Bruce knocked his knuckles against DeMile's head and asked if he was at home.

Later, James DeMile swallowed his hurt pride and, responding like a martial artist rather than a mere brawler, asked Bruce to teach him some of his skills.

Also in the audience that day was Jesse Glover, an African-American judo exponent who discovered, to his delight, that he and Bruce Lee attended the same school. Glover became one of Bruce's first serious students.

Doug Palmer now works as an attorney in Seattle. His diaries recall his own experience of meeting Bruce around this time:

> I saw him give a *gung fu* demonstration during a street fair and was mesmerized by his blinding speed and obvious power, by his lithe fluidity and his perfectly executed moves imitating the praying mantis and other forms. The brother of a friend of mine was taking *gung fu* lessons from him and I mentioned that I'd like to learn too. A week or so later, in the middle of a crowd milling around outside the Buddhist temple, I felt a tap on my shoulder. When I turned, a handsome Chinese man a few years older than I stood facing me with a hooded expression. 'I heard you wanted to see me,' he said.
>
> I introduced myself and said I was interested in learning *gung fu*. He shrugged noncommittally, then told me where they practiced. 'Come by and watch sometime,' he said. 'If you're still interested, we'll see.'
>
> Twice a week, until I left for college, I worked out with the class, sometimes in a backyard and, through the winter, in a garage.

The class was small, made up mostly of men older than Bruce. Many of the students were proficient in judo; I had boxed for a number of years. All of us were enthralled by a form of martial art that seemed the ultimate in efficiency and deadliness . . . No one had heard of *gung fu* then. Comedians had a lot of fun with it – 'Is that like egg fu yung?' One of my high school teachers, a hulking ex-football player, asked me if it would 'stand up to a good ol' Minnesota haymaker.'

Bruce's natural talents and outgoing personality soon attracted other students. Impromptu training took place in Ruby Chow's parking lot after Bruce had finished work. In these sessions he learned as much as he taught, trying out various moves on his new students.

Along with some of the others, Jim DeMile used to drop in at a local supermarket owned by Takauki Kimura – known to his friends as Taky – a Japanese-American who had been held in an internment camp during the Second World War. While in the camp, Taky had taken judo lessons from a fellow internee. Knowing that he would be interested, Jim DeMile told Taky about the incredible young martial artist they had got to know.

Now approaching seventy, Taky Kimura is a soft-spoken and likeable man who still runs his business in Seattle. He recalls how he met Bruce Lee:

> They told me I just had to go and see him. Now, I'd seen martial artists in Japan who were older and more experienced so I didn't see how a young kid could be any better, but they kept insisting. So I went down to a training session being held on one of the playing fields near the university. As soon as I saw what he could do I asked if I could join their club – although it was his thinking that impressed me, even more than his speed and power. There was a small group of us: Jesse Glover, Jim DeMile, Ed Hart, Pat Hooks, Doug Palmer. We used to work out in parks, or anywhere that there

was an open space. I worked out with Bruce quite a lot by myself. He would encourage me to socialize with him, but I was already taking time off work to train, and besides, I was twice his age.

At thirty-eight years old, Taky Kimura was twice as old as most of the others, a sad-eyed man whose confidence had taken many knocks. Bruce was only eighteen and restless yet the two warmed to each other. For the next year they met and trained in parks for several hours every Sunday and talked afterwards over a cup of tea in a Chinese restaurant. A close friendship developed.

Taky Kimura says:

Remember, Jesse Glover was black; James DeMile had ethnic origins. There were a couple of white guys but most of us were from minorities. I was brought up in one of the few ethnic families in our neighbourhood and we encountered a lot of prejudice . . . I couldn't get served in restaurants, couldn't get a seat on a bus. I tramped the streets for six months, looking for a job. It destroyed my whole sense of being a person. Fortunately I didn't take to drink under the whole stress of it all. Finally, I had to say, 'Am I a man, or what!' and get a hold. Later I married a Caucasian woman, who loved me and who treated me like everyone else.

Bruce would say to me, 'You're just as good as they are.' Then he would say, 'Jesus, Taky! You dress like an old man, you look like you're sixty. Get yourself some clothes.' He didn't only build me up physically, he built up the emotional and mental aspects – and I got myself back.

Training sessions were sometimes held behind Taky's supermarket. As the group worked out and joked around, Bruce would suddenly become serious and start lecturing them. This meant only one thing: there was a girl around. As Bruce's lecture continued, Jim DeMile tried to slide away. It was DeMile's misfortune to look more menacing and murderous than any of the other guys, and if there was a girl who Bruce wanted to impress then he was the natural choice: 'Now what I do in my system is . . . Ah, Jim!'

Bruce began a relationship with Amy Sanbo, a Japanese-American girl, who like Taky, had also been in a US internment camp during the war. While Amy recognized Bruce's abilities and positive qualities, she also saw his immaturity. At a social gathering Bruce would do one-finger push-ups to attract a crowd. When Amy accused him of being a show-off, he countered that he only wanted to see how people would react. She told Bruce that although he quoted wisdom he did not live up to it. And while Amy showed compassion for others who were less fortunate, Bruce's response was that anyone who wanted to get out of a hole could do so. Bruce would often dominate their conversations with his favourite subjects: *kung fu* and his dreams for the future. Although Amy had her own ambitions to become a writer and dancer, Bruce seemed uninterested and told her that she would find fulfilment through helping him.

Bruce Lee had difficulty understanding that not everyone could share his ambitions or his abilities. He could be an impatient teacher: he would show a move only once or twice and if you didn't catch it, it was unlikely to be repeated. He thought that if he could do it, so could anyone else. Taky Kimura was one of those who couldn't always keep up. He told Bruce that he was quitting, adding that it was easy for the teacher but not the student. Bruce replied that Taky 'had the talent, but refused to recognize it'.

Taky takes up the story:

I was working twice as hard as the other guys because I was older than them. One day I was looking out of the corner of my eye to see if I was making any impression on Bruce. Of course he knew exactly what I was doing and I heard him say to one of the others, 'He'll never make it.' That hurt me to the bone. But because I'd always been a quitter, it drove me to try that much harder, and even though I was clumsy I think he saw that I was dedicated and sincere in what I was trying to do. Then he started to work with me and kind of took me aside and showed me lots of extra things. The next thing I knew, he was grooming me to be his assistant.

Yet Bruce also played on Taky's difficulty in asserting himself by having him act as an unpaid chauffeur. 'I was happy to take him on his dates,' says Taky, 'because he was doing something for me. But my family wasn't so happy when I had to get up at 2 a.m. to go and collect him.'

To earn a bit of ready cash and gain new students, Bruce Lee started giving regular demonstrations in the area. These included a series of television programmes for Seattle's KCTS-Channel 9, the educational station. But no matter how much Bruce rehearsed his students for these displays, things would sometimes go wrong. Then Bruce's temper would flare as he was embarrassed at being part of a display that appeared unprofessional. In one routine Jesse Glover forgot what he was supposed to do. Finding himself face to face with Bruce under the hot lights and in front of the cameras, he panicked and hit Bruce in the face. Suddenly it was no longer a display. In an instant Jesse Glover was flat on the floor and there was a steely look in Bruce's eyes.

'I was with Bruce at some of his demos,' says Taky, 'and he would put away some big guys. But his strength was not plain brawn. He used to tell us this story about an old lady whose house caught on fire. Her most precious possession was a piano which was on one of the upper floors. Without stopping to think about how she was going to do it, she carried the piano out of the house to safety. Later, it took four men to lift it. Bruce could call up and harness that kind of energy at will. His power came from a tremendous base of internal energy which he knew how to bring out.'

Just as in childhood, Bruce was still fond of practical jokes. 'One of the guys in the class was an optometrist,' recalls Doug Palmer. 'Bruce had a whole bunch of contact lenses made. One pair had red veins in them – he used to put them in and goof around. He would stumble into a restaurant and be led up to a table by one of us, then fumble for a menu, pass his hands across the page and start ordering in Chinese while one of us interpreted.'

'He was a unique young man,' says Taky. 'He could turn his personality from one segment to another. One minute he would be telling us a raunchy joke, the next he would be talking about Zen and Taoism. He was very flexible and could change depending on who he was talking to.'

Although Bruce was capable of deep and genuine insight in one moment and great humour the next, he could also suddenly explode with anger.

Taky Kimura recalls:

There was a guy called Eddie Pearce who used to hang around outside the store. I befriended him and he became almost like my younger brother. Now Eddie had a bad stutter, and Bruce occasionally used to stutter when he talked although, in his case, I think it was due to difficulties with a new language rather than a speech problem. When I introduced Eddie to Bruce, of course Eddie began stuttering and I saw Bruce tense up and his fists begin to tighten, thinking that he was being mocked. Once Eddie realized what was going on he quickly tried to explain, 'I-I-I really d-d-do stutter,' which only made the problem worse and I had to step in.

Bruce was a very intense young man and more than once there

might have been trouble if I hadn't been there. One Sunday afternoon, Bruce and I were driving through Seattle being followed by a motorcycle cop. We drove on, stopping at every red light, for four or five blocks until the cop pulled us over. 'You guys are having a really good time, driving at twenty-nine in a thirty-mile-an-hour zone.' The cop was trying to stir something up – it was a discriminatory thing. I could feel Bruce tensing up and I know that if I hadn't been there, he would have gone for him.

James DeMile recalls one occasion when Bruce and his friends were strolling through Chinatown when they saw a young Chinese girl being harassed by some men in a car. Bruce walked over to the driver's door and told the guy to cut it out. As the guy leaned out of the window to threaten him, Bruce snapped a backfist into the man's face, breaking his nose, before the car sped off.

Taky saw Bruce's character as 'flexible'. But there was a darker current running deep beneath it all, a powerful force that was about to break through into his life.

5
THE SHADOW

AS HE DEVELOPED as a martial artist, Bruce Lee was
also undergoing the inner challenges and changes that accom-
pany such a way of life. Bruce's sister Agnes related how he
had sleepwalked regularly since childhood. His brother Peter
recounted how Bruce even fought in his sleep. Taky Kimura
spoke of the tremendous accumulation of internal energy that
Bruce could draw on. Now it all came to a climax.

In his room at the Chows', in the middle of one night,
Bruce Lee fought with a 'black shadow' that held him down
for several minutes. The effort of resisting defeat left him
drenched in sweat. Since it takes little imagination for the hack
journalist or scriptwriter to turn the event into a wild tale
about a demon or a curse, this has become the most cheapened
and distorted incident in Bruce Lee's life.

This event needs to be seen from its correct perspective:
there is no doubt that Bruce had begun to generate (or open
up access to) powerful energies outside the realm of the
ordinary everyday way of functioning. But energy is neither
inherently good nor bad; it is both. It is both *yin* and *yang*,
light and dark. Energy contains all possibilities.

That night, Bruce was not fighting a ghost but was being

brought face to face with aspects of his personality that he had previously been reluctant to acknowledge: his anger, his cockiness and his insecurities. Bruce had simply met himself. He underwent an intense confrontation with his own unconscious self in which all the contradictions, the darker sides of his nature, were made apparent to him. It may well have felt as if he were fighting a dark force.

In the Tarot, the Devil card depicts this archetypal experience and speaks of the powerful psychic energies that are set loose. Here, the Devil represents not an evil force, but impulsive instincts and energy in a disordered state. The Devil teaches the Fool (the naïve spiritual seeker) to recognize and accept all aspects of his nature, both light and dark.

The psychologist Jung presents this archetypal force not as the Devil, but as the Shadow. The Shadow is the blocked energy that comprises repressed or negative feelings which, when removed, can allow the release and integration of a great deal of energy for positive purposes.

Indeed, it was soon after this incident that Bruce Lee embarked on a course of serious self-improvement. At Edison, he gained a high school diploma with good enough grades to secure a place at the University of Washington in Seattle, which he started attending in March 1961. Initially, he enrolled in subjects that were of immediate practical interest to him: English, gymnastics and wrestling. But with a strong intuition of where he was now heading, he also signed up for classes in theatre speech and speech improvement. Over the years he spent at the university, he also took courses in drawing, composition, social dancing, Chinese philosophy, Chinese language, the Far East in the modern world, general psychology, the psychology of adjustment, personal health and leadership. Bruce also began to soak up self-help books on the development of potential, 'making luck', and positive thinking.

This sudden surge in Bruce's ambitions was backed up by a powerful conviction that he could achieve them. Meanwhile, he struggled with equally strong feelings of homesickness by writing essays about life in Hong Kong.

Bruce was now attracting more and more students. But James DeMile doesn't believe that Bruce was intentionally setting out to teach:

> It was more like he was saying, 'Here's what I have to offer – you take it. In the meantime, I'm going to be training and developing myself.' Fortunately, I absorbed a tremendous amount of his philosophy and technical skill because I was interested. I also became more focused and aware of myself, and more in control of my movements. It helped in my evolution as a person, and with my confidence. Meanwhile, Bruce was changing as he developed more flow, more energy and more intensity. His time in Seattle was one of experimenting with various stances and techniques to overcome his limitations.

In Hong Kong, Bruce had fought with people who were his own size. Now he was faced with opponents seventy pounds heavier and six inches taller than him – what he called 'trucks rolling in'. Bruce knew that if he was hit by someone like DeMile or, even worse, by someone at a public demonstration, then he would be hurt and so would his reputation. It wasn't simply a matter of pride, it was a matter of survival. As his students' skills improved, they challenged Bruce to increase his own. He maintained his edge due to his understanding of the root concepts and principles of fighting.

Jesse Glover explains:

> There were several factors that made Bruce what he was. First, was his ability to simplify – to take something complex and render it down to its basic essence. Second, was his natural speed and his

ability to imitate any movements he saw, even if he saw them only once. Third, was the motivation that drove him to higher levels: the fear of being beaten and the desire to be the best – fear that he might meet someone with his own ability but who was bigger and stronger – and the fact that if he was the best, such a thing couldn't happen.

Bruce Lee had found Yip Man's traditional approach painfully slow in giving out information. In his teaching, Bruce adopted a simple motto: 'Use only that which works, and take it from any place you can find it.' Jesse Glover continues:

> During the first two years that I knew him, Bruce Lee was a split individual who sometimes raved about the attributes of various *kung fu* arts during one conversation, only to put them down during another. During this period in the early '60s, Bruce travelled through California and the West Coast, as far as Canada, to look at and talk to *kung fu* masters.

Whenever they did permit him to watch or showed him some technique, Bruce quickly saw how he could make it more efficient, something that seldom endeared him to the host. A series of these encounters began to make him think that much of what was being taught was ineffective.

'Bear in mind,' continues Glover, 'that during this period Bruce was training forty or more hours a week. He was approaching his peak time of development and his actions reflected the great gains he was making. The better he became, the less regard he had for tradition, and he said so whenever he had a platform to speak from. And he could back his words with actions.'

A Japanese black belt karate student by the name of Uechi, who had been at Edison with Bruce, had taken exception to Bruce's opinion of karate and had been making a nuisance of himself for some time. At one of Bruce's demonstrations, the karate man kept contradicting Bruce in front of the audience. Bruce explained that nothing was meant personally and repeated that it was not his intention to downgrade other styles but simply to clarify his own approach.

'Bruce tried to dismiss it but eventually it got to him,' says Taky Kimura. 'The next time the guy did it Bruce told him they would have to have it out.'

After deciding on a suitable place to fight, the two headed for the handball court at the local YMCA, accompanied by a small crowd filled with anticipation. Makeshift rules were quickly established: there would be three rounds of two minutes, with Jesse Glover acting as referee.

Bruce took up a *wing chun* stance. Uechi adopted a karate forward stance then switched to a cat stance and snapped out a front kick to Bruce's stomach. Bruce parried the kick and instantly closed in with a rapid series of straight punches before Uechi could get any counters going. The Japanese never managed to land another blow as Bruce drove him to the ground. As he fell to his knees, Bruce kicked him in the face and Jesse Glover ran in to stop the fight. 'It lasted about ten seconds,' adds Taky Kimura.

The karate man reappeared a week later, telling his friends that he had been involved in a minor car accident. 'Bruce was quite generous about the whole business,' says Taky. 'Rather than embarrass the man in front of his friends, Bruce just let it go at that. Later, the guy became a pupil. Bruce showed a lot of class; he didn't hold a grudge, he let him in and just moved on.'

'What Bruce could readily demonstrate at the drop of a hat,' says Jesse Glover, 'he was advocating for everyone. The problem for everyone else was that his ability was based on a great many factors which they didn't possess. Few people had the physical background to make Bruce's ideas work. What Bruce presented to the public was only the tip of the iceberg. One of the requirements for learning these arts is intensive practice spread over the appropriate time period. You cannot learn them overnight and you cannot learn them without effort. In order to successfully use any of Bruce's ideas, you had to develop more than a little of Bruce's skill.'

James Lee (the Oakland *kung fu* teacher whose brother Bob had taken a dancing lesson from Bruce) had a friend named Allen Joe who happened to be travelling to Seattle for the 1962 World's Fair. 'Since you're going,' said James Lee, 'why don't you check out this guy and see how good he is?'

Allen Joe tracked Bruce Lee down to Ruby Chow's restaurant. He waited till late in the evening and was sitting there drinking a Scotch when Bruce showed up dressed 'real sharp'. Allen mentioned James Lee and they began talking *kung fu*, eventually moving outside, where Allen started to show Bruce his classical moves. Without smiling, Bruce told him it was no good and to try them on him. Every time he tried a move on Bruce he ended up 'flying all over the place'. Bruce then showed him the practice form on his wooden training dummy, which he had nicknamed Bodhidharma.

'I was really impressed,' said Allen Joe. 'He was so smooth that everything I had learned seemed stiff and clumsy in comparison.'

After he returned home Bruce wrote to Allen and about two weeks later James Lee wrote to Bruce, who then went down to Oakland for a visit. James Lee finally had to agree, 'This guy is good. He's unreal!'

Bruce Lee made an equally powerful impression on a student at Garfield High School, where he was an occasional guest lecturer. Now twenty-two years old, Bruce arrived one day, looking cool with Amy Sanbo on his arm, to give a talk on Chinese philosophy. He didn't notice Linda Emery, an athletic girl of seventeen, but she was taken enough to ask the girl beside her who he was. Her friend, a Chinese-American girl named Sue Ann Kay, replied that Bruce was the guy who was teaching her *kung fu*.

In the three years that he and Amy had been dating, Bruce had proposed marriage several times and been turned down every time. In the summer of 1963, Bruce was planning a trip back to Hong Kong, where he hoped to tell his family that he and Amy were to be married. He made one final proposal hoping to clinch it by offering her a ring that had belonged to his grandmother. Bruce knew that Amy had been offered a job in New York and he was pushing her into marrying him or turning him down for good. Amy turned him down one last time and disappeared from his life. For a while he tried, unsuccessfully, to find her.

At the same time Bruce got a letter from the draft board, which was not at all keen to let him leave the country as his American citizenship made him eligible for military service. Bruce asked his English professor Margaret Walters to write a character reference assuring the draft board that he was an honourable man. Although his life in the States had recently been shadowed by disappointment, Bruce had no intention of running out on it.

6

SUMMER IN
HONG KONG

IN THE SUMMER of 1963, the Lee household in Nathan Road consisted of Bruce's mother and father, his sister Agnes, brother Robert, a cousin and an aunt, a servant – and the chicken living on the veranda. Bruce's friend and student Doug Palmer had studied Mandarin at college and he jumped at the chance when Bruce invited him to come along on the visit home.

One evening, as the family sat around the table, Doug Palmer was introduced to the subtleties of Cantonese. In his notes, he recalls:

> Cantonese, the Chinese dialect predominant in Hong Kong, is a tonal language. Sounds which are otherwise identical can have a radically different meaning with a different tone. By then I could speak Mandarin, which has four basic tones, reasonably well. But Cantonese has seven and, for me, the differences were sometimes impossible to hear.
>
> One night, the family sat around the dining table playing a simple game which consisted of rolling a die with the figure of a different animal on each face. Whoever was quickest to yell out the correct animal after the die was rolled advanced his marker. One of

the animals was a shrimp, pronounced '*haai*' in a low tone. In the excitement of the game my voice would rise and I found myself shouting '*hai*' with an even higher pitch every time the shrimp was rolled. The ladies of the household thought this was most amusing and giggled each time. Finally, Bruce took me aside to explain the difference in tone between the word for shrimp and the word for cunt.

Bruce Lee and Doug Palmer found no shortage of things to do that summer. They went swimming at the sand beaches, went to the movies (as long as they remembered to buy a reserved seat well ahead of time), visited amusement parks, ate in restaurants or simply soaked up the atmosphere and energy of the bustling streets. Bruce also got Doug involved in his practical jokes. One target of these jokes was the Hong Kong police, who were quite corrupt and who, along with British soldiers, made up the two categories of humans that Bruce disliked most. Bruce would select a Chinese policeman wearing a red bar on one of his sleeves, signifying that he spoke (somewhat rudimentary) English:

> Once we spotted one of the cops with a red bar, my job was to walk up to him and ask if he could tell me the way to the Canton Theatre. Since there was no Canton Theatre, but there was a Canton Road, the cop would invariably ask, in heavily accented English, 'Canton Road?' 'No!' I'd say I was supposed to meet a friend at the Canton Theatre and, thereupon, I would launch into a non-stop monologue of double-talk. Each time the confused cop would repeat 'Canton Road?' I would give another burst of double-talk. Finally, I would demand loudly, in Cantonese, 'What the hell are you mumbling about?' At that point, Bruce would stroll up helpfully and ask what the problem was. I would explain that I was looking for the Canton Theatre. Bruce would say that he was going that way and would accompany me and we would walk off leaving the cop with an even more confused look on his face.

One night Bruce was returning home to the Kowloon side on the Star Ferry. Two street punks had been goading him, but he endured their comments and ignored them. After the ferry docked they continued to follow Bruce and insult him. Finally, Bruce spun round and snapped out a low straight kick to the nearest punk's shin. The second one quickly backed off. Bruce left it at that and continued home. When he heard about the incident, Bruce's cousin Frank, who was a few years older, shook his head in disbelief and laughed. 'A few years ago, he would have beaten them both up.'

Bruce also took delight in faking fights with Doug Palmer in front of a crowd of onlookers.

> We practised our routine: two roundhouse swings from me, which he blocked with his forearms; then a stiff uppercut to my stomach, which I had to make sure I'd tightened in time. We would time it so that we would emerge from an elevator, arguing loudly, then swing into our skit in front of the crowd waiting for the elevator.
>
> I'm not sure whether Bruce's sense of humour was Chinese or uniquely his own. Bruce used to act like a geek and let a street punk goad him. When the punk swung, Bruce would block it awkwardly and snap at the punk's groin and incapacitate him with a blow that appeared to be an accident. As the punk rolled in pain, Bruce would cover his mouth with his hand and titter effeminately, then walk off. 'A person can accept getting beaten by someone who is stronger or bigger than he is,' Bruce would explain, 'but if he thinks he's been beaten by a nerd, he'll be pissed off for the rest of his life.'

While in Hong Kong, Bruce also continued serious training and sought out Yip Man, taking Doug Palmer along only to watch, cautioning him not to let on that he knew any *kung fu*.

> Although he had kicked over the traces in the States, teaching *gung fu* to anyone who was interested, without regard to race and to the consternation of many people in Seattle's Chinatown, he was not

ready, out of respect for his teacher, to 'come out of the closet' in Hong Kong.

Yip Man was a smiling man with a twinkle in his eyes, slight and getting on in years, but still fit. He and Bruce would practise sticking hands in his apartment at the top of a high-rise. There were no other students present, and the two of them, in their undershirts, would go at it for long periods.

'We hung out together all that summer,' says Palmer, 'except when we had dates.' When Bruce's childhood sweetheart Pak Yan heard that he was in Hong Kong, she called him. In the five years he had been away she had featured in one picture after another. Now, she told him, she would soon begin work on a new film in which she was to play 'a bad girl'. She wanted to know if Bruce would be able to help her prepare for the part. Over the next few weeks, he helped her prepare several times.

Whether or not his father knew about Pak Yan, a week before Bruce was due to return to Seattle Lee Hoi Cheun decided that Bruce, at the age of twenty-two, should now be circumcised. Even more astonishingly, Bruce agreed, returning to the apartment one day walking carefully. He quickly changed from the tight pants he normally wore into a pair of loose-fitting traditional ones, borrowed from his father. Each morning the purple organ was inspected until it had taken on a more normal appearance. 'I remember him hobbling about,' chuckles Palmer. 'If he'd known how painful it was going to be, I think he would have had second thoughts.'

By the time Bruce Lee and Doug Palmer took off for the United States, Bruce was able to walk normally again.

On the way back we stopped in Tokyo for a couple of days, then again in Hawaii. Through a friend, Bruce was asked to give a demonstration at a *gung fu* school in Honolulu – by then he had completely recovered from his operation. At that time, the *gung fu* schools in Hawaii, as elsewhere, were still strictly Chinese; so it was quite a surprise when I climbed on to the stage with Bruce to give a demonstration to fifty students and their teachers. Afterwards a number of people gathered around to ask questions. One of them asked if Bruce was teaching me *gung fu*. From the way he asked and since from the demonstration it was obvious that I'd had some training, his implication was clear: he considered it heresy that Bruce would be training a non-Chinese.

The same fellow, with a cigarette dangling from his mouth, now approached Bruce with questions about his technique. He asked Bruce how he would block a front kick and Bruce offered to demonstrate. The man kicked at groin level and Bruce blocked it with a slapping palm block, then resumed his explanation. The man kept his leg extended in the air, after the kick was blocked, and flicked his foot feebly after Bruce had withdrawn the block. 'See,' he said, 'you were open there.'

Although Bruce was smouldering, he had become adept at handling this type of person without hurting them. He continued his explanation and offered to demonstrate a different block. The man obliged and threw a punch, but of course this time Bruce did not withdraw after blocking it; he trapped it and followed with a counter of his own, just slow enough to allow the fellow to block it with his free hand. Bruce grabbed the second hand too, and tied up both of the man's arms. The force and speed of the second pull was so great that the man's cigarette went flying from his mouth as he was jerked forward. The whole time Bruce continued calmly explaining each move, his head turned to the growing audience, as he kept the man's arms pinned and demonstrated several more alternative moves. Then, satisfied, he let the man go.

When Bruce returned to Seattle, the US government had their own plans for him. He was called to take a physical exam for the draft board as a prelude to possible service in Vietnam.

Surprisingly he was considered to be physically unacceptable to the US Army (due to an undescended testicle).

If Bruce Lee was unsuited for work as a waiter, then he was hardly cut out to be a soldier. He probably would have been court-martialled within a week of being inducted into the armed forces. Not only did he hate routine and regimentation but his temper was on a hair trigger.

That summer, Linda Emery graduated and took a summer vacation job. In September she started at the university while Bruce began his junior year there as a philosophy major. One Sunday her friend Sue Ann Kay invited her along to her *kung fu* lesson. They went to Chinatown, where Bruce's class was held. Although it took place in a bare concrete basement, the atmosphere was buoyant. Linda had expected to make only this one visit, but she surprised herself by both enjoying the class and becoming one of the regular students.

Sunday afternoons were the social highlight of the week for the *kung fu* class. They were usually spent in Chinatown, where Bruce would crack jokes throughout lunch before they moved on to a cinema, often to see a samurai film. On the journey between the restaurant and the cinema, Bruce would walk in front. Suddenly, objects like an orange might come flying back at them, thrown by him. They learned to reach out and catch these without comment; it had to be instinctive. During the film Bruce would analyze the action, pointing out mistakes in the way it had been filmed. Later he would quiz everyone to see if they'd been paying attention, asking about minute details of the film, about people who'd been in the restaurant, or about the weather. Bruce used everything as an opportunity to teach his students to become more aware, and to make them aware that they could become more aware.

Bruce asked the university for permission to use the men's gym to give demonstrations, and these soon attracted more students. People began missing classes to spend time in the student union building where Bruce showed *kung fu* moves, explained the philosophy behind them and cracked jokes in between.

At other times they would train outside on a grassy area lined with trees. During one afternoon session, Bruce chased Linda Emery to one side and suggested dinner; without the others.

7
LINDA

LINDA EMERY WAS the perfect date for Bruce; she was a good listener. As they sat in the Space Needle's revolving restaurant, with the lights of Seattle turning slowly below them, Bruce overflowed with his plans for the future.

He was still living at Ruby Chow's, and was feeling both stifled and restless when Taky suggested that Bruce begin looking for premises where they could all meet and train. The students would each pay him around four dollars a week so that he could support himself and pay the rent. Bruce found a suitable place and in October 1963 he handed Ruby Chow his notice and opened the Jun Fan Gung Fu Institute on 4750 University Way, not far from the campus. A school prospectus was printed. Bruce was offering a martial arts method that was fast, efficient and economical, but he also warned that it couldn't be mastered overnight. The school occupied the entire ground floor of an apartment building where there were showers already installed. Bruce camped out in a windowless room at the back, sparsely furnished with things he'd brought back from the summer trip to Hong Kong.

While she had to keep the relationship secret from her mother and stepfather, Linda spent most evenings there with

Bruce. Linda came from a white Protestant family, and while her mother could hardly object to her having Asian friends in a school where over half the student population was black or Asian, she did draw the line at dating. Linda's mother would certainly have strong feelings about the affair but it was now obvious to Linda that her own feelings for Bruce had become even stronger.

Toward the end of 1963, when Doug Palmer returned home to Seattle for the Christmas vacation, he accompanied Bruce Lee on one of his demonstrations, this time at Garfield High School from where Palmer had graduated one year ahead of Linda's class. Here, Bruce gave the first demonstration of the 'one-inch' punch. Palmer recalls:

Garfield was a tough, inner-city high school, over half black and Asian. The class that Bruce began speaking to had several football and basketball players in it, who lounged in their seats, never having heard of *kung fu*. Bruce started out by contrasting the karate-style punch (delivered from the hip) with the *wing chun* centreline punch delivered straight from the solar plexus. He then confided that there was a punch with far greater power which could be delivered from a distance of a single inch. Some of the students were stirred from their boredom to briefly register mild amusement at the idea. Bruce asked for a volunteer to demonstrate the 'one-inch' punch on. While guys smirked at each other, Bruce singled out the biggest kid, sprawled out across his chair at the back of the class, and asked him to step forward.

The class perked up a little, giggling as Bruce stood dwarfed by his volunteer. Bruce placed his knuckles against the big guy's chest and steadied himself. 'Wait a minute,' said Bruce, suddenly. He then made a production out of finding a chair and placing it about five feet behind his stooge. 'Okay,' said Bruce, as he resumed his position. 'Now we're ready.' This had the desired effect: the students were now watching in anticipation. The big guy glanced back over his shoulder at the chair five feet behind him. Up till then, he had been laid back about it; now that it looked as if he were going to be laid out, he was damned if he was going to let a skinny little Chinese guy make a fool out of him. The big guy braced himself, one foot back. Bruce, the showman, kept up a constant patter, his arm extended and his fist touching the kid's chest. Suddenly, his arm shimmered, nothing more, and mouths fell open as the kid flew off his feet and into the waiting chair, knocking it over backwards as he sprawled ass over kettle onto the floor. Bruce now had the attention of the class.

Bruce had continued to keep in touch with James Lee, and in June 1964 they began making plans to open a second branch of Bruce's Jun Fan Institute in Oakland. Bruce had by now lost interest in completing his philosophy doctorate at the University of Washington and at the end of the term he sold his '57 Ford and shipped his furniture to Oakland. Linda drove Bruce to the airport wondering how, or even if, she fitted in with his plans. Bruce told her he wanted to have some money behind him before even thinking about marriage or a family.

The air was thick and muggy in the Long Beach Sports Arena on a July day in 1964. The air conditioning wasn't working and the crowd, there to watch the annual International Karate Tournament, was restless after sitting through hours of matches. Then Ed Parker, the sponsor of the event, went to the microphone to introduce Bruce Lee, who was to put on a demonstration of the little-known Chinese art of *kung fu*.

Ed Parker recalled, 'He was very broad-minded about things, very anti classical *kung fu*; he felt that they were all robots. So I told him that if he were to come down to the tournament and demonstrate, people would have a better cross-section of the martial arts world.'

Wearing a simple black *kung fu* suit and slippers, Bruce took the floor. Just as he had done with the students at Garfield, he drew the audience into his presentation, which climaxed with the one-inch punch as his victim flew back and gasped for breath.

Although they were impressive, Bruce was against simply doing tricks like this if they had no real point to them. The real purpose of the inch punch was to show that there is a far more powerful way of striking someone than simply by using the strength of the arm and shoulder muscles. The more relaxed the muscles are, the more energy can flow through the body. Using muscular tensions to try to do the punch, or attempting to use brute force to knock someone over, will only work to opposite effect.

Competing in the black-belt division of Ed Parker's championships that day was Filipino martial artist Dan Inosanto. Apart from studying *kenpo* karate with Parker, Inosanto also trained in the Filipino arts of *escrima* and *kali*. After the match he went to meet Bruce back at his hotel room to talk and exchange ideas and techniques. Inosanto was less than satisfied with the results of their short session.

Nowadays, Dan Inosanto still has a characteristic slightly worried look. Now approaching sixty, he still runs every day and looks as fit as he did twenty years ago, and he continues to teach at his academy in Marina del Rey, California. He recalls:

> I was completely flabbergasted! He controlled me like a baby; I couldn't do anything with him at all. He didn't really have to use much force either; he just sort of body-controlled me. I'd lost to other people before but not in the way that I lost to him; he was dominating the action completely, calling all the shots like it was a game! I couldn't sleep that night. It seemed as though everything

I'd done in the past was obsolete. He countered everything I knew without really trying. It was very frustrating.

After Ed Parker's karate tournament, Bruce and Dan Inosanto spent a lot of time together, sometimes just walking and talking or exploring old bookshops. Inosanto took over Taky Kimura's role and helped Bruce give demonstrations in the San Francisco area. These shows now followed a familiar format, including lightning-fast finger jabs, kicks and punches that stopped within a whisker of their target, Bruce testing his reflexes against a challenger, doing thumb push-ups or board-breaking. Dan Inosanto spent four days taking falls and punches for Bruce in demonstrations at the Sing Lee Theater in Los Angeles. In the evenings, at the Statler Hilton, Bruce taught him some of his fighting method, what Inosanto called 'a devastatingly improved version of *wing chun*'.

Bruce and Linda wrote to each other regularly. Linda used a post office box so that her mother wouldn't find the letters.

Soon marriage was on the cards and Bruce wondered how he was going to deal with his future mother-in-law. Facing a karate black belt was one thing; facing Linda's mother was quite another. So the formidable fighting machine suggested that they get married first, make a tactical retreat to Oakland, and then call Linda's mother with the news.

On 12 August 1964, Bruce returned to Seattle with a wedding ring lent to him by James Lee's wife. Unfortunately, after applying for the licence at the county courthouse the details of the forthcoming wedding were published in the local newspaper, as required by law. When Linda's aunt saw the announcement she phoned the Emerys to ask what had happened to her invitation. The immediate family rallied in a show of strength designed to pressure the couple into calling it off. But Bruce met them with economy and directness, telling them, 'I want to marry your daughter. By the way, I'm Chinese.'

In trying to talk the couple out of it, Linda's uncle suggested that it wouldn't be a Christian marriage, while telling Bruce that Linda couldn't do anything! 'She'll learn,' he countered.

It may have been the revelation that she was soon to become a grandmother that had Linda's mother making quick arrangements with the minister at the Seattle Congregational Church. Taky Kimura was the best man – 'the only person outside the family to be invited' he recalls proudly – while Linda's mother and grandmother gave her away. It was all so rushed that Bruce had to rent a suit for the ceremony and Linda didn't even have a wedding dress, nor was there a photographer present.

'He could at least have bought flowers,' sighed Linda's mother.

8
FIGHTING FIT

SOON AFTER BRUCE and Linda moved into James Lee's home in Oakland, James's wife died of cancer, leaving him with a young son and daughter. The five were soon one family.

A dishevelled man with iron-hard hands, James Yimm Lee was twenty years older than Bruce and a former state weight-lifting champion, amateur boxer and judo brown belt who now worked as a welder while teaching *kung fu* part-time. He was also one of the few people in the United States with any knowledge of Chinese martial arts. He had trained for years in traditional *kung fu* but had become dissatisfied with its set patterns and lack of practical training, and had developed his own informal style.

It was natural then, that James Lee realized what Bruce had to offer. Indeed, James said he learned more in the short period after they met than he had in all his former training experience, because Bruce didn't teach obsolete routines but only the essence of self-defence in situations that weren't prearranged.

James and Bruce became partners and opened the second branch of the Jun Fan Gung Fu Institute on Broadway in

Oakland. There were few students at first, but Taky Kimura subsidized their income by insisting that they receive all the takings from the Institute in Seattle.

Neither of Bruce's schools was ever conceived as an out and out commercial venture. Bruce wasn't simply trying to attract as many paying customers as possible; he wanted students who showed both ability and commitment, not overnight wonders. What he offered had to be taught on a one to one basis; it wasn't simply a matter of lining up students and practising moves. Bruce needed to understand each student's particular natural physical advantages and weaknesses, temperament and attitude. Each student had to progress in a different way. So Dan Inosanto, for example, was able to realize that he first needed to free himself from mental tension in order to progress further.

Bruce explained that mere technical knowledge is only the beginning of *kung fu*; to master it, one must enter into the spirit of it. To this end he refused to offer ready-made moves but encouraged his students to be alert and to experience what was actually happening so as to 'solve the problems' for themselves.

For a while Bruce succeeded in his hope of avoiding the kind of conflict he'd had with the students of other martial arts schools in Hong Kong. Rule 9 of the institute called for discretion when explaining the school's training methods to others, so as not to stir up ill feeling and rivalry with other schools. Ironically, the first trouble came early in 1965 from a Chinese *kung fu* instructor just across the bay in San Francisco.

Wong Jak Man had recently arrived from Hong Kong to teach *kung fu*. Seeking to make a name for himself, he presented Bruce with a written challenge to fight, with the loser having to close his school. Behind this challenge there also lay the traditional martial arts community's objection to Bruce teaching their secrets to Westerners who already had the natural advantages of size and strength. Wong and several colleagues turned up for the appointed fight with a long list of rules for the contest: no eye jabs, no groin kicks and so on. Bruce was incensed by this and became so eager to meet the challenge that Wong quickly suggested a more formal sparring match to decide the issue. But Bruce would have none of this and, unable to back down in front of his colleagues, Wong apparently had no choice but to see it through.

According to the reports of onlookers, the fight was anything but smooth, fast or efficient. After a scrappy exchange Wong turned to run and his entourage tried to step in, but were intercepted by James Lee. Bruce went after Wong, punching him on the back of the head, but was unable to land a finishing shot.

As Bruce later told Dan Inosanto:

> I chased him and, like a fool, kept punching his head and back; my fists were already swelling from his hard head. Then I did something I'd never done before: I just put my arm round his neck and knocked him on his ass. I kept whacking him as he lay on the floor until he gave up. I was so tired I could hardly punch him.

Bruce turned the delegation off the premises and they left without another word.

Linda found Bruce cooling off on the back porch, looking despondent and anything but satisfied with his victory. Bruce was deeply annoyed that what should have taken a few seconds had taken over three minutes, leaving him winded and facing the fact that he was in less than optimum condition. In public Bruce admitted to no faults, but in private he was mercilessly self-critical.

As a result of this fight, Bruce began to examine both his fighting and his training methods. As he searched among the traditional styles and within himself, he realized that every martial art was essentially incomplete. What was required to go beyond the mere technical confines and shortcomings of any martial art? This was the question which had now taken root in him.

Encouraged by James Lee, Bruce began an intensive programme of physical conditioning. He started every day with an early-morning run of several miles, often with Bobo, the Great Dane he had named after his childhood pet Alsatian, Bobby. For Bruce, running was also a kind of meditation, an opportunity to let things flow. Houses, cars and trees passed along with his thoughts, feelings and sensations. After lunch there was another run or an hour on the exercise bike.

Conditioning exercises were included in the regime, centred mainly on the abdomen, using the tried and tested boxing method of having a heavy medicine ball thrown at his midsection, along with sit-ups and leg raises. As Bruce's new approach took shape, he lost no time in criticizing the old guard: 'There are lots of guys around the world that are lazy. They have big fat guts. They talk about *ch'i* power and things they can do, but don't believe it.'

James also started Bruce on weight training. At first he did reverse curls all day to develop his forearms, but once he saw how it might add strength to his speed, he bought a full set of weights and used them consistently. Bruce did everything he could to maintain his muscular gains, and also began experimenting with high-protein weight-gain drinks that he blended himself and supplemented with ginseng, royal jelly and massive doses of vitamins.

Once committed to a course of action, Bruce would take it to the limit. His workout schedule listed the number of repetitions of the exercises he had set himself to do; beside some was the note 'INF' – meaning to infinity. He would keep going until he could go no further – and then keep going.

Even out of the gym, Bruce never stopped training in some way or other. Back in the 1950s, every schoolboy had cut out a newspaper coupon to send away for details of a bodybuilding method known as Dynamic Tension. Charles Atlas had built a mail-order empire by promising to help 100-pound weaklings get revenge against bullies who'd kicked sand in their faces. Dynamic Tension was in fact an exercise system known as isometrics in which one group of muscles works against an opposing group – for example, by gripping the hands in front of the chest and trying to pull them apart without letting go – or by working against a dead weight. Standing next to a wall in casual conversation with someone, Bruce would push against it with the back of his hand to 'flow the energy' in his triceps.

Bruce utilized whatever was to hand: he practised kick power by kicking trees until they were jarred by the force; he practised accuracy by kicking at pieces of litter that had been blown up by the breeze. And where no particular training equipment existed to meet his needs, he would invent it and then call on James Lee's welding skills to construct it.

Go into any modern well equipped martial arts school and you will find a variety of practice apparatus. There will be a 'heavy bag' for punching and kicking at full power; a 'top-and-bottom speed bag' which springs back only if punched in a straight line; a selection of smaller bags (with various fillings); and padded mitts to practise punching with accuracy and power. You might also find air-filled kicking shields to practise depth of penetration and kicking on the move; and there will almost certainly be a loop-and-pulley device to stretch the legs.

All these types of equipment were assembled in James Lee's garage. Yet even with the most comprehensive array of training equipment to be found anywhere at that time, Bruce was still finding ways of getting even more from it to increase both his own and James Lee's skills. The *wing chun* wooden dummy was adapted with a spring-loaded head; bags were mounted on spring-loaded platforms so as to fly back unpredictably, or built oversize so that extra power was needed to make any impact.

Bruce also tried to get a little more out of the equipment by investing extra energy in his approach to it. The heavy bag wasn't punched 'passively'; Bruce visualized it as an opponent he actually had to fight – ducking and sidestepping, moving in and out. What was most valuable, he felt, was real sparring against an untrained and uncoordinated fighter, who added to the problems to be solved by his sheer unpredictability.

By this combination of methods, the basic attributes of stamina, strength, flexibility and economy were gained by running, weight training, stretching and a sparring method designed to find the most direct route to the target. Bruce tried always to add an extra element to his training, yet he knew perfectly well that it wasn't merely force and vigour that made an effective fighter but also the degree of timing and relaxation he could bring to all his physical skills.

For Bruce Lee, the spirit in which everything was carried out was as important as technique, and this required harnessing one's mental and emotional forces. The secret of this emotional content was a kind of purposefully directed anger. Once, while Bruce was showing Taky a move, he wasn't satisfied with the way Taky was doing it and casually slapped him hard across the face. Taky's eyes narrowed; forgetting it was Bruce, he moved in aggressively. 'Yes!' said Bruce, laughing. 'That's what I want!' Bruce tried anything in training that would add some of the emotions of anger and fear stirred up in real confrontation, while trying to remain centred under the stress by heightening the senses and searching for a simple flowing approach to combat.

Before long, Bruce had become so powerful and effective that he could only go all out on the wooden dummy; it became too dangerous to do so on a person. Anyone holding an air shield for Bruce to kick would usually end up on his back; one unsuspecting visitor who held a punching mitt for Bruce had his shoulder dislocated with the force of the blow. Even so, the power that Bruce could channel wasn't merely the result of conditioning and training methods but arose, at its source, from regular periods of meditation – the wellspring of *ch'i*. Bruce was less inclined to talk about meditating than fighting, but the first item on his daily list of things to do was always 'Meditation and Mental Training'. In this time, he simply sat and focused his attention throughout his body, allowing his mind to settle and his senses to register what is present everywhere. To use the Zen expression, he would 'empty his cup' so that it might be refilled.

One evening after a long day's training and teaching, Bruce and Linda went out to dinner at a restaurant in San Francisco. After being shown to a table, Bruce thought he recognized one of the waiters on the other side of the room. Sensing Bruce's gaze on him, the man looked up and his eyes widened as the tea he was pouring for a customer spilled over the edge of the cup and ran onto the table. The waiter was Wong Jak Man.

9
SCREEN TEST

ALSO PRESENT AT Bruce's demonstration at the Long Beach tournament in July 1964 was Jay Sebring, the owner of a Beverly Hills hair salon, who also trained with Ed Parker. What he saw that afternoon impressed him as much as it did everyone else. One of Sebring's clients was William Dozier, a TV producer whose credits included the *Gunsmoke* and *Perry Mason* series. Once when Dozier was getting a haircut, he mentioned to Sebring that he was looking for someone to play the part of Charlie Chan's son in a new series about the Chinese detective. Sebring suggested he get in touch with Bruce Lee.

On 1 February 1965 at East Oakland Hospital, Linda gave birth to a son, Brandon Bruce Lee. Three days and as many sleepless nights later, Bruce found himself in front of the cameras at the studios of Twentieth Century-Fox, to take part in a screen test for a possible role in the *Charlie Chan* TV series.

On a chair in the centre of what looked like a smart suburban living room sat a young man, wearing a neat black suit that looked a size too small, a white shirt and a black tie with a small tight knot; his hair was short and neatly brushed. He sat with his legs crossed and his hands clasped together, and smiled nervously – a quiet and unassuming man whose face might even have been said to look slightly chubby. Suddenly he glanced somewhere over to his left where from the darkness a voice instructed: 'Now, Bruce, look into the camera lens and tell us your name, age and where you were born.'

'My name is Lee, Bruce Lee. I was born in San Francisco. I am twenty-four right now.'

'And you worked in motion pictures in Hong Kong?'

'Yes, since I was around six years old.'

'And when did you leave Hong Kong?'

'1959, when I was eighteen.'

'I see. Now look over to me, Bruce, as we talk,' continued the director. 'I understand you've just had a baby boy and you've lost a little sleep.'

'Yeah.' Bruce laughed. 'Three nights.' His voice fluttered with nervousness and his facial expressions were all a little exaggerated.

'You told me earlier today that karate and ju jitsu are not the most powerful forms of Oriental fighting. Which are the best?' asked the director.

'Well, I think *kung fu* is pretty good,' came the untypically modest reply. After further prompting, Bruce continued. '*Kung fu* is a more complete system and it's more fluid.'

Recalling the time that Yip Man sent him away from the school to think things over, the day he had spent walking by the water, Bruce began to compare the principle of *kung fu* to the nature of water. 'You cannot punch it and hurt it, you cannot grasp hold of it. Every *kung fu* man is trying to do that: to be flexible, to adapt to the opponent.'

'What's the difference between a karate punch and a *kung fu* punch?' came a further question.

'Well,' replied Bruce, 'a karate punch is like being hit by an iron bar – whack!' He paused for a moment and smiled. 'A *kung fu* punch is like being hit by an iron ball swung on an iron chain – WHANG! – and it hurts inside.'

After a fresh reel of film was loaded, Bruce acted out some of the characters from classical Chinese theatre, demonstrating the moves and gestures that represent the scholar and the warrior.

'Now show us some *kung fu* movements,' said the director.

'Well, it's hard to show it alone, but I'll do my best.'

A middle-aged man with silver hair and spectacles, a member of the studio staff, was 'volunteered' as Bruce's stooge, to the delight of his sniggering colleagues. Bruce caught the atmosphere and suddenly warmed to the situation, joking, 'Accidents do happen!'

'There are various kinds of fights,' he began. 'It depends on where you hit and what weapon you will be using. To the eyes, you will use the fingers.' Bruce threw a lightning *bil jee* strike towards the man's eyes. The old man looked more than worried. 'Don't worry,' Bruce assured him, and whipped out another jab to his eyes. 'And to the face,' added Bruce as his punches made an audible rush of air, lashing within an inch of the man's nose as he explained that the power of the punches came from the waist.

The director stepped out in front of the camera for a moment to adjust Bruce and the old man more towards the camera.

The subdued chuckles from the floor became belly laughs and Bruce joined in the conspiracy with the studio technicians, trying to hide his laughter with his hand across his face. The director, sensing the hapless volunteer's rising desperation, asked Bruce to back off a little.

'You know, *kung fu* is very sneaky,' said Bruce, 'just like the Chinese.'

The old man was jumping like a rabbit. 'These are just natural reactions,' he pleaded.

Bruce patted him on the shoulder to reassure him. 'Right!' said Bruce, who had spent years of training to replace such 'human reactions' with more useful ones. 'Then there is the jab, the punch, the backfist . . . and then low!' he exclaimed as he whipped out three strikes that had the air whistling around the man's head, and then dropped low to strike at the groin as soon as the man's hands had automatically moved up to protect his face.

'Then there are the kicks, straight to the groin, then up!' And, just as fast as the punches, there came a front kick to the groin, a roundhouse kick and a hook kick to the head. 'He looks kind of worried,' added Bruce casually, now in complete command of the situation.

Everyone realized the speed and accuracy of Bruce Lee's movement. The technicians laughed openly, both at their colleague's predicament and in amazed disbelief at something none of them had ever seen before.

'He's got nothing to worry about,' said the director confidently. 'Now show us how a good *kung fu* man would coolly handle it and walk away.' But before Bruce could demonstrate this, the reel of film ran out.

Although the Chinese use the different attributes of various animals as the basis for their system of casting horoscopes and understanding character types, martial arts' imitation of animals puts us more in mind of the American Indian relationship to 'power animals'. The Native American calls upon his spirit ally to empower his actions – whether it is the keen eye of the eagle, the swiftness of the deer or the healing ability of the bear that he wishes to embody. In the same way, martial arts' animal forms originated from the dances of a shaman imbued with the animal's spirit. As with any true mythological tradition, the emphasis is not so much on the actual physical form of the animal as on its vital energy. In the Shaolin tradition imitating each animal developed a particular attribute. For example, the tiger strengthened bone; the dragon brought strength of spirit. Bruce Lee's first experience of the animal fighting styles was watching Master Kwan's films as a boy.

'Practising alone involves forms – imitating, for instance, a crane, a monkey or a praying mantis,' said Bruce, when filming recommenced. Now, despite the tight suit he was wearing, Bruce completed his screen test by demonstrating the crane form, stretching his arms and weaving them in a fluid motion which at one moment suggested both the neck, head and beak of a great bird and its flapping wings. Suddenly he stabbed out a strike and then kicked high above his head, '*Biaah!*' an animal shriek followed by another fierce jab, before slowing the routine and looking over, almost bowing for a second, to the director, who said, 'Show us one more and then we're all finished.'

As Bruce tried to pull his shirtsleeves and suit jacket back into shape, he continued, taking a forward stance with his hands extended and the fingers curled into claws as he ran through the tiger form.

'Thank you very much.'

A week later, Bruce's father died in Hong Kong. With the new baby just arrived, Bruce decided to go alone to the funeral. While he was away Linda visited her mother, who had still not entirely accepted her daughter's marriage. When Linda arrived in Seattle with baby Brandon in her arms, her mother greeted her with 'How could you have done this?'

In Hong Kong, Bruce arrived at the mortuary where his father's remains lay and crawled from the front door to the coffin, wailing loudly for good measure. Chinese tradition requires penance from a son who was not present at his father's death. Bruce's noisy atonement perhaps brought some peace to Lee Hoi Cheun's soul.

Two weeks later, when Bruce and Linda were back together in Oakland, William Dozier called to say that the *Charlie Chan* series had been shelved. But he added that a good audience reaction to his new *Batman* series would allow him to follow it with an entirely new series, *The Green Hornet*, using the same formula of an adventure series hero and his sidekick. Bruce was signed to a one-year option.

In May 1965, the Lee family boarded a plane back to Hong Kong. In one of those little ironies that life sometimes arranges, the combined airfare came to $1,800, the exact amount that Bruce had just been paid by Dozier.

Life at Nathan Road was not smooth. Grace Lee was still suffering from the death of her husband while Linda was struggling with a baby who cried most of the night in the sweltering heat. While Linda didn't encounter the same prejudice that Bruce had endured from her family, she was unable to speak more than a few words of Cantonese and felt left out. Bruce tried to smooth things over by joking that the new member of the family was the only blond-haired Chinaman in the world, while adding to Linda's problems by promising everyone that she would cook them a wonderful meal.

Batman was well received and *The Green Hornet* was to follow it into production, but William Dozier still had no idea when. Bruce made regular calls to the States about the series from Hong Kong, but made no attempt to contact any of his friends and colleagues in the Hong Kong movie industry, even though most of them were still active in the business. This indicates that it was in America that Bruce intended to make something of himself.

During the four months Bruce and Linda spent in Hong

Kong, Bruce settled the details of his father's estate. He and Linda went on occasional outings or shopping trips and went sightseeing. And Bruce took Brandon to visit Yip Man, to ask a favour of him.

Hawkins Cheung was back in Hong Kong at the time and the two of them happened upon each other in the street. Says Cheung:

> I was just about to say Hello when Bruce stepped in very quickly – I was surprised at his fast movement. His character hadn't changed at all: he still wanted to be top dog. Bruce told me, 'I have to train very hard to beat my opponents, so I've come back to learn more of the dummy techniques from the Old Man. I want to film him so that I can show my students in America. I'm on my way to see him now.'
>
> A few days later, Bruce gave a demonstration on a popular TV chat show. He didn't say anything about *wing chun* or Yip Man and I suspected that something had happened between them. I knew Bruce's character: if he wanted something, no one would stop him. If they did, then Bruce would go out on his own and then come back and show you. I found out that the Old Man had refused to be filmed doing the wooden dummy form. His traditional thinking had come up against Bruce's Western thinking.

For the rest of his stay Bruce continued his intense training regime at a local gym. The activity alternated with long periods of deep thought as he considered a complete break with tradition to forge his own martial arts way. At the same time, he was starting to feel concern about how he was going to earn enough to provide for his family.

10

THE GREEN HORNET

IN SEPTEMBER 1965, Bruce, Linda and baby Brandon returned to Seattle where they went to stay with Linda's family. Brandon was still not sleeping through the night. His howling throughout most of the day was punctuated by remarks from Linda's mother, who was given to wondering out loud when Bruce was going to get himself a proper job.

For Bruce, this was a time of having to turn inward even though the need to push forward with his ambitions was becoming more intense. He read everything he could about all aspects of fighting, while he also studied the teachings of the Buddha, Lao Tzu and Krishnamurti. During these months of relative inactivity, Bruce also began to suffer from backache.

The Lee family hardly had time to settle back into James Lee's house in Oakland when the call came through from William Dozier that *The Green Hornet* was to start shooting in three months' time.

In March 1966 the Lees moved to Los Angeles, into a small apartment at Wilshire and Gayley in Westwood, an upmarket area in the west of the city. It was Bruce and Linda's first home of their own since they'd married. Realizing that he was now going to be paid $400 for each episode of *The Green Hornet*, Bruce did what any man would do: he went out and bought a new car, a modest blue Chevy Nova.

The Green Hornet had been one of America's most popular radio serials of the 1930s. Created by writer George W. Trendle, the character was the nephew of another of Trendle's fictional characters, Dan Reid, better known as *The Lone Ranger*. At night, Britt Reid (played by Van Williams) changed his business suit for green clothes and a mask to become the scourge of criminals. Bruce was cast as the hero's chauffeur and sidekick, Kato. He wore a chauffeur's uniform and a mask and drove their own version of the Batmobile, the Black Beauty.

Thirty half-hour episodes were planned. Bruce was naturally most concerned about how the action was to be staged. At first the fights were planned to be like the slugging matches seen in westerns. Perhaps recalling the Wong Jak Man fight, Bruce refused to take this approach, saying that the essence of his *kung fu* was efficiency. As compensation, he suggested that the fights be shown in slow motion, an idea since used many times. When it came to filming the fight scenes, Bruce was actually forced to slow down his movements because they only registered as a blur when filmed at normal speed. At the director's insistence, Bruce agreed to some flashy flying kicks for visual impact, but not before he'd pointed out that, in a real fight, moves like that would get you into serious trouble.

The series premiered on 9 September 1966. Over a jazzy version of 'The Flight of the Bumble Bee', a voice intoned dramatically: 'Another challenge for the Green Hornet, his aide Kato, and their rolling arsenal the Black Beauty! On police records a wanted criminal, the Green Hornet is really Britt Reid, owner-publisher of the *Daily Sentinel*. His dual identity is known only to his secretary and the district attorney. And now, to protect the rights and lives of decent citizens rides The Green Hornet!' The narrator, the same as the one who opened the *Batman* shows, was the producer himself, William Dozier.

The first episode introduced the American television audience to *kung fu*. In the opening scene of act two, the Hornet and Kato are surprised by three hoods. Kato kicks a wooden box into their midst, distracting them for the instant that he needs to act. The fight is short and sweet – a few fast kicks and powerful punches. In a following fight scene Kato overcomes gun-toting criminals by flinging poison darts at them.

Along with Kato's poison darts, the Hornet carried a gun that shot a powerful but non-lethal sleep-inducing gas. The Hornet's 'sting' was a collapsible device that fired an ultrasonic beam powerful enough to shatter metal. Kato mainly used his fists and feet, though in one episode he introduced a Chinese weapon, the *nunchaku*: two short sticks joined together by a linking cord. The team's rolling arsenal, the Black Beauty, was a matt-black 1966 Chrysler Imperial adapted by Hollywood car customizer Dean Jeffries at a cost of $50,000. The car was armed with rockets and other deadly devices; its headlights were green, allowing the heroes to see four miles ahead at night with the aid of a built-in camera. The car was stored underground in Britt Reid's garage, suspended upside down on a rotating platform ready to replace his convertible when he set out as the Green Hornet. Access to the Hornet's stronghold was through a hole in a Candy Mints poster, an early bit of product placement.

The series marked the first time that *kung fu* had been seen in the West outside the movie theatres of the Chinatown districts, and younger viewers were astonished by what they saw. The real star of *The Green Hornet* was Kato, and Bruce, in character, was soon making personal appearances all across the country, sometimes several stops in one day. He did the usual round of local radio guest spots and TV shows, opened supermarkets and appeared at fairs, in public parks or at martial arts tournaments.

Although Bruce was a natural showman and often an outright show-off, he put limits on how far he was prepared to exploit his skills even at the then handsome fee of $1,000 or more per appearance. He exclaimed again and again that he had no time for tricks like breaking boards, adding 'boards don't hit back'. Although he was mobbed by enthusiastic fans on these public appearances, he was hardly getting his face known by appearing as Kato, wearing a mask!

Surprisingly, nearly half of Bruce's fan mail was from young girls. In reply to one of these letters, he wrote:

> *Dear Vicki,*
>
> *The art I use on TV is not* karate. *It is the ancestor of* karate *and is known as* gung fu, *which is of Chinese origin (so is* karate*).*
>
> *Breaking boards and bricks are mere stunts and are not recommended for anyone, especially a girl like you. Technique is the main goal you should work at. If you want to break something, use a hammer.*
>
> *Thank you for writing. I enjoyed your letter very much.*

Younger audiences loved the show but, because it was played straight, adults weren't as enthusiastic, preferring the more camp *Batman*. As 'real' characters, Kato and the Green Hornet were simply unbelievable, which was particularly ironic given that this was probably the first time any real fighting skills had been seen on TV outside the boxing ring.

The Green Hornet closed on 14 July 1967, after twenty-six weekly episodes, finishing with an additional two-part show in which the Green Hornet and Kato teamed up with Batman and Robin in a crossover episode to launch the second *Batman* series.

At first, the Green Hornet and Kato battle Batman and Robin (who manages to match the skills of the world's pre-eminent martial artist). The director, not wanting to upset fans of either series, had Batman and Robin fight the Hornet and Kato to a draw. Eventually, all four combine their resources to defeat the villainous stamp thief, Colonel Gumm. As he read the script for the final episode, an ironic grin spread across Bruce Lee's face.

On the day of the filming, Bruce maintained an icy silence but his eyes burned through the holes in the mask he wore. Once or twice actor Burt Ward, who played Robin, cracked a feeble joke. When the cameras rolled for the fight scene, Bruce began to stalk his opponent menacingly. Ward backed away, spluttering that it was only a TV show. Bruce ignored him and closed in. Offstage someone squawked like a chicken. Bruce exploded into laughter, unable to keep up the act any longer. 'Lucky it is a TV show,' he added with a wry smile.

The Hornet and Kato made one other TV appearance, on the *Milton Berle Show* during the 1966–7 season. They appeared in a comedy skit in which Berle was cast as a stuntman supposedly working on an episode of their show.

With the cancellation of *The Green Hornet*, the Lees were soon on the move once more. Although the large twenty-third-floor apartment in nearby Barrington Plaza was one they could hardly afford, Bruce arranged to give martial arts lessons to the landlord in return for a rent reduction. The landlord, as it turned out, had similar arrangements with many of the tenants and soon both he and the Lees were uprooted.

Despite the fact that it was Bruce who had generated almost all of the fan mail for *The Green Hornet*, further roles did not materialize. Now he felt as if he'd taken a step backwards. While continuing to make occasional appearances as Kato,

Bruce again directed his energy into what he knew best – teaching *kung fu*.

As a teacher, Bruce's role was to expose his students' vulnerability. But privately he was now having to endure his own. Introspection and inactivity had been followed by success and then disappointment. As he would have to do again and again, Bruce was now forced to strike a tenuous balance between his ambitions and his art.

11
JEET KUNE DO

ONE DAY BRUCE LEE and Dan Inosanto were driving along, talking about swordsmanship. Bruce said that the most efficient way of countering in fencing is the 'stop-hit', in which you parry and counter all in one move; that is, when the opponent attacks, you intercept the move with a thrust of your own. The idea is to score a hit in the middle of your attacker's action, making it the most economical of all counters.

Bruce then said, 'We should call our method the stop-hitting fist style, or the intercepting fist style.'

'What would that be in Chinese?' asked Inosanto. 'That would be *jeet kune do*,' said Bruce.

More than once, Bruce Lee came to regret coining the phrase *jeet kune do*. 'It's just a name, don't fuss over it,' he said. 'There's no such thing as a style if you understand the roots of combat.' Bruce Lee certainly had no intention of creating a new martial arts style.

As someone once remarked about religion, 'Put every great teacher together in a room, and they'd agree about everything; put their disciples in there and they'd argue about everything!'

The same is true of the martial arts, and Bruce Lee anticipated this might well be the fate of his own teaching. He often commented on the similarity between the martial arts and religions: that the classical arts were just as restricting and out of touch with life as were dogmatic and fundamentalist religions.

In the same way, Bruce Lee did not believe that one should put one's faith in others or wait passively to be shown 'the way', but considered that each person must take individual responsibility. Once, when asked if he believed in God, he replied, 'If there is a God, he is within. You don't ask God to give you things, you depend on God for your inner theme.'

Centring his own approach in the timeless precepts of Taoism and Zen, Bruce was more concerned with embodying the living spirit that flows through all real art, religion and philosophy. But this spirit is only alive at the very moment that it is being experienced. Spiritual enlightenment or philosoph-ical insight can only be understood in the very moment of its actual experience and not by someone who later reads (or writes) a description of it. Bruce Lee knew that a martial art can only be understood through actual experience. Any description, including the following, must not be mistaken for the lived experience.

In essence, this experience involves the intimate relationship between the physical and spiritual aspects of energy (for which Bruce used the expression 'body feel') echoing Bodhidharma's teaching that in reality body and spirit are inseparable.

The first requirement lies in developing an overall feeling of relaxation. The more subtle universal energies can only be experienced in the body once all personal tensions – physical, emotional and mental – have been allowed to fall away from every part of the body. Essentially, this is the process of meditation, which can be practised both in stillness and in movement; even, eventually, while sparring and fighting. To this end, relaxation is practised initially to get the feel of it and then repeatedly so it may be called on voluntarily even in the most stressful situations.

At the same time that Bruce was discovering all this, Western body-mind therapists such as Wilhelm Reich and F. M. Alexander had also become aware that the revelations of the spirit take place in the body. Awareness of posture and balance and feelings of gracefulness or awkwardness serve as a constant and accurate guide to one's psychological state. It is interesting that the English word 'grace' itself implies both ease of movement and the descent of spiritual energy. As the *I Ching* says, 'By adopting a certain physical posture, a resonant chord is struck in Spirit.'

Bruce Lee described how a student learning a martial art passes through three stages. In the first stage, he or she understands very little about the art of combat. In a fight, all of the student's blocks or strikes would be instinctive and automatic reactions; but, at the same time, they would be uncontrolled and mostly inaccurate. For example, in the event of a surprise attack in a dark street, the untrained reaction is to withdraw defensively or to lash out wildly, to freeze or flail, rather than to fight efficiently. Action at this stage is often no more than an angry or fearful reaction.

The second stage involves a long period of training in which the student learns various techniques of striking, kicking and blocking. The student finds that he or she must move and breathe in a completely new way, which means that one's thinking and feeling will also change. In fighting or sparring there will at times be moments of 'psychic stoppage', where the student freezes for a moment to analyze what is happening and calculates a response. For the time being, the student loses the ability to fight instinctively.

The final stage, when the right moves happen automatically, involves a combination of factors. The transition from uncoordinated effort to skill is made only through repeated practice of the actual technique. This opens and then refines the appropriate bioelectrical circuits in the nervous system. Before fighting strategy can even be considered, basic technical skill combined with a relaxed feel has to be established.

Although relaxation is a physical state, it can only take place when the mind directs attention to the body. Both relaxation and repetition are effective only when allied to what is even more essential: the process of paying attention. The mind must direct attention to the physical movement being practised in order to stop it becoming a mechanical gesture. In this way, the movement may become more refined and efficient.

At first, then, attention allows the development of 'body feel'. Eventually, while being maintained in the body, it must also be extended out to one's external world. This peripheral awareness can then become the basis of strategic fighting. Only then can attention be devoted to solving the problem of the opponent's attacks and defence.

Attention is an increasingly rare commodity in modern times. The fast cuts of MTV videos and the politicians' sound bites on TV news are designed for an audience with a minimal attention span, who are either unwilling or unable to invest the energy needed to really see and listen. Bruce Lee knew that the difficult process of developing strong and continuous attention is essential to the martial artist.

Fighting skill depends on registering shifts and lapses in the attention (and thus intention) of our opponent, so that we can sense where and how to respond or initiate our own attack. Ultimately, strategy depends on being able to control our opponent's body by controlling his attention. But until we can master our own awareness, how can we have any chance of influencing another's?

To summarize, the objective of training is to supersede wrong or inappropriate reflexes with right ones. At first the student will punch any old way. Then he or she practises for a long time to discover a new way. Eventually this new way becomes instinctual.

This is the essential meaning of an aphorism which Bruce took directly from Zen tradition (and in which he simply replaced 'clouds and mountains' with 'kicks and punches'):

> Before I practised the Way, a cloud was just a cloud and a mountain was just a mountain. After I'd studied the Way, a cloud was no longer a cloud, a mountain no longer a mountain. Now that I understand the Way, a cloud is again just a cloud, a mountain is just a mountain.

The three stages of learning are not unique to the martial arts. Anyone who has learned to use a computer, drive a car, or play a musical instrument will recall the same process taking place.

At first one can do nothing much at all – maybe get a few noises out of an instrument or type a painfully slow letter. After some instruction and practice, things improve a little. But movements will still be stiff, too exaggerated or too tense. There will also be occasional moments when one has to stop and think about it. This is the stage where the musician learns the scales and can play simple pieces or is able to copy a few simple phrases from different records, and maybe even string one or two of them together while managing to stay in tempo.

After a lot of practice and experience, the subconscious mind begins to take over the process. When I am driving a car and someone runs out into the road, I don't have to think about how to brake or take evasive action; there is an instant reflex. In the normal course of events, I can drive without thinking about it; I am able to hold a conversation and at the same time have a peripheral awareness of what is going on in the world at large, further down the road.

At a similar stage, the musician is able to improvise tunes with different moods or play written music with some individual expression. He may even have developed a recognizable style. At this stage if he plays a simple piece, it is no longer stiff or clumsy, there is both a flow and an authority to it, perhaps even some spirit. He may even surprise himself by playing something he's never heard before. He may even begin to know, to feel that in some places it might be best to leave a silence.

Dan Inosanto likened the process to that of learning to read. 'Eventually, you learn to read groups of words. Where a student will see three motions, the experienced man will see one, because he sees the overall energy path.'

Interestingly, a professional golfer said in a recent interview that he knew he was really on top of his game when, just before he played a shot, he could 'see the energy lines' that ran from the ball to the hole.

Bruce Lee was aiming to instill in his students the physical, emotional and mental coordination that would allow the spontaneous and spirited flow of the appropriate actions in combat. In short he wanted people to fight as naturally as catching a ball thrown to them.

At this level of ability, the martial artist is beyond trying to 'do' techniques, everything just flows, simply and directly, according to the training that has been experienced. Now, there is no separation between the fighter and the fight itself.

I am reminded of a line by the poet W. B. Yeats, who asks, 'How do you tell the dancer from the dance?' The answer is you can't. In the same way, how can a dancer separate his or her own experience of dancing from the dance itself? Again, the answer is that it can't be done. The same applies to fighting.

At this level of experience, technique and strategy mean simply fitting into the opponent's movements and intentions, neither opposing any attacking force head-on with too much resistance or aggression, nor giving way completely. Pliable as a spring, the fighter becomes the complement of the opponent's energy. Understanding and experiencing the inter-play of energy involved, the fighter no longer feels himself separate from either his opponent or the fight itself. He no longer opposes or struggles but simply completes his own half of a single whole. The fighter and the fight take on an ego-less impartial quality in which the conflict resolves itself naturally.

This is a level of ability that can neither be anticipated nor imitated. It can only unfold from within. It is not reached by learning more and more techniques, but by moving to an entirely new level of perception where things are in essence much simpler.

Bruce Lee firmly rejected the idea that learning is a process of accumulation. Mastery is approached, he said, not through acquiring more and more knowledge, but through stripping away the inessentials. A stone sculptor, rather than building up with clay, instead chisels away everything not needed, revealing the underlying form hidden inside the material. In line with this analogy, Bruce often referred to his kicks and punches as 'tools'.

Bruce found it both difficult and frustrating to try and teach people right from the beginning. *Jeet kune do* was a conceptual approach, a philosophy. As such, it was of use only to people like himself: experienced martial artists who were willing to search further.

12
STUDENT/MASTER

AFTER IMPROVISING FOR several months in various temporary locations including Wayne Chan's pharmacy in Chinatown, Bruce Lee opened his third school in February 1967 at 628 College Street in the Chinatown district of Los Angeles, just a few blocks from Dodger Stadium. The institute, like those in Seattle and Oakland, was in an anonymous building. On Bruce's orders, no visitors from outside were allowed in the school. To ensure complete privacy the windows were painted over with red enamel paint. Dan Inosanto was appointed Bruce's assistant instructor and membership was strictly limited to martial artists who showed talent. If Bruce found a martial artist who already had some grounding or someone who could use what he had to offer, then he was prepared to teach for free.

Jerry Poteet, an early student in Los Angeles, recalls, 'I was short of money and unable to pay for training. Bruce wrote me a letter saying, "Come on in. Forget about paying until you can. You're sincere and that's what counts."'

Bruce encouraged his students to train in their street clothes, saying this is what they would most likely be wearing if they were involved in a fight. While he liked to keep things relaxed and friendly, he could be strict when the situation demanded. He once addressed the whole class: 'I know that a lot of us are friends and, outside of the school, I'm Bruce. But in here you call me *sifu*. Because of the informality, there has to be some discipline. If this school was in China, there would be a lot of people here now missing their front teeth.'

Classical martial arts training combined the development of strength with testing a student's patience and sincerity by having him spend considerable time standing in the deep wide horse stances. But Bruce saw this practice as being divorced from the reality of fighting and as pointless as learning to swim on dry land. Yet the first few months of training with him saw a similar kind of probationary period. Each week included several gruelling sessions of physical conditioning, and quite a few fell by the wayside. Serious teaching began for those who remained.

Dan Lee, now a *t'ai chi* instructor in Pasadena, California, was an electrical engineer and language instructor and the Los Angeles school's first pupil in 1967. 'Part of the high standards that Bruce maintained involved giving everyone a personal fitness programme,' says Dan. 'He looked at you and saw what area you needed to work on most. He really meant business and worked very hard. He was the one person I respected most. He was a straightforward person, intense but most of all honest. He didn't hold back any punches.'

Dan Lee's last remark has a double edge to it. While Bruce insisted on discipline in his classes, he was still struggling to harness his own volatile temper. One night after class, Dan Inosanto, Dan Lee and Bruce were in Bruce's kitchen at home. Bruce got out some boxing gloves and challenged Dan Lee to a knockabout. While they were jabbing at each other, Dan got through with a lucky punch. Bruce went after Dan Lee for real and as Dan Inosanto recounts, 'broke his jaw as he followed him, hitting him with short punches, all the way down to the ground. He must have hit him fifteen or twenty times, or at least it looked that many. It was all incredibly fast, but he did control the blows.'

'Yes, it happened,' says Dan Lee. 'It was a long time ago. I was very privileged to work with Bruce Lee.'

Dan Inosanto adds, 'If Bruce had one drawback, I think it was that temper he had. He told me once that it was because he was in a rush to educate people and wanted fast results.'

Bruce didn't have years to spend on building the foundation that he himself had received in Hong Kong. He simply could not spend the time needed on one-to-one sticking hands practice to induce the required awareness. Bruce would work at the highest level from the moment students walked through the door. With no previous experience of these methods, students must have been left overwhelmed and bewildered.

Yet Bruce could also be compassionate. 'I was in a sporting goods store with Bruce,' says Dan Inosanto, 'when I saw a set of weights I wanted to buy, until I realized that I only had twelve dollars on me. Bruce said that while we were there, he should probably buy a set of weights for Brandon. I thought, "He's starting Brandon a bit early; he's far too young for weight training." Later that day, when we arrived at my house, Bruce turned to me and said, "I really bought these weights for you, so you'd better start using them." I almost started to cry because of his generosity.'

Just as had happened in Oakland, shortly after the Los Angeles school opened there was a confrontation, this time with two local martial artists who wanted to fight. Bruce explained that they were in the middle of a class and that if they wanted to fight him they would have to wait until the class was over. He quickly rearranged the class so that Dan Lee, one of the best students, was working out in front of the two challengers.

During a break in the class, Bruce sauntered over to the two spectators and said that if they still wanted to fight he'd be more than happy to let them spar with his students. The pair politely turned down the invitation and left. Bruce had used what was, for him, a new kind of strategy, 'the art of winning without fighting', says Dan Lee.

Because Bruce could teach only small classes, he decided to boost his income by taking on private students who paid $50 per hour instead of paying the regular monthly fee. Jay Sebring had already put Bruce in contact with Steve McQueen and the movie star became one of Bruce's first celebrity pupils. A growing reputation meant that Bruce also attracted many professional fighters, including several karate champions, for special training.

Karate was introduced into America by former World War Two servicemen who had learned the art while stationed in the Orient. The first karate school in the United States was opened by Robert Trias in 1946. A decade later, karate was popularized by Ed Parker, the man who organized the Long Beach tournament where Bruce was discovered. Yet up until this time even Western teachers were at great pains to adhere to the Oriental tradition they were passing on. In abandoning tradition, Bruce Lee anticipated and set the stage for a new breed of martial artist. Traditionally, the mixing of martial arts was frowned upon. But things changed when Chuck Norris mixed Korean and Japanese arts to his own advantage, out-kicking Japanese stylists and out-punching the Korean stylists.

Joe Lewis first met Bruce Lee at Washington's Mayflower Hotel while both were guests of the 1967 National Karate Championships. Bruce had appeared as Kato; Lewis was the defending champion. But it wasn't until they were back in

California that they had a chance to speak when they met again in a parking lot outside the offices of a martial arts magazine. Joe Lewis recalls:

> As I left the building to get into my car, Bruce Lee called me over and gave me this pitch about becoming my instructor and showed me various moves. Here was this little *kung fu* guy trying to tell me something about fighting and I'm saying to myself, 'I'm an international karate champion and this guy's going to tell me about fighting?' What he was saying just went in one ear and out the other. He spent a long time trying to convince me about some of the things he was doing, but I just had a blank screen up.
>
> Anyway, I was in partnership with Bob Wall and Mike Stone [also karate champions] and one day, some time after this meeting, Mike started telling us about this guy Bruce Lee who was phenomenal with all the different techniques he was doing. For him to compliment somebody unknown like Bruce Lee was strange because I couldn't remember hearing Mike Stone ever compliment anyone. Mike Stone sold me on Bruce's theories which came from utilizing fencing footwork and *wing chun* to make it applicable to kickboxing, which is what I was into.
>
> So Bruce set it up so that Mike Stone, Chuck Norris and I would visit his house once or twice a week. He showed me a lot of fighting principles and emphasized footwork to me and the importance of using distance and mobility against an opponent.
>
> Bruce had hundreds of books on all the fighting arts; he had hundreds of boxing manuals and dozens of films. We used to sit and analyze boxing and wrestling films.

The 1951 championship fight between Willie Pep and Sandy Saddler was a particular favourite of Bruce's. In this fight Pep used interesting footwork borrowed from judo. During the course of the fight, which Pep was losing, he was not averse to using an open hand to jab Saddler's eyes with his thumb. Once or twice on the blind side of the referee he used a judo leg trip to unbalance his opponent, along with many other non-boxing techniques.

Joe Lewis continues,

> We would study the strategies on film, and also go to tournaments and watch guys fight. Then I would go out in a tournament and prove whether it worked or not. You can't have a better set-up than that. I thought it was the greatest life that ever existed. And I don't think there was ever anything like it before, or ever will be again.
>
> In person, Bruce had a charm that didn't come across on the screen. I guess you could use the word 'magic'. What does the word magic mean? There's a spark of enthusiasm in everybody's mind. Bruce used to ignite that spark. He could explode that sense of imagination in you. You'd say, 'Wow! That's what martial arts is all about! Yeah, Bruce, you're right on the money!' It had that kind of flavour. He could just inspire you to love martial arts. The word ought to be 'inspiration'. He was an incredibly encouraging, inspiring spark of energy.

It should be noted that Bruce Lee's karate star students were formidable fighters before they met him. In Okinawa, where he was stationed with the Marine Corps prior to serving in Vietnam, Joe Lewis became a black belt in an unprecedented seven months, then won his first national tournament in 1966. Bruce Lee would claim that even great champions recognized his genius and, really, he was right. But Bruce was also shrewd enough to realize that he had as much to gain from the relationship as anyone.

Joe Lewis says:

> Bruce wanted people who would go out and represent what he stood for. He figured he'd get the biggest names at that time and build up his credibility as an instructor. The masters on the Chinese *kung fu* circuit were looking down at him. Bruce resented it because he felt that most, if not all, of these *kung fu* masters couldn't fight.

I think he wanted the prestige of being able to say that he was a master and that his students were champions. He didn't get any respect from the *kung fu* masters at that time and felt very misunderstood by people around him. He needed attention and a sense of people looking at him and feeling he was significant. He didn't just want to be looked on as a *kung fu* expert. That was the label he had and it was hard to shake it.

He'd come to me and say, 'Joe, I'm not a master. I'm a student-master, meaning that I have the knowledge of a master and the expertise of a master, but I'm still learning, so I'm a student-master.' That was the term he used to my face.

Dan Inosanto adds, 'Bruce never really believed in the word "master". He considered the master as such when they closed the casket. I don't think he ever wanted it because he realized that.'

Bruce Lee had now been training in *kung fu* for over half his life and had reached such a level of mastery that there were only a handful of people around who could give him a serious workout. Yet many of the traditional martial arts fraternity saw Bruce Lee as an upstart whose methods were little more than glorified street fighting. Bruce himself certainly had no misgivings about his abilities and took great delight in pointing out the shortcomings of the more traditional approaches to the fighting arts. He even had a mock grave, complete with tombstone, installed in the school. The inscription on the stone read: 'In memory of the once fluid man, crammed and distorted by the classical mess.'

In a letter to Dan Inosanto, Bruce wrote, 'Use your common sense to see what is the real thing and what is merely a lesson in routine dancing. *Gung fu* is simply the direct expression of one's feelings with the minimum lines and energy.'

He once showed Dan Inosanto what he meant by this, surprising his friend by flinging an object at him without warning. As Dan reacted and caught it, Bruce pointed out how Dan had simply acted, directly and naturally, without adopting any special stance or needing to wear a special uniform.

From the outset, Bruce stressed that training had to relate as much as possible to actual combat and to situations that might be met with on the streets, using only the simplest and most effective moves. Bruce said that the best way to develop the power to punch and kick was simply to keep punching and kicking. Likewise the best training for fighting was to fight, or at least to practise the nearest thing, which was to pad up and spar all out. There was nothing sophisticated about it, and certainly no rules.

When he was dismissed as a brawler by many of the traditional martial arts fraternity, Bruce would explain that not adhering to set methods didn't mean that he was unskilled or without form. It meant that he was not limited to what he had practised but could improvise and adapt.

Bruce's attitude to fighting brings to mind a scene from the film *Butch Cassidy and the Sundance Kid*. Cassidy, played by Paul Newman, is about to fight a rival for the leadership of an outlaw gang. Just as they are squaring up, Newman asks innocently, 'Just a minute, what rules are we having?' His tough opponent replies indignantly, 'No rules!' The words have hardly left his lips when Cassidy's boot hits him in the groin. As he buckles in pain and drops to the floor, we can see him trying desperately to say that he hadn't meant it like that, coupled with the awful realization that he had been outwitted. Bruce Lee would certainly have enjoyed that scene.

The difference between the classical martial arts and Bruce Lee's evolving fighting method had become as radical as the difference between eighteenth-century soldiers fighting in line and column and the methods of modern guerrilla warfare. Bruce Lee practised and taught what was necessary to win, simply and scientifically.

Throughout the 1960s Bruce assimilated as much knowledge and experience as he could about every aspect of fighting that he could use. He had amassed an extensive library, paying as much as $400 for a rare book. As long as a book had something to do with fighting, Bruce bought it. He placed great value on his books; he didn't regard them merely as possessions, but as treasuries of knowledge. He would study a new book intently, analyzing the fighting techniques to find the weaknesses by acting them out. Although he never practised karate, he knew the names of all the techniques in Japanese and could demonstrate them. Not only did Bruce have books on every type of hand-to-hand fighting, but also on archery, ballet and fencing. His books on philosophy concerned not only the insights of Chinese sages like Confucius and Lao Tzu; there were also works by Krishnamurti, Spinoza and Kahlil Gibran's *The Prophet*, along with pop psychology books on self-help and positive thinking by writers like Norman Vincent Peale and Napoleon Hill.

Bruce also collected films of Joe Louis, Rocky Marciano, Max Baer, Jack Dempsey, Muhammad Ali and other great boxers. Bruce used to watch Ali's films over and over to analyze and imitate his movements. An orthodox boxer, Ali led with his left hand. Since Bruce was experimenting with a right lead stance he set up a mirror so that he could watch Ali's movements and practise them the appropriate way.

The first time Bruce put on boxing gloves, as a teenager, he became an interschool champion, beating the three-year title holder. He had fenced with his brother (a Commonwealth Games champion) and done some *t'ai chi* with his father. He had trained intensively in *wing chun* while being involved in almost daily street fights in Hong Kong. Before coming to America he learned forms from other styles of *kung fu*, such as the praying mantis, *choy li fut*, eagle claw, and *hung gar*. In the States, he had practised judo with Taky Kimura, 'Fred' Sato and Jesse Glover. He had trained in Filipino martial arts with Dan Inosanto and travelled to meet instructors in other styles. The champion wrestler Gene LaBell played Bruce's patsy in many episodes of *The Green Hornet*, and the two had become close friends and traded techniques. Bruce had met Wally Jay, a judo and ju jitsu exponent responsible for many innovations in those fields. He had worked with karate champions Bob Wall, Chuck Norris, Mike Stone and Joe Lewis. He tried Thai boxing, Western boxing, *savate* (French footfighting), and had learned a few dirty tricks for good measure. From this potent cocktail of diverse influences emerged his modern and unorthodox fighting method.

Doug Palmer says:

> After I went back to college on the East Coast and Bruce moved, we saw each other only occasionally on vacations. Each time there was a notable change. I watched him evolve over the years. I couldn't see how he could ever have any more than he already had, but each time he had new theories and techniques that became part of an expanded vision.

Adds Dan Inosanto:

> But Bruce kept a lot of things to himself . . . He was into *ch'i* development. The first thing on his schedule was meditation. What I'm trying to say is that he sort of pointed his students in one direction and pointed himself in another. He was heavily into what I call 'esoteric studies'. I know that he had a lot of literature on it and he studied acupuncture, but he kept a lot of these things to himself.
>
> He also programmed his mind by repeating affirmations over

and over again to raise his martial art skill to the highest level. He showed me one affirmation he had written down saying that by 1970 he would be the biggest Chinese star in the world and make ten million dollars.

The fact that Bruce could teach only a handful of people at any one time meant that he had long ago given up the idea of opening a nationwide chain of *kung fu* academies. At the same time, while he had been striving both to perfect his art and convey its essence to others, he was again being driven to fulfil his ambitions.

He realized that he had to break out of teaching and bring his art to a wider audience. He knew he had to make it as a film actor.

13
THE WARRIOR

ALONG WITH HIS partner Tom Kuhn, Fred Weintraub runs an independent production company in Century City, Los Angeles. In 1968, Weintraub was head of Warner Brothers' film division and Kuhn was in charge of television.

'At that time,' says Weintraub, 'I used to spend time looking at Chinese movies. They were four hours long and boring as shit, but in the last thirty minutes a guy in white would come in and defeat all the bad guys. Because of that interest, friends introduced me to Bruce Lee and we also became friends. I hired two young writers [Ed Spielman and Howard Frielander] and tried to put a feature together for Bruce, but I could never get anything off the ground.'

Bruce himself had already spent some time working on an idea concerning the adventures of a Shaolin warrior-priest who used *kung fu* skills against the outlaws of the old West. Eventually his idea found its way to Tom Kuhn, who suggested a TV movie as a pilot for a possible series with the working title of *The Warrior*.

By now Bruce had attracted several more celebrity students including actor James Coburn and screenwriters Stirling Silliphant and Joe Hyams. Silliphant was one of the most highly regarded and successful writer-producers in Hollywood. He had written the cult TV series *Route 66*, and his credits were to eventually include *The Towering Inferno*, *The Poseidon Adventure* and an Oscar for *In the Heat of the Night*.

Silliphant is now semi-retired and lives in Bangkok with his wife Tiana. Despite the fact that he hired lots of actors, Silliphant has talked about the difficulty he had in getting to Bruce. To become his pupil, he had to go through what was in effect an audition.

Bruce Lee first came to Silliphant's attention through a story making the rounds in Hollywood. The story went that Bruce had met the singer Vic Damone in his Las Vegas hotel suite after one of the singer's performances. Damone had an interest in the martial arts, but he insisted that a tough Italian street brawler would always beat a slightly built Oriental. Damone had two huge bodyguards who also had a low opinion of the martial arts and they were enlisted to prove the point. Bruce agreed to be tested. He asked that one guard be placed behind the door to the suite, with the second man about five feet behind him, smoking a cigarette. Bruce explained that when he came through the door, the first man was to try and stop him. The cigarette was there to represent a holstered gun. Bruce told Damone that before the singer could count to five, he would be through the door and would have knocked the cigarette from the second guy's mouth, 'disarming' him. Bruce was further giving them the advantage of telling them exactly what he was going to do, forfeiting the element of surprise.

'If I succeed,' said Bruce, 'will you take this as an acceptable example of the effectiveness of martial arts?'

'Sure,' came the disdainful replies.

Bruce left the room. The singer told his guards to go easy on the little Chinese guy. 'Just knock him on his ass with one good shot.'

Suddenly there was a loud wrenching noise as the door flew clear off its hinges, taking the first guard with it. Bruce followed through in one motion and kicked the cigarette out of the second guard's mouth while he was still frozen in place. The singer managed the comment, 'Holy shit.'

After a three-month search, Silliphant succeeded in finding Bruce by contacting *Green Hornet* producer William Dozier.

When they finally did meet, Bruce was appalled to find that the writer was fifty, though he conceded that at least Silliphant was still in good shape. While Bruce admitted that there were people in China who began training in martial arts in their sixties, he wasn't sure if he wanted to teach anyone of that age, adding that it would depend on the writer's speed and commitment. What Bruce didn't know was that in his youth Silliphant had been a state university fencing champion with fast reflexes and a competitive attitude. He told Bruce that he was quite simply 'a winner'. Warming to Silliphant, Bruce put him through his paces and accepted him as a student.

In order to discourage celebrity dabblers, Bruce charged high fees. In the beginning Silliphant elected to share the cost of his $100 private lessons with fellow writer Joe Hyams, who had also just become involved with Bruce. 'Had I trained directly with Bruce,' says Silliphant, 'it would have been futile. That was one of the reasons he put Joe Hyams and me together.'

Bruce's fees now began to rise steadily until he was eventually charging $250 an hour, though only to a handful of students. The director Roman Polanski had Bruce flown to Switzerland for a few private lessons. Bruce would not have gone had he not needed the money. It must have been as frustrating an experience for him as it was a fruitless one for Polanski. A student who had trained regularly for a few years might benefit from a master class such as this. But for a complete beginner to think that he could buy even a brief insight into Bruce Lee's skill was as unrealistic as expecting to become a virtuoso musician by buying a guitar and engaging Eric Clapton for an hour-long lesson.

Students like Coburn and Silliphant showed more commitment and so gained more insight. Bruce Lee explained that studying a martial art holds up a mirror to the self and that it is a path of self-study which leads ultimately to self-knowledge. For example, in learning to find a way into fighting range without being hit, Coburn discovered that there wasn't just a physical problem to be solved, but he also had to cross mental and emotional divides. Silliphant also spoke of a 'resonant chord' that was struck in his own spirit when he found that his training raised the quality of his writing as he gained more insight into human emotions.

When movement and energy are intentionally brought into one's awareness, then not only do martial art techniques become more efficient but the whole of life is similarly affected. The levels of the practitioner's outer skill and the inner state reflect each other. Understood like this, every art and skill can be a way to inner development. There is a Japanese saying: 'Archery and dancing, flower arranging and singing, tea drinking and wrestling – it is all the same.' From the ordinary point of view, this makes no sense, but once the underlying significance is grasped, the meaning is clear.

During 1968 and 1969, some of Bruce's film industry students got him bit-part work. He made minor appearances in episodes of the TV detective series *Ironside* (in which he played a martial arts teacher) and in the sitcom *Blondie*. In *Here Come the Brides*, Bruce had a non-fighting guest role in an episode called 'Marriage, Chinese Style'. The series was set in the 1870s when Seattle was a village with a population of around 150; the village menfolk imported boatloads of marriageable women from the East. Bruce was also the technical advisor for the Matt Helm detective thriller *The Wrecking Crew*, which starred Dean Martin and Roman Polanski's wife, Sharon Tate.

Bruce's contacts were willing to help him, but there were not that many opportunities. There were very few parts in Hollywood that called for Chinese actors outside of the stereotypes. In particular, Stirling Silliphant realized that something special would have to be written for Bruce. Then they would have to overcome the problem of getting a studio to back the idea with hard cash.

Meanwhile, Silliphant had written *A Walk in the Spring Rain* for Columbia, with Anthony Quinn and Ingrid Bergman set to star. Although it was a love story, the writer had contrived to include a fight sequence. The problem was that the story was set in the mountains of Tennessee, where there were not many Chinese martial artists! Silliphant managed to get Bruce involved by having him choreograph the fight scene. This was not simply for Bruce's benefit but so that Silliphant could continue his training routine.

As with Vic Damone's bodyguards, Bruce's ability was openly doubted by the two rough rednecks whose fight Bruce was there to supervise. Silliphant elected to clear a few things up straight away and organized a demonstration which resulted in the two stuntmen being sidekicked, in turn, almost clear across a swimming pool.

Silliphant did manage to write an acting part for Bruce, that of Winslow Wong in the 1969 detective feature *Marlowe*. The film starred James Garner as the hard-boiled private detective Philip Marlowe in a script based on Raymond Chandler's novel *The Little Sister*.

In the story, Bruce works as a heavy for the villain of the piece. One scene was specifically written to show off Bruce's athleticism: he comes in to smash up Garner's office, culminating in a stunning kick high above his head to shatter a light fixture. Marlowe's later handling of Bruce Lee's character is quite unrealistic. Standing on the edge of a balcony he taunts Wong by casting doubts on his manhood, then simply steps aside to avoid the flying kick that sends Wong sailing off the edge of the roof to his death. After witnessing the precise aggression of the office attack, more people laughed at this unconvincing scene than chuckled at the craftiness of Marlowe. Although Bruce was in only a couple of scenes, this marked his first appearance in a full-length Hollywood picture.

Aside from these jobs cooked up by Stirling Silliphant, Bruce's only income was from his teaching and a trickle from *The Green Hornet*. Yet despite his money problems and with Linda pregnant again, Bruce decided to buy a new house. At first he set the budget at $30,000 but soon realized that it fell far short of what he had in mind. Bruce was feeling the need to provide a good life for his growing family, and it was difficult for him to admit that he couldn't afford to. He felt he belonged with his successful friends in the movie business. Reasoning that it was only a matter of time before he joined them, he went to look over a bungalow just off Mulholland Drive in the upmarket Bel Air area.

Mulholland Drive winds and dips for twenty miles along the crest of a ridge that runs from Hollywood to the Pacific coast at Malibu through some of the most desirable real estate in Los Angeles. To the north there are views across the San Fernando Valley, while to the south lie the canyons and spectacular vistas of the city and the ocean. Bel Air Estates is entered through gates on Sunset Boulevard or Mulholland Drive. Roscomare Road is lined with detached bungalows, with gardens of cypress, bougainvillea and hibiscus. There is no pavement, because no one walks in Bel Air. The air is warm and still and there is a feeling of space and calm. There can't be many better places to live in a city.

Although it needed some work, Bruce bought the bungalow at 2551 Roscomare Road and hung his training bags under the eaves at the back. But at nearly $50,000 he was in way over his head and was soon struggling to meet the mortgage payments. On top of this, the household costs were much higher than he was used to. He didn't have the money to furnish it properly. And now the Internal Revenue Service was knocking on the front door – which had yet to be repainted. Yet when Bruce received a windfall of $8,000 from the sale of one of his father's properties in Hong Kong, instead of buying furniture or paying the bills he bought a red Porsche and went racing along Mulholland Drive with Steve McQueen.

In a letter dated 6 January 1969, Bruce Lee wrote to William Cheung, who was now living in Australia:

> During the last ten years, Chinese martial art has been a major part of my activity, though I am now in a new field: the field of acting. My achievement in the martial art is most satisfying and the word 'Chinese' has come a long way in the circle of martial art, due to the fact that all three of the US karate freestyle champions are studying under me. William, I've lost faith in the Chinese classical arts – though I still call mine Chinese – because, basically, all styles are a product of 'land swimming', even the *wing chun* school. So my line of training is more toward efficient streetfighting with everything goes, wearing head gear, gloves, chest guard, shin and knee guards, etc. For the past five years now I've been training the hardest and for a purpose, not just dissipated hit-miss training. I'm running every day, sometimes up to six miles. I've named my style *jeet kune do* – [my] reason for not sticking to *wing chun* [is] because I sincerely feel that this style has more to offer regarding efficiency.

I mentioned all the above because it is a major event in my life and [I'd] like to fill you in with it.

I've been doing good too in the field of acting. I don't know whether or not you've seen my TV series *The Green Hornet* in Australia, but I've worked for a year in it, setting up a good foundation. Occasionally I appear on TV and movies. The latest one is an MGM production *Little Sister* with James Garner that should be coming out in a few months. I'm in the process of forming a production company with a few important backers here in the States, concentrating on producing martial art movies, TV series, etc.

I've just bought a half-acre home in Bel Air on top of a hill – plenty of fresh air – like living out in the country, but tough on the calves running around the hillside.

Well my friend, all in all, that's what happened to me . . .

Despite the upbeat tone of his letter, Bruce was only too aware that he had more to do than simply convince his old friends that he was now a great success. He had always taken a fiercely positive attitude to his life, but whether he called it faith, confidence, determination, ambition, or a vision that things would work out, no longer mattered. Bruce Lee had spent sixteen long years developing his skills and perfecting an art that, so far, no more than a handful of people had benefited from. And now he had just spent $50,000 on a new home. Now, things just *had* to work out.

14

THE SILENT FLUTE

IN THE HABIT of making predictions about his future, Bruce Lee said that he would make *kung fu* known throughout the world. But he also knew beyond any doubt that the only way he could do this was by making films. Bruce had both allies and ambition, and others agreed that he had all the necessary qualities. Yet he could find no outlet for his abilities and visions, and this only made things worse. Bruce also had the same disarming tendency in the film world that he had with the martial arts fraternity – to say exactly what he thought. This didn't win many allies in an industry whose wheels tend to run smoother when oiled by bullshit. Nobody knew quite what to do with him. More to the point, nobody was willing to risk money on an unknown actor who also happened to be Chinese. It must have made Bruce question more than once the time he had spent fighting his fellow countrymen for the right to teach *kung fu* to Westerners.

If no opportunity was going to arise naturally, then just as his motivation had created his abilities, so it would also create the opportunities to use them. In short, he would go to Hollywood with a film. Bruce realized that a starring role was out of the question, but reasoned that a stronger supporting role than the one he'd had in *Marlowe* would reveal enough of his talents to open the door further. He already had an idea for a film which he had quite literally dreamed up.

For some years, Bruce had been having a recurring dream about a 'seeker', a character who he had come to realize was himself. These dreams had left enough of an impression for him to have made a few notes about them. Bruce wanted to use these notes as the basis of a screenplay which he now asked Stirling Silliphant to write.

The film was to be called *The Silent Flute*. The flute itself was a metaphor for the call of the soul, which only certain people can hear. It was a 'hero's quest' story, tracing a martial artist's evolution towards self-understanding. On the way there would be trials and revelations, battles with others, and battles with his own doubts and fears. Bruce decided to play several supporting roles, as animal and elemental characters that the hero would have to overcome on his journey. Bruce would also appear at various times as the hero's guide, playing the flute. At first only animals could hear it, but by the end, the hero, the seeker named Cord, would also be able to hear it. Although the lead role would be played by a star name, it was already clear that Bruce was going to dominate the action.

Bruce wanted Steve McQueen to play the starring role and he and Silliphant went to talk to the actor. McQueen, who had never really stuck to the discipline of training with Bruce, said he was too busy. But as Bruce became more and more enthusiastic and pressed him to become involved, the real reason emerged.

'Be honest,' said McQueen. 'This is a film to make Bruce Lee into a star. I like you, but I'm not here to make you a star. I'm not going to carry you on my back.'

Bruce said nothing and he and Silliphant left soon after. McQueen's words had burned deep into Bruce, and they would never be forgotten. Outside, he turned to Silliphant and said, 'I'm going to be bigger than he is.' Then, more quietly, he repeated the same vow to himself.

The two went to James Coburn and told him the situation. Coburn said he was 'with them', meaning that he was offering to play the lead role himself. But now it was Silliphant's turn to get cold feet and he tried to pull back from the project, saying he was already up to his ears in writing commitments.

The Silent Flute had begun as an idea to make a definitive martial arts film that would give Bruce the exposure he needed. Now other pressures were starting to build and there was more at stake. Not only was he becoming increasingly concerned about getting his break in pictures, Bruce also needed to make some money or he would be in danger of losing the house. *The Silent Flute* went from being a good idea to a necessity and then to an obsession. When it began to look as if the whole project was about to be abandoned, Bruce was distraught. He would lose both his chance of stardom and his ability to provide for his family. Bruce always tried to picture the best possible outcome of any situation and not dwell on the more fearful possibilities. But his concerns were made more acute with the birth of his daughter Shannon on 19 April 1969.

In an attempt to solve everybody's problems it was agreed to hire a scriptwriter to develop Bruce's ideas, with Silliphant and Coburn putting up the $12,000 fee. The writer managed to lose most of Bruce's plot by turning it into mainly science fiction and sex. He was fired and Silliphant's nephew had a try. Again, none of the three was happy with the outcome.

As Silliphant saw Bruce becoming increasingly desperate, he finally gave in. He proposed a regular writing session three nights a week to dictate their ideas to his secretary. No excuses for absence would be accepted. Although this work was purely speculative, they met without fail at the appointed times. Before long, a story began to come alive and there was excitement in the air.

Despite the always financial crisis looming, things moved along well. Then one morning, as Bruce began his daily workout, he felt a stab of pain in his lower back and the barbell across his shoulders went crashing to the floor. Over the following days, heat and massage treatment brought no relief. The pain grew steadily worse until a doctor's examination became vital. The final diagnosis was not good: Bruce had damaged a sacral nerve and experienced a severe muscle spasm. He asked the obvious question: how long would it be before he could start training again? The doctor advised complete rest.

The damage wasn't simply physical; it was total. Bruce now found himself flat on his back unable even to hold himself upright let alone support a family, in a house he couldn't pay for as the bills piled up. It wasn't simply that Bruce could no longer train or practise as a martial artist; he felt he had no future at all. To anyone, let alone someone with Bruce's energy and ambition, such a situation would be a nightmare. For perhaps the first time in his life, Bruce Lee was truly frightened.

Only a few months earlier, it was Hollywood that had had no idea what to do with Bruce Lee. Now Bruce Lee had no idea what to do with himself. For several weeks he lived between the bed and the chair at his desk, fighting depression by drawing plans for a bed that would help him to rest his injury better.

Unable to fight physically, Bruce now had to battle his own fears and doubts using the strength of his will and emotions, just like the hero of *The Silent Flute*. He believed that only through his belief would things ever work out. And so Bruce battled every negative thought as it arose, by 'seeing' it written on a piece of paper which he then mentally crushed into a ball and burned to a crisp. Every inner voice that said, 'I can't,' was replaced with one that said, 'I can.' Every image of failure was replaced with one of success. Bruce once told Joe Hyams that he considered the mind to be like a fertile garden in which anything that is planted – flowers or weeds – will grow. As Bruce tried to acknowledge and go with his injury rather than resist it, he felt both his autonomy and his self-esteem being eroded. At times, he was close to exploding with frustration.

Unable to train, Bruce now turned adversity into advantage by using this time to write down the precepts by which he lived and worked. In the years that Bruce had been in America his ability to express himself had matured almost beyond recognition. He began collating his notes, usually written in succinct paragraphs derived both from his own experiences and from books in which he'd found vital information or inspiration.

When Bruce could tolerate the situation no longer, he began to train and teach again. While everyone assumed that he had recovered, he was still in chronic pain, but had simply willed himself to act as if everything was all right.

Around this time, *The Silent Flute* was presented to Warner Brothers. The studio was willing to give it a shot, but only so long as the film was made in India, in order to use up money that previous Warner pictures had earned there but which the Indian government would not allow out of the country. Bruce began planning the trip to India; Coburn and Silliphant shot each other a sidelong glance.

Almost a year since the idea for the film was first dreamed up, Bruce, Coburn and Silliphant flew to India to scout locations. They landed in Bombay, flew on to New Delhi and then hired a car and driver to take them north over dirt roads in the searing heat. From the moment they started looking, they knew there would have to be enormous changes to make the script fit in with what they found. An ominous feeling came over Silliphant and Coburn. Drawing on their extensive experience, they had to admit that filming in India wasn't going to work. Bruce had never before travelled outside Hong Kong and the West Coast, nor did he have any idea of the production problems involved. He would not allow the others to dissuade him as he urged them to keep looking. They continued driving north. Through long hours of heat and dust and bumpy roads, Bruce suffered from constant back pain while Coburn and Silliphant sat with heavy hearts. When the friendly humour had worn a little thin they would sleep for a while until Bruce began to talk about the film again. Tensions began to surface.

During the trip, James Coburn always sat up front with the driver while Silliphant sat in the back with Bruce. Bruce had a habit of singing quietly to himself as they travelled. His favourite tune at the time was 'Yesterday'. No doubt he was thinking about the time when all his own troubles seemed so far away. Bruce's singing continued to irritate Coburn until he snapped, 'Stop that! You're driving me crazy!'

Bruce joked with Coburn that his voice was rich because it was 'Well, off!' But as Coburn turned to look down the long road ahead, Bruce shook his fist at the back of Coburn's head. As the trip wore on, the two drifted further apart.

When they reached the northern border of India, Silliphant and Coburn were more than ready to call it quits, but not Bruce. He was feeling desperate now; everything – his career, his dreams, his whole life – was at stake. For this reason, the other two got on a plane with Bruce and flew south to Madras where he was convinced they would find the locations they were looking for. From Madras they went to Goa; all they found there were hippies from all over the world on the beach.

The martial arts had first been brought to China by the Indian monk Bodhidharma, but hundreds of years later there weren't any even vaguely competent martial artists to be found in India. When Bruce put on an impromptu display of his skills for some local martial artists, they stared in disbelief. In their own exhibition they had fallen through ineptitude; now they fell to their knees, quite literally, in astonishment.

Wherever there was any kind of audience, Bruce Lee the entertainer would come alive. This became a source of further tension between him and James Coburn. Coburn wanted to keep a low profile, while Bruce looked for any opportunity to show off. In airports, Coburn would sit quietly reading while Bruce would attract an audience of children and put on a quick show of fighting moves or tricks. Unused to seeing Chinese people, they would gape at him as he ran through a few moves, and then burst into applause.

Suffering from terrible back pain, and seeing his future dissolving before his eyes, Bruce had to do something to prove to himself that he still had some appeal. These incidents also revealed another facet of his character: while James Coburn was simply an actor and movie star, Bruce Lee was a natural performer whose innate talent allowed him to entertain any-where, with or without a script.

The three returned from Goa to Bombay and to the Taj Mahal Hotel. Bruce was given a room not much bigger than a broom closet, while Coburn's room was bigger than the hotel's dining room. Coburn was an international star who was accustomed to this kind of treatment from hotel management, but Bruce could no longer stand the blows to his pride, confronted with the reality of his situation and how far away he was from where he wanted to be. That evening, Bruce Lee vowed that he would be a bigger star than both Steve McQueen and James Coburn.

For nearly a month, the three had travelled the length and breadth of India. Now that they were going home the only thing they could agree on was that the trip to India had failed. But while Stirling Silliphant and James Coburn had successful careers to resume, Bruce Lee had nothing. He was even more desperate now; this had been his only hope and he couldn't let it go. To hell with locations, he said; his attitude alone would make it work. James Coburn was against making the picture in India, citing artistic reasons. Stirling Silliphant thought they should still try and pull something together because his instincts told him that the time was right to make a martial arts picture. Bruce simply needed the picture to be made, at all costs. But in the end, James Coburn's decision not to remain involved caused Warner Brothers to withdraw.

Back in America, with no money coming into the Lee household, things had turned to an even darker shade of black. Both Coburn and Silliphant offered Bruce financial help but he would have none of it. His pride took a further blow when Linda suggested that the only way out of the hole would be for her to go out and work. Being Chinese, the injury to his pride in being offered charity and being unable to support his family was doubly painful. But in the end he had to agree that there was no other way. To save Bruce's pride further, an elaborate conspiracy was set up so that no one else would find out about the arrangement. With neither qualifications nor experience, Linda could only get a minimum wage job. After a day of parenting and managing the household, she then worked from late afternoon to midnight. Linda's health soon began to suffer.

Once Bruce had put Brandon and baby Shannon to bed, he spent the long evening hours alone reading, writing or in enforced contemplation, his back still racked with pain.

It was not the best of times.

15

LONGSTREET

DESPITE THE FAILED trip to India, Stirling Silliphant again tried to help lift Bruce Lee's career by writing a part for him in the pilot show for a new TV series called *Longstreet*. Silliphant had actually begun work on a script especially for Bruce before they left for India, when Bruce was still exasperated with the delay of *The Warrior*. The *Longstreet* episode was even entitled 'Way of the Intercepting Fist'. Written with help from Bruce, the story portrayed him as a martial arts instructor who teaches a blind detective how to protect himself. Silliphant then approached the head of Paramount TV, Tom Tannenbaum, who was in charge of developing the series.

Tannenbaum had trained in karate with Ed Parker and had seen a Bruce Lee demonstration at the 1966 Long Beach tournament. 'I was very impressed with him and wanted to meet him,' says Tannenbaum:

> The *kung fu* or *jeet kune do*, whatever he was doing back then, I had never seen before. Someone else in the industry had seen him perform at an earlier tournament and had tested him for the role in *The Green Hornet*. I got hold of a copy of that screen test and,

again, was very impressed. He had an intensity in his eyes and he was extremely confident.

I called him up and told him I'd like to take lessons. Bruce said, 'Come on down to my school in Chinatown at nine o'clock on Sunday morning. Knock twice on the door.' So I did. There was a little spy panel on the door which slid open, and Bruce let me in. There was a small class going on. As I waited I saw a notice on his desk which read: 'Show me a classical karateist and I'll show you a dead man.'

Then he came over and said, 'I'm going to hold this catcher's mitt and you hit it.' Now, I weighed about 200 pounds and Bruce at that time weighed about 132. I hit it, and I hit it hard. Bruce said, 'Now you hold it.' Without even pulling his striking hand back, and using just the torque of his body, he literally knocked me across the room. In fact, I hit the wall so hard that a picture fell down. It was embarrassing because all the students in the class looked at me. Still, I was fascinated because I had never met a man who weighed almost seventy pounds less than me who could knock me across the room. Bruce said, 'That's the power. Now I'll show you the speed.' He put a nickel in my palm and said, 'Close your fingers before I grab it out of your hand.' He moved like lightning and I quickly clenched my fingers. When I opened my hand, the nickel was gone and in its place was a dime. That's all I had to see. I said, 'That's fine, I'm yours.' So I started taking lessons from Bruce.

In Silliphant's script, Mike Longstreet (played by James Franciscus) is present during a murder, but he is blind and can't make a positive identification on the evidence of his hearing alone. He tracks down the killer, a tough longshoreman, and plans to unmask him. Bruce plays an antique dealer named Lee who saves the blind detective from being forced off the dock by a gang. Longstreet wants to know how Lee managed to do it and wants to learn how to fight like him and go after the killer. Lee refuses, saying that he has the wrong motives. But as the story develops, Lee begins to teach Longstreet, working both on his attitude to life and on a fighting method in preparation for the coming confrontation. Now Bruce only had to wait, yet again, for the filming of the show to begin.

In the meantime, Bruce took Brandon with him to Hong Kong to arrange for his mother to come and live in the United States. When he arrived in Hong Kong, he was astonished at the welcome he received. Twentieth Century-Fox, anxious to turn a profit from what had been a relatively unsuccessful TV series in the States, had recently marketed *The Green Hornet* in Hong Kong and throughout Southeast Asia, three years after it had first been aired in America. When dubbed into Mandarin, the show broke ratings figures in Singapore and the Philippines, and Kato, not the Hornet, was its acknowledged star. Much to Bruce's surprise, when he stepped off the plane he was surrounded by TV and newspaper reporters ready to boast of the local boy made good.

Hong Kong newspapers, radio and TV stations clamoured for interviews. Bruce, along with Brandon, appeared on talk shows on Hong Kong's two TV stations. One show host, Joseph Lau, persuaded Bruce to overcome (once again) his aversion to doing tricks and Bruce leapt, kicked and broke four one-inch boards dangling in the air. Then five-year-old Brandon managed to break one almost as big as himself. After a year of inactivity, dreading that it might all be going wrong, all of Bruce's charm, wit and star quality were suddenly on tap again.

Seizing the moment, Bruce immediately got his boyhood friend Unicorn to probe his employers, the Shaw Brothers film studios, about a possible film offer. Bruce gave Unicorn information about his schools and copies of magazine articles to take to Shaw Brothers. But all the information was in English, and Unicorn first had to set about getting it translated.

*

129

The Hong Kong film industry made films the way Detroit made cars: on an assembly line. They could wrap up a production in three days; a big-budget extravaganza might require a week. The Shaw brothers – Runjy, Runme and Run Run – had almost singlehandedly set up the Hong Kong industry. Shaw Brothers Studios was a mixture of purpose-built sets and sound stages where everything from pagodas to concentration camps were perched on a windy hillside overlooking Clearwater Bay. Shaw Brothers was the biggest studio outside Hollywood and Europe, accounting for two thirds of the Chinese films produced in the world. An average of seven features was always in production, while the dubbing rooms were shared on a tight schedule of three shifts daily.

The secret of Shaw Studios' success was a hard-nosed policy geared to speed and economy. Films were shot without sound and, like Italian spaghetti westerns, later dubbed into whatever language was required. The films were often shot without a written script, more or less made up by the crew as they went along and edited directly on camera with few retakes. Stories were lifted straight from Western films with little or no adaptation, what the Cantonese call 'warming up yesterday's cold rice'. The emphasis was on 'fist and pillow' – violence and sex. A director was lucky if he earned half of the amount budgeted to pay for the fake blood required for the violent scenes. Like the directors, writers and production crew, actors and actresses were overworked and underpaid.

Even so, there was still a waiting list to join Shaw Brothers' contract players. For a reasonable fee, Run Run Shaw would enrol would-be actors in the Southern Dramatic School (his own acting academy). Actors were expected to provide their own lunch and transport to and from locations. Contracts were ironclad; they could only be broken by leaving the profession or leaving the country. With an air of benevolent paternalism, Run Run Shaw told one interviewer that a number of actors' suicides and breakdowns over the years had been caused by the sudden pressures of fame, adding that he was always available to assist if it looked as if anything like that was about to happen to one of their stars.

Shaw Brothers films were guaranteed good distribution, as the studio owned 140 cinemas throughout Hong Kong, Singapore, Indonesia, Malaysia, Taiwan and parts of Vietnam and Burma – known as the Mandarin circuit. They also booked for an additional 500 cinemas, including those in the Chinatowns of San Francisco, Los Angeles and New York. The Shaw dynasty embraced thirty or forty companies throughout Southeast Asia, with interests in real estate, banking, insurance, breweries and amusement parks. In 1970, they were estimated to be worth between $40 million and $200 million.

The Singapore-based Cathay organization had been Shaw Brothers' only serious film-making rival. Cathay was looking ready to give them a run for their money until a plane crash over Taiwan claimed the lives of several of Cathay's top executives.

A slight, dapper and bespectacled man, Run Run Shaw was as sleek as he was slick. He ran his empire from behind a desk that dwarfed him, in an elegantly austere office decorated with modern Chinese art. Brushing aside accusations of low wages and bad conditions with an elegant hand, Shaw was quite direct about his approach to film-making: 'If audiences want violence, we give them violence. If they want sex, we give them sex. Whatever the audience wants, we'll give them.'

Unhappily, it would appear that Run Run could not apply the same simple credo to his own requirements. He regretted that he could not spend more time with his grandchildren because he was compelled to spend a lot of time with some of his actresses out of a strong sense of duty to the company. Lavish parties were thrown in a house surrounded by lush gardens on a quiet corner of the huge studio lot. Shaw owned several houses and country villas, and naturally he required several Rolls-Royces, Cadillacs and Lincoln Continentals to travel between them. Run Run did note with great wisdom that he could only travel in one of his cars at a time.

With Bruce Lee's translated publicity material in hand, Unicorn approached one of Shaw's senior executives, Mona Fong. She had not heard of Bruce Lee, and neither had a director who was also present in her office. So Unicorn went directly to Run Run himself with Bruce's proposal to do one picture for the studio for a fee of $10,000. In addition, Bruce insisted on the right to make script changes where necessary and to be solely responsible for arranging any fight action in the proposed film. The bemused mogul did not know what to make of such a strongly worded proposal. Ironically, Hollywood thought Bruce was too different from everyone else, while the Hong Kong studio thought he was just the same as all the other actors in the Mandarin martial arts films that were their stock-in-trade.

By the time Shaw did respond to his proposal, Bruce had already returned to the States. Bruce was wired a counter-proposal from the studio in which Shaw graciously noted Bruce's 'modest' success in the United States and offered him a seven-year contract for $2,000 a film – in other words, their standard junior actor's contract. Bruce politely declined.

Bruce now began work on the episode of *Longstreet*. He virtually plays himself. Long sequences of the script amount to a lesson in his fighting method and philosophy. This performance ranks as some of his most important work on screen.

Mike Longstreet is getting a lesson in how to sidekick. Lee asks Longstreet to hold the air bag so that he can feel the depth of the kick. One of Longstreet's colleagues arrives just in time to see the detective sailing backwards through the air, landing in a flower bed.

'Now what exactly is . . . this thing you do?' says the colleague.

'In Cantonese,' replies Lee, '*jeet kune do*, the "way of the intercepting fist".'

'Intercepting fist?'

'Or foot,' adds Lee. 'Come on, touch me anywhere you can.' As his opponent steps forward to throw a punch, Lee snaps out a low sidekick to his kneecap. 'You see,' explains Lee, 'to reach me, you must move to me. Your attack offers me an opportunity to intercept you. In this case I'm using my longest weapon, my sidekick, against the nearest target, your kneecap. It can be compared to your left jab in boxing, except it's much more damaging.'

'I see,' says the friend, nonchalantly. 'Well, speaking of a left jab—'

But Lee blocks the sudden punch, having read the intention a split second before the punch is thrown. 'This time I intercept your emotional tenseness. You see, from your thought to your fist, how much time was lost.'

Bruce often explained to his students that a lot of martial arts are taught in the block-hit, one-two manner, when it is more efficient to perform a simultaneous block and hit. At an even more efficient level, awareness is more attuned so that as soon as the opponent moves, he is intercepted and struck. At the most refined level, even the intention of being attacked can be felt and neutralized before it is begun.

In the story, Bruce also teaches Longstreet to listen to what is going on around him, not just to move for the sake of moving but to relate it to what is going on. Lee asks Longstreet if he can hear the bird that has been singing quietly in the background throughout their conversation. Because Longstreet is blind, Lee cannot get him to become more aware of his peripheral sight, but he can get him to expand his overall awareness through listening more attentively.

In writing *Longstreet*, Silliphant based the blind detective's lessons with Lee on his own experiences. 'The first thing he'd done with me,' says Silliphant, 'was to concentrate on body movement and understanding the relationship between you and your opponent. At first, Bruce blindfolded me and made me move in conjunction with what I felt his movements might be, on all sides. We practised that for weeks before we began anything specific.'

The same exercise was a natural one for the character Lee to teach the blind detective Longstreet, just as Bruce had got Silliphant and Joe Hyams to develop their kinaesthetic awareness by practising sticking hands while blindfolded.

At one point Longstreet observes, 'It's funny that out of a martial art, out of combat, I feel something peaceful, something without hostility, almost as though if I knew *jeet kune do*, it would be enough to know it and not use it.'

But at a later training session, Longstreet does find himself unable to use what he is being taught. Lee tries to get his student to practise the finger jab to the eyes. 'Don't worry, I've covered them,' says Lee, who is wearing a pair of goggles.

'I can't do it,' says the detective.

'Why?'

'I don't know, I just can't do it!'

'Why, because you're blind? The finger jab is one of the most effective attacks . . .'

'Well, let's just forget that attack, shall we?'

'That man who attacked you,' says Lee, 'would he have hesitated to gouge out your eyes?'

'Well, that's his problem!'

'A bird would, or a cat would, without any hesitation, without thinking.'

'I'm not a bird, I'm not a cat,' says Longstreet. 'And I do think.'

'That's your problem!' says Lee.

Later Longstreet is still having problems trying to remember everything he's been taught.

'If you try to remember, you will lose,' says Lee. 'Empty your mind. Be like water. Put water into a cup, it becomes the cup. Put water into a teapot, it becomes the teapot. Water can flow; it can flow or creep or drip or crash! Be water, my friend.'

Longstreet asks why he doesn't just stand in front of his opponent and recite what Lee has just told him. 'Maybe he'll faint or drown.'

'You are not ready,' says Lee.

'I know.'

'Like everyone else, you want to learn the way to win, but never to accept to lose. To accept defeat – to learn to die – is to be liberated from it. So, when tomorrow comes, you must free your ambitious mind and learn the art of dying. May it be well with you tomorrow, Mike.'

Now, more than ever, despite all the obstacles he faced, Bruce Lee was convinced that his future lay in America. The Paramount executives were pleased enough with the *Longstreet* episode to decide to open their new autumn season with it. At the same time, Hong Kong radio stations were still phoning Bruce and broadcasting his conversations over the air 8,000 miles away. One of the people who was listening was Raymond Chow of Golden Harvest Studios. Chow was a former employee of Run Run Shaw who had now become his bitter rival.

For several years, Raymond Chow had been one of the top executives at Shaw Brothers. When Run Run had been exercising his 'sense of duty' with a young singer, Mona Fong, she impressed him so much with her own, equally devoted application to her career that he found a position for her in the company. Soon, Fong had manoeuvred herself into a position of authority, eventually ending up as Chow's superior. This provoked Chow into leaving the company and raising enough money to set up on his own. But Chow and his partner Leonard Ho were barely surviving, finding it difficult to get their films shown due to Shaw's virtual monopoly of the distribution circuit. The Golden Harvest studios were little more than a cluster of old shacks perched on a Kowloon hillside. So far, Chow had not been in a position to improve his lot or to strike back at Shaw, but he saw in Bruce Lee an opportunity to change all this.

Chow sent one of his senior producers, Liu Liang Hua, to make Bruce an offer. Liu was also Mrs Lo Wei, the wife of one of the directors whom Chow had pirated away from Shaw Brothers. Chow improved Shaw's offer enough to make Bruce bite. It was a simple deal: two pictures for a straight fee of $15,000. Chow also included a generous one-way ticket to the location as part of the deal. Coburn and Silliphant advised Bruce against accepting the offer, saying that he should hold out for more, but Bruce was tired of waiting. After seeing previous opportunities slip away he was determined not to lose this one. He signed the deal.

Bruce did his homework and viewed Golden Harvest's current batch of releases, then called Raymond Chow and asked him if that was the best he could do. If there was one thing Bruce knew beyond doubt, it was that no one fights the same as anyone else. His whole fighting philosophy was based on that very observation. What bothered him about the films he'd just seen was that they were one-dimensional. Bruce had no problem with fighting people and playing a character at the same time. Whether it was acting or action, it made no difference.

Once Run Run Shaw heard about Bruce's decision to work for Golden Harvest he countered with an improved offer. But Bruce had already signed and intended to honour the contract. Even so, a worried Chow tried to insist that Bruce fly directly to Bangkok, rather than going via Hong Kong.

On arrival in Bangkok, Bruce was driven north to the filming location in the remote village of Pak Chong. In the middle of the hot season, the small hotel was a hellhole with no air conditioning to alleviate the soaring heat and humidity, polluted water, no mail service to speak of and no fresh food. Pak Chong was a place for which only insect lovers might find some enthusiasm. Yet Bruce did not complain; he was here to make a film to be called *The Big Boss*, and that was good enough.

16
THE BIG BOSS

MARIA YI, LEADING actress in *The Big Boss*, looked down from the window of her hotel room, slightly puzzled. Several times she'd seen Bruce Lee lying in his trunks beside the pool but she'd never seen him swimming. What she didn't know was that Bruce had never overcome his childhood aversion to swimming that resulted from his sister Phoebe holding his head underwater after he'd shoved her into a pool.

Later, at dinner, Maria watched Bruce struggle with a tasteless steak as hard as the plate he was eating it off; this was one fight he gave up on. A few days earlier Bruce had broken a glass in his hand, resulting in a gash that required ten stitches. While at the hospital in Bangkok he had caught flu and rapidly lost ten pounds. Now, with one hand bandaged, he held his fork in the other and raced to finish his meal before the cockroaches and lizards got to it.

The simple plot of *The Big Boss* concerns the Chinese community in Bangkok who live in fear of Thai gangsters run by a Japanese boss. The film's budget was less than $100,000, which at the time wouldn't even have paid for a sixty-second TV commercial in the States.

In *The Big Boss*,* Bruce Lee plays Cheng Chao An, who has left behind a troubled life in China to start afresh in Thailand. In turning over a new leaf, Cheng has vowed to his mother that he will not get into any more fights and wears her locket to remind him of his promise. Cheng is met in Thailand by his cousin, played by James Tien. As they stop at a roadside drink stand to refresh themselves, the serving girl (Nora Miao) is harassed by a bunch of louts. As his cousin drives them away with some fighting moves, Cheng fingers the locket and looks on wistfully. Arriving at his uncle's house Cheng meets his other cousin, the pretty Mei Lin (Maria Yi).

Once settled in, Cheng gets a job in the local ice factory. Shortly afterwards, two of the factory workers discover that some of the ice blocks are being used to transport drugs, and when they refuse to join in the operation they are killed. Suspicious about the missing pair, the other workers go on strike, demanding an explanation. The boss of the ice factory (a mean Japanese named Mi) calls in his Thai goons to put down the restive workers and a battle breaks out between the Thais and the Chinese. At first Cheng is torn between his impulse to help his fellow workers and his promise to his mother. But when he is struck by a metal hook wielded by one of the thugs he enters the fray, and in a series of stunning set pieces wipes out the enemy. At the end of the fight Cheng finds the locket, broken in two.

This makes Cheng the workers' hero, but the crafty factory manager promotes him and later invites him to a party at Mi's house. There, the naïve Cheng ends up drunk and chases some

---

* *The Big Boss* was released in the US as *Fists of Fury* (see also the note on pages 367–8). Throughout this book, Bruce Lee's films are referred to by the titles under which they were known on their initial release.

whores, hired by the manager, around the table in a comic scene. Cheng ends up in a bedroom with a woman but he falls asleep before she is even undressed and wakes in the morning cuddling her like a teddy bear.

Now Cheng is shunned by the other workers who believe he has sold them out. Later, Mi's prostitute takes Cheng to the brothel where she works and tells him the truth about Mi's operations. When he returns to the factory, Cheng discovers that some of the ice blocks do contain packages of drugs. In two other blocks of ice he also finds the frozen bodies of the missing workers.

At that moment Mi's son arrives with his gang. Cheng, now alone, fights twenty thugs wielding knives, clubs and chains in a series of remarkable fights. Moments of bloody violence (he kills a thug by splitting his head with a saw) are followed by cartoon-like violence as he punches one of the gang clean through a wooden fence, leaving a gap in the shape of a man.

Cheng then returns to Mi's mansion for a final showdown on the lawn. In the knife fight that follows, Cheng's shirt is ripped off and he is cut by a villain's blade. He pauses and tastes the blood from the wound before the climactic and cathartic final scene. Having killed all of Mi's men, Cheng realizes that he will have to pay. In the closing scenes, he gives himself up when the police arrive.

In the first week of filming Bruce found it harder and harder to keep his impatience in check. The equipment used for filming was old and in bad repair and the 'script' consisted of a few basic ideas scribbled on scraps of paper. The director, Wu Chai Wsaing, had a violent temper and screamed and ranted at the entire cast and crew until the production manager – the same Mrs Lo Wei who had signed Bruce to the Golden Harvest contract – could take no more. Mrs Lo Wei called

Raymond Chow and demanded that Wu be replaced. By a happy coincidence, one of Chow's directors, a certain *Mr* Lo Wei, had just finished a film in Taiwan and he was duly dispatched to Thailand to work on *The Big Boss*. The new director, however, proved to be no better than the first.

A compulsive gambler, Lo Wei was far more concerned with what was going on at the racetrack than what was happening on the film set. Because sound was not recorded at the same time as the action was filmed, Lo Wei arranged to have the commentary of the horse races booming across the set while the actors were attempting to play a scene. Bruce was incensed by Lo Wei's lack of involvement in the picture.

Bruce sprained his ankle badly when landing awkwardly from a jump. He could not move properly and was also racked with aches and fever and was having difficulty keeping food down. Even so the filming continued. His twisted ankle meant that he had to drag his injured leg, so in several scenes he had to be filmed in close-up. The cut on his hand had still not healed and he needed rest and injections for back pain after every scene. Lo Wei considered Bruce a hypochondriac.

At the same time Bruce was also trying to improve the poor script as he went along. Although Han Ying Chieh, the actor who played the boss, was also the official fight coordinator of the film, Bruce took control over his own fight scenes almost immediately. When there was some dispute, he would disrupt filming by some little strategy such as 'losing' one of his contact lenses while filming in the ice-cutting factory where there were thousands of tiny ice chips on the floor.

Other scenes were filmed in a local brothel which was dirty and smelly. The prostitutes, accustomed to getting less than a dollar a trick, were paid $10 to do nothing except keep out of the way. At least they would be able to recall one day's work when they didn't get screwed.

*

While Bruce was isolated deep in Thailand, *Longstreet* opened the autumn TV season in the United States to good reviews. At last, Bruce Lee and Stirling Silliphant had realized a small part of what they had been hoping to achieve together for many years. Bruce's episode generated more fan mail than the rest of the series and most of it was addressed to Bruce. Stirling Silliphant was quite right when he said that it was Bruce's first good film and one of the best martial arts shows ever seen on TV.

Tom Tannenbaum immediately tried to track Bruce down to get his agreement to appear in further episodes of *Longstreet*, but no one could get a message to him, hours away from the nearest city. This situation worked to Bruce's advantage. As the telegrams kept arriving, Golden Harvest executives were not slow to notice that US producers were chasing their new actor.

Ploughing through the pile of telegrams waiting for him on his return to Hong Kong, Bruce found offers to appear in three further episodes of *Longstreet* for $1,000 a show. Knowing that a second picture for Golden Harvest was already in the bag, Bruce asked Paramount to double their offer, and they agreed. Linda could now quit her job, but they were still in deep trouble over the house payments.

When Bruce returned to Los Angeles, it turned out that the three *Longstreet* episodes in question had long been written; in view of Bruce's surprise success in the first episode, Paramount had tried to work him into more stories. Bruce found himself making brief, hastily written appearances that were little more than walk-on parts.

Despite this, there was still a feeling that something was about to break. Paramount made a new option offer. Warners revitalized the prospect of developing a TV series for him. What was the best course to take? How were audiences going to react to *The Big Boss?* Should he keep his options open? There were more questions to be considered. Yet Bruce was feeling certain about one thing: his time had come.

Although only a Boy Scout band welcomed Bruce on his return to Hong Kong, there was a big enough crowd of journalists to indicate that even before *The Big Boss* had opened something was happening. In October 1971, together with Raymond Chow and his partner Leonard Ho, Bruce and Linda sat and waited for the midnight premiere of the film. They joked a little, trying to ease the apprehension they were all feeling. Hong Kong audiences would openly jeer a film they didn't like; they were even known to attack the seats with knives if it was really poor.

When the film ended, a stunned silence lasting a few seconds was followed by complete uproar. Bruce was mobbed as he tried to leave the theatre. The next day's press was equally ecstatic.

From the opening credits, *The Big Boss* is obviously a film made on a shoestring budget. The credits themselves were drawn by a rather shaky hand and there are enough wobbly camera shots in the film itself to suggest that most of it was shot without any retakes. Canned cocktail jazz muzak adds a bizarre note to the death scenes. But *The Big Boss* was both better acted and plotted than any comparable film and a half-credible storyline strung together realistic action sequences.

To Western tastes, Chinese films were either too understated or over the top. When watching Bruce Lee's Chinese films one must remember that they are not acted realistically as are films in the West. Mandarin film-making stems from a long theatrical tradition. The plots, set designs, costumes, gestures and expressions are rooted in the mime traditions of theatres like the Cantonese Opera Company in which Bruce's father used to act as he too pursued a career in films. If a comparison can be made, similar elements can be seen in the silent films made in the early days of Hollywood.

To Western eyes, *The Big Boss* may have seemed like just one more in a long line of cheap exploitation films streaming from Asia. But in the context of the Hong Kong film industry, whose staple fare was windmilling fistfights and buckets of blood, the film was revolutionary. Bruce Lee had used his American experience and given his and the other characters a few human touches. What to the West might appear over-stated, clumsy or even camp was the closest anyone had come to realism in the Asian film world.

More importantly, Mandarin audiences had a genuine star. Bruce Lee was not a jobbing actor who had been put through Shaw's drama school, he was a natural. Bruce Lee had the same charisma that made James Dean a star, and without which someone like Robert de Niro is merely a skilled actor.

The fight scenes alone would have been enough to make Bruce a star in the East. The moves are all executed with a fluidity and discipline born of nearly two decades of practice. To prove that the fights were not merely the result of camera trickery or slick editing, Bruce insisted on long takes, letting the camera run for up to half a minute on a single shot. Though the exaggerated feats of the old style Mandarin films are not entirely absent, Bruce managed to keep the action more organized and to reduce the emphasis on weapons in order to showcase the kind of action that had never been seen on film before.

Within three weeks of its release, *The Big Boss* smashed the local box office record, earning over $HK3 million. The film was shown 875 times in Hong Kong before going on to break records throughout the whole Mandarin circuit. From the audience reaction at the premiere Bruce knew that the film would earn well, but he hadn't anticipated a runaway hit. Neither, of course, had Run Run Shaw, who was left to bemoan his fate. 'Bruce Lee was just another actor,' he sighed heavily. 'How could I have known?'

While Bruce prepared to make his second film, Golden Harvest provided a small furnished apartment at 2 Man Wan Road in the Waterloo Hill area of Kowloon. The elevators in the building rarely worked and rather than have everyone trudge up and down the stairs, Bruce turned it into a game in which they ran up the thirteen flights of stairs.

Wu Ngan, Bruce's adopted brother, lodged with the family and soon became Bruce's steward. Later, when Wu Ngan married, his wife joined them. Two-year-old Shannon started attending a local nursery school, while six-year-old Brandon went to La Salle, the school from which Bruce had been expelled some years earlier.

17
FIST OF FURY

IN 1971, BEFORE the premiere of *The Big Boss*, Bruce Lee had already started work on his second film. *Fist of Fury** is a hymn of revenge which played on the deep animosities between the Chinese and the Japanese.

The story begins with a real historical event, the death of a Chinese martial arts teacher, Ho Yuan Chia, in 1908. At the turn of the twentieth century the Japanese had established a strong political presence in Shanghai. Ho was a stevedore of extraordinary strength and ability who once routed an entire troop of Japanese challengers. Bruce Lee plays Chen Chen, a former student of the old master, who arrives back at the Ching Wu school to pay his respects to his teacher only to find that he has just died. At the funeral a distraught Chen flings himself into the grave and tries to claw open the coffin. 'How can a healthy man die?' he wails.

The master's memory is insulted when Mi Wu, a reptilian Chinese who works as a translator for the Japanese martial arts association, presents the students with a tablet inscribed 'To

---

* Originally entitled *The School for Chivalry*, it was renamed *Fist of Fury* and later released under the title *The Chinese Connection* in the United States.

the Sick Nation of Eastern Asia'. He goads Chen to retaliate with one of the worst unintentional dubbing puns ever heard in a film: 'What's the matter; are you yellow or something?' Chen is so enraged by this insult that despite his teacher's code he goes to the Japanese club where he single-handedly wipes out the entire membership and smashes the insulting tablet. The Japanese association's president demands Chen's arrest and he has to go into hiding.

In the meantime Chen discovers that two spies had a hand in poisoning his teacher. Not immediately obvious to Western audiences is how Chen achieves this by noticing the difference between Chinese and Japanese styles of underwear. Chen kills them and hangs their bodies from a lamp post outside the house of the Japanese consul. While Chen is hiding out in a graveyard eating a roasted cat, the Japanese wreck the Chinese school, showing no mercy to the women students and desecrating the shrine to the master's memory. Chen's fiancée finds him in the graveyard and they make plans to run away together and start a new life. But later Chen decides to seek out the instigator and avenge his teacher's murder.

Lo Wei, who was again directing the film, also played the detective on Chen's trail. Meanwhile, the Japanese school is holding a welcome party for a Russian wrestler (Bob Baker) who has found it necessary to leave his country. Leering at belly dancers and guzzling sake, they insult their Chinese collaborator, Mi Wu, who crawls away drunk. Once outside he staggers to a rickshaw that happens to be driven by Chen, now in one of his many disguises. Chen picks up the whole rickshaw, holding it and its passenger several feet in the air, and hears him confess that it was Suzuki, the head of the Japanese school, who had ordered the murder of his teacher. As Chen kills Wu, more badly translated dialogue has Wu whining, 'Why is everyone always picking on me?' before he too is hung from a lamp post.

Now disguised as a telephone repairman, Chen gains entry to the Japanese school. (Bruce posing as a Japanese was something that sent the Chinese fans wild with delight.) Once inside the school, Chen fights his way past a swordsman and the Russian wrestler to the inner sanctum, where he avenges his teacher by killing Suzuki in combat. Chen returns to his own school and sees that a massacre has taken place, but when the police arrive and threaten to close the school down under pressure from the Japanese authorities, Chen emerges from his hiding place and surrenders to the Shanghai police, with the assurance that his fellow students will be spared and his school's honour will remain intact.

At the school gates, a row of armed police level their rifles at him. Bare-chested and defiant, Chen runs headlong at them, launching himself in a glorious death leap into a hail of his persecutors' bullets.

As with *The Big Boss*, this second picture went into production with the story little more than an outline of how the action might develop. Equipment and facilities at Golden Harvest proved to be no better than in Thailand. The already strained relationship between Bruce Lee and Lo Wei now went from bad to worse. Bruce was furious at Lo Wei's continuing lack of attention. Silent and patient forbearance was not Bruce's most prominent quality and there were several clashes as the film progressed. In Thailand this had not been too damaging, but now that Bruce was a local star and the filming was taking place in the heart of Hong Kong, the local press was quick to make the feud public knowledge.

Lo Wei himself had started in the film industry as an actor in 1948 before becoming a director in 1957. He had made over eighty low-budget feature films, mostly for Shaw Brothers, before Raymond Chow brought him to Golden Harvest. He was not going to be told his business by a young upstart who was only making his second film. Soon, the two could not agree on anything.

Even so, *Fist of Fury* was completed in six weeks. Many of the faces seen in *The Big Boss* appeared again. Like the previous film, *Fist of Fury* was made for $100,000. Much of the budget was spent on creating the two Japanese buildings and gardens with bridges and pools. One week was spent on location at a nearby park. There, Lo Wei had to contend with local street gangs, whose leaders would demand payment for using 'their bit' of road. The protection money was usually paid, much to the annoyance of Bruce, who had to be restrained from attacking the hustlers.

The production values of *Fist of Fury* were higher than those of *The Big Boss*. Spaghetti western soundtrack music was added. But far more evocative were the sounds made by Bruce during the fight scenes in which the fist of the title appears at times almost to have a will of its own. Although offscreen Bruce fought with silent efficiency, in *Fist of Fury* he lets out strangely beautiful cries that sound like a wild cat or a screeching bird, adding to the effect of his animal grace. In the English-language version, some of the effect is spoiled by the ludicrous voice used to dub the speaking parts, but at least the animal cries are Bruce's.

Stunts (like the ten-foot trampoline-powered leap in *The Big Boss*) were again included at Lo Wei's insistence. These also detract from Bruce's real abilities. The scene where he picks up the rickshaw and passenger and holds them several feet in the air is an impossible feat and denies his real skills, which were themselves only slightly short of miraculous.

Adding to the power of his fighting action and cries, some of Bruce's facial expressions have an almost elemental power to them. At times his face registers an extraordinary blend of emotions: the shock at taking a life, the ecstasy of revenge, regret that it has to be this way, the strange gaze that enters his eyes as he kills an opponent. Yet perhaps all of this was overshadowed by Bruce's introduction of the weapon that will forever be associated with him, the *nunchaku*. Although the *nunchaku* had made a brief appearance in *The Green Hornet*, *Fist of Fury* marks its first real use in film.

The *nunchaku* are two short hardwood sticks connected by a flexible chain or cord. When one of the clubs is grasped the other can be swung to strike with up to 1,600 pounds of force at the point of impact. The shock of this impact is not transferred to the club held in the striker's hand, isolated by the short connecting cord.

The *nunchaku* that Bruce Lee uses on screen are lighter than the heavy wooden weapons normally used for combat. These lighter 'chucks' could be spun and switched even faster, adding to the excitement. When the swooping noises of rushing air were overdubbed later the scenes became even more impressive. Although Bruce was not the film's official fight coordinator, his influence is overwhelming, and nowhere more than in the *nunchaku* scenes.*

The chucks did not start out as a weapon but as a tool. They were used originally by farmers on the island of Okinawa, in the East China Sea, for flailing rice to separate the grain from the husk. When the Japanese invaded Okinawa they confiscated all the weapons on the island. The islanders, a melting-pot community at the heart of several trading routes, had over the centuries merged fighting skills from China with those of other Asian cultures. Now they resourcefully developed a system of fighting by employing their farming tools as

---

* These *nunchaku* scenes were edited out in the UK version. In the US *nunchaku* were banned in some states, including Bruce's home state of California. There is some irony in this, given the availability of guns and the number of shootings that occur in the States.

weapons. Also on the island were many Chinese families, including several monks who had set up home there. Okinawan rebels persuaded these monks to teach them the secrets of Chinese hand-to-hand combat.

Eventually the Japanese discovered this method and absorbed these fighting techniques into their own culture. By the 1930s schools were flourishing all over Japan. This new style was called karate, a literal translation of 'Chinese hand', although its meaning was later changed to mean 'empty hand'.

Karate, barely twenty years old, was far better known in America than *kung fu*, which was many centuries old, due to karate being brought back by US servicemen after the war. The fact that karate originated with Shaolin monks who had taught their skills to the Okinawans in order to help them repel their Japanese invaders was not wasted on Bruce Lee.

The opening scenes of *Fist of Fury* dug deep into Chinese popular feeling. The Chinese had been plundered and exploited for centuries by stronger foreign powers. For hundreds of years the relationship between the Chinese and Japanese had been one of open hostility punctuated by regular periods of war. Japan had been responsible for the territorial division of China at the turn of the twentieth century and had gone on to humiliate China, Hong Kong, and the rest of Asia during the Second World War. Despite his years in the United States, Bruce was well aware of national feelings, and played shamelessly on them. He also derived great satisfaction at portraying a lone *kung fu* artist wiping out an entire school of karate practitioners.

When Bruce Lee slowly cast his gaze over his Japanese opponents and declared, 'Now you listen to me, and I'll only say it once: we are not sick men,' audiences went wild, leaping to their feet or onto the seats to howl their approval and delight.

Another key scene sums up the mood of the picture: Bruce rips down a sign that reads 'No Dogs or Chinese' from the entrance of Shanghai Park, and using a flying overhead kick smashes it to pieces. This is no cinematic fabrication; such a sign actually hung there. For good measure, en route to the film's climax where Bruce dispatches the samurai who had killed his master, he also finishes off the Russian played by Bob Baker.

By the end of his second film Bruce Lee had advanced from being a supreme screen fighter who was genuinely as good as he appeared, to becoming much more. He had done something dreamed of by every politician: he was now a household name. He had become a national hero.

In the weeks following the release of *Fist of Fury*, the atmosphere on the streets of Hong Kong must have resembled that in England after the English football team beat Germany in the 1966 World Cup final. It wasn't simply a matter of winning a game of football, just as what was happening on the streets of Hong Kong in 1971 was more than popular reaction to an exciting new movie. It was a matter of national pride, of triumph over a bitter rival. In this sense, *Fist of Fury* was no worse than the great rash of war films that came out in the 1950s in which the Germans and the Japanese were always villainous caricatures.

Bruce Lee had struck a nerve that ran right into the heart of his countrymen. He had replaced a sense of self-doubt and inferiority with one of dignity, identity and victory. To their astonishment, the new hero of the Hong Kong Chinese was Chinese!

In its first four-week run, *Fist of Fury* broke the record set by *The Big Boss* by taking in over $HK4 million. Outside the cinemas, tickets changed hands for $50. In Singapore, the film had to be withdrawn for a week while traffic police found a way of dealing with the numbers of people clamouring to see it. In the Philippines, the government withdrew the film in order to give some of their own films a chance to earn some money.

Even though hardly a soul in the West was aware of it, Bruce Lee was undoubtedly the fastest rising star in the world and the industry's hottest property. Suddenly he was unable to walk down the street or eat in a restaurant without quickly drawing a crowd. While young men everywhere in Southeast Asia wanted to be like Bruce Lee, it also seemed that every young girl wanted to marry him. And it wasn't only young people who were suddenly made aware of Bruce's unique skills. A middle-aged Englishman in a neat business suit who was interviewed as he left a theatre showing the film said, 'He's in a league of his own. It's a question of body movement and choreography, the timing, the overcoming of human limitations.'

There were troublesome aspects of Bruce's instant celebrity, including a rapid increase in the number of challenges to fight made by every street punk who wanted a moment of glory. Already photos of Bruce Lee were appearing every day in the Chinese newspapers alongside articles linking him to every local starlet or revealing the latest twists in his running battle with Lo Wei. The director had now taken to calling himself Hong Kong's first 'millionaire director', while claiming all credit for the success of Bruce's films. Lo Wei managed to destroy any credibility he might have had by claiming that he had taught Bruce Lee to fight on the set of *The Big Boss*, saying that while Bruce was a good street fighter, he had found it necessary to teach him how to fight on film.

The truth of the matter was that Bruce Lee had not only propelled Lo Wei to his ten minutes of glory, but had single-handedly saved Golden Harvest and Raymond Chow from obscurity. And now that Bruce had fulfilled his two-picture contract for Chow he was free to negotiate a new contract. Producers from all across Southeast Asia were desperate to get his name on a contract. People would stop Bruce in the street and hand him cheques for large sums, which he immediately tore up, knowing that if he had cashed any of them he would have found that he had committed himself to some project or another. Run Run Shaw, who only a year previously had thought that $10,000 was too much to pay Bruce, now proposed the biggest pay rise in history by offering him twenty times that much. When Bruce refused, a blank cheque followed. Some producers were offering a reward of $10,000 to anyone who could get Bruce Lee's signature on a contract. One of Bruce's distant relatives, Yu Ming, was suddenly inspired to seek out his long-lost cousin. All of this served only to make Bruce very wary. Suddenly, he no longer knew who to trust or who was trying to take advantage of him.

One thing was certain: Bruce Lee would no longer work like a hired hand for wages. He went to see Raymond Chow and suggested they become partners. Chow, realizing that Run Run Shaw was still waiting just down the road, rightly figured that half of the profits an association with Bruce was sure to generate was a lot better than none. The two men formed Concord Productions, with Bruce in charge of creative decisions and Chow making the day-to-day business decisions.

Unfortunately, Chow's first decision was to ask Lo Wei to direct a new film with Bruce, to be called *Yellow-Faced Tiger*, which was set to start filming in Japan in January 1972. Again there was no script for the film, and Bruce refused to commit himself until there was one. Although they went through the charade of several abortive planning sessions, in truth Bruce had no intention of ever letting Lo Wei anywhere near another of his films and had already said so in public. Bruce declared that he wanted to write his own scripts, he wanted to direct his own films, and he wanted a share of the profits too, because it was his ideas and his appearance in the films that drew the crowds. No Hong Kong film actor had ever done this before. He took this line not because he thought he was the best writer or the best director around, but because he had no confidence in, or respect for, hack directors. Bruce believed his own enthusiasm would result in a better film than one that came off Lo Wei's conveyor belt.

As Bruce began to write a script and prepared to direct a film to be called *Way of the Dragon*, ripples started to spread through the Hong Kong film industry. Before Bruce decided to write and direct, actors had just taken their wages and done what they were told. No matter how well a film did only the producers saw any profit; everyone else took a salary, and usually not a very good one. Now that Bruce had opened the door, other leading actors pressed for better pay and conditions, and the effect filtered all the way down the line to the technicians and crews. Not only did Bruce think it was fairer that key people had some profit participation, he also reasoned that it would increase everyone's enthusiasm and involvement in a project which would in turn raise the standards of the films being made. That Bruce Lee's films came to international attention and that Hong Kong films became more competently made was in no small part due to his revitalizing effect on an industry whose methods had become stale and perfunctory. One Hong Kong newspaper commented: 'Bruce Li is clearly an asset amid a local film industry bankrupt in everything but quantity.'

It was during this period that Bruce gave interviews and wrote articles for an extensive series in the Far Eastern press. Taken together, they reveal both his ambitions and his dilemmas.

Bruce found himself answering charges of glorifying violence in scenes like the one in *The Big Boss* where he splits a man's head in half with a saw (the scene was censored in the UK version). Bruce claimed that the way he portrayed it was bordering on fantasy. The real violence, he said, was the slaughter happening in Vietnam. For Bruce the problem was that all his audiences wanted from him was action, and they saw him only as a 'superhero'. Bruce complained to the *Hong Kong Standard* that if he really expressed what he wanted to in his films then audiences wouldn't understand him most of the time. His ambition, he said, was to make films that were both serious, philosophical and entertaining, and to take some responsibility for educating his audience.

Bruce saw the root problems of the Hong Kong film industry as its lack of quality and commitment and a lack of basic professionalism. He found Mandarin films overplayed and the scripts poor. He told *New Nation* (an English-language newspaper in Singapore) that often he was the only one who turned up to work on time, while others drifted in up to an hour later. He declared himself willing to invest as much energy in film-making as he had in martial arts. He saw his twelve years in the United States as a period of preparation and growth. To those who said he was simply lucky, he countered that he had made his own luck by being aware of opportunities and taking advantage of them, and by spending thousands and thousands of days perfecting his skills.

But even as Bruce basked in the attention, continuing to clarify his intentions and pour out his ambitions to the press (who now called him the King of Hong Kong), early in 1972 he had to sell the Bel Air home that had drained his money faster than it could be earned. It was sold at a small profit, in need of some repair.

18

WAY OF THE DRAGON

BRUCE LEE HAD made two successful films in the East but his ambitions lay in the West. Even as he planned his third film he still anxiously awaited a decision from Warners and the ABC network about *The Warrior*. He wanted the part desperately and had set his mind on it so much that he told his friends and the local press that matters were virtually settled.

But towards the end of 1971, an interview he did for Canadian TV indicated that things were not going his way at all. The Canadian news reporter Pierre Berton, who was one of the first in the West to realize that a new phenomenon was happening, flew to Hong Kong to interview Bruce.

> **Berton**: Are you going to stay in Hong Kong and be famous, or are you going to the United States and be famous?
>
> **Bruce**: I'm gonna do both. Because I have already made up my mind that in the United States, I think something of the Oriental, I mean the true Oriental, should be shown.
>
> **Berton**: Hollywood sure as heck hasn't.
>
> **Bruce**: You better believe it, man. I mean, it's always the pigtail and the bouncing around, chop-chop, you know, with the eyes slanted and all that.

Berton: Let me ask you about the problems that you face as a Chinese hero in an American series. Have people come up to you in the industry and said, 'Well, we don't know how the audience is going to take a non-American.'

Bruce: Well, the question has been raised. In fact, it is being discussed, and that is why *The Warrior* is probably not going to be on . . . They think, business-wise, it's a risk. And I don't blame them . . . If I were the man with the money, I would probably have my own worry whether or not the acceptance would be there.

Berton: How about the other side of the coin: is it possible that you are – well, you're fairly hip and fairly Americanized – are you too Western for Oriental audiences?

Bruce: I have been criticized for that.

On 7 December 1971, Bruce received a telegram from Warners saying that 'due to pressures from the network regarding casting' he had been dropped from *The Warrior* TV series, by now renamed *Kung Fu*.

Here was a story with a Chinese background, with a Chinese man as the lead character, and one of the reasons that Bruce was given for his being dropped was that he looked too Chinese! Other reasons were offered: he was too short; he had too strong a Chinese accent; he was not a big enough name to carry a weekly TV show; he didn't have enough experience. But as Warners' head of television Tom Kuhn admitted, 'Although we knew that he wanted it, Bruce Lee was never seriously considered.'

On 22 February 1972, ABC-TV's *Movie of the Week* was the pilot for the *Kung Fu* series. The accompanying publicity release explained the theme:

Kwai Chang Caine, a Chinese-American fugitive from a murder charge in Imperial China, becomes a superhero to the coolies building the transcontinental railroad, through his mastery of an ancient science-religion.

Kung Fu told the story of a wandering Shaolin warrior-priest, a man of peace yet one who was capable of inflicting instant death. It repeated the familiar theme of a hero who tries at all costs to avoid fighting until there is no other course.

The lead role in the series was offered to actor and dancer David Carradine (who looked only a little Chinese) despite the fact that Carradine's only knowledge of *kung fu* was that he had heard the expression – twice. Most of the early action of the series featured judo moves because the technical advisor David Chow also knew little about *kung fu*. Eventually a new technical director, Kam Yuen, was brought in.

Joe Lewis, the karate star who trained with Bruce Lee, recalls Bruce's own idea for the opening of what became the *Kung Fu* series: a heavily ornamented Chinese-looking stagecoach pulls into a dusty main street. As the local cowboys amble up to look it over, the doors fly open and out jumps a man in a *kung fu* suit. Lewis says that when Warners gave the part to David Carradine, Bruce decided that he would concentrate on Hong Kong to begin his climb to success, just as Clint Eastwood and Charles Bronson had needed to go to Europe first to become stars. Lewis adds, 'It hurt Bruce when he failed to get the *Kung Fu* series. He experienced a lot of rejection.'

Bruce Lee had been thinking about writing and directing long before he had gone to Hong Kong to make his first film for Golden Harvest. Joe Lewis says during the time that he and Chuck Norris were training with Bruce, he would often mention ideas for films. Although Joe Lewis and Bruce worked together when Bruce choreographed the fights for *The Wrecking Crew*, Lewis declined to get involved in Bruce's new venture. Lewis felt that in this film Bruce was aiming to show that the Oriental martial artist was superior to the Caucasian.

Lewis claims that Bruce wanted to cast him as 'a big, strong, muscular, blue-eyed, blond-haired, all-American punch bag'. But Bruce countered that the problem was finding Western martial artists (who were almost always of much bigger physique) who were fast enough to fight him convincingly. Bruce said that he asked Chuck Norris to appear in *Way of the Dragon* because Norris was one of the few martial artists who was fast enough. Bruce observed that he had worked on his own speed because a smaller man who can swing faster hits as hard as a heavier man who swings slowly. 'And besides,' he added, 'you can't keep fighting midgets.'

Joe Lewis obviously felt that the power of the stronger and heavier Western martial artist would ultimately prevail over the speed of the faster and lighter Oriental martial artist, and that is why he declined to act to the contrary.

Lewis continues: 'Bruce knew that he was asking me to get involved with a movie in which I got my butt beat by a little 128-pound Chinese guy who had never been in the ring.'

A succinct comment from Bruce's mother shows that Joe Lewis was not so far off the mark. Grace Lee recalls: 'Bruce told me, "Mom, I'm an Oriental person, therefore I have to defeat all the whites in the film." I don't believe he had ever mentioned this to Chuck Norris.'

Joe Lewis and Bruce Lee never fought in earnest, so the outcome of such a contest is open to debate. Lewis does acknowledge, however, how he won his contest against heavyweight karate champion Greg Baines in Los Angeles, on 17 January 1970: 'I used a lot of the stuff Bruce Lee had shown me.'

An African-American Muslim, whose rippling muscles testified to his years of dedicated training, Baines was the favourite. As the fight started, Baines took the traditional deep wide stance of the *karateka*. There were a few subdued chuckles as Lewis began bobbing around the ring, darting in and out scoring points against the nearly stationary Baines. Each time Baines would attempt a kick, Lewis intercepted and jammed the kicking leg then countered quickly with combination punches. When Baines threw a karate punch, Lewis trapped the striking hand while countering with his own strike. The audience were at first bemused and then stunned.

In the next round Baines did no better. Although he was doing nothing wrong according to traditional karate methods, Lewis wasn't observing any of the traditions. His stance was light and fast; he deflected punches instead of blocking them; he kept his hands high not low. And instead of locking his arm out rigidly like an iron bar, his punches whipped in and out 'like an iron ball on a steel chain – WHANG!' Then, in an unprecedented move, Lewis faked to go one way but changed his attack, tumbling Baines to the canvas.

Says Lewis, 'I set the guy up with the forward hand strike that Bruce had shown me in *jeet kune do*, then I came across with a good ol' boxing right hook. It finished the match.'

Nobody in the audience could justify any longer the domination of traditional karate. Some of them refused to see the obvious and blamed Baines for lack of spirit, yet it was the tools that he had been using that were lacking, not Baines himself. Just as the karate champion had been stopped in his tracks, so had the smug superiority of the traditionalists.

In early 1972, in preparation for filming *Way of the Dragon*,* Bruce Lee bought and read a dozen books dealing with all aspects of film-making. Placing incredible demands on his energy, he intended virtually to make the entire picture himself:

* To add to the confusion, because *Way of the Dragon* was released in the US after *Enter the Dragon*, it is known there as *Return of the Dragon*.

to write, produce, direct and star in it; to scout the locations, cast it, choose the wardrobe and choreograph the fight scenes. In the process he lost several pounds of hard-won weight.

For the storyline, Bruce drew on his memories of leaving Hong Kong for San Francisco in 1958 and on his experiences as a waiter at Ruby Chow's restaurant. When he had first arrived in the United States, Bruce had bought a Chinese-English dictionary; he now found himself referring to it to help him find the appropriate Chinese words rather than English ones so that he could express his ideas in planning meetings with his assistants.

Way of the Dragon was the first Hong Kong-based picture to be shot in Europe. At $130,000, the budget was slightly higher than his previous films but production costs were covered by pre-sales to Taiwan. On 4 May 1972, the first team arrived in Rome. It consisted of Bruce, Raymond Chow and Nashinoto Tadashi, a Japanese cameraman Bruce hired because he considered the Japanese to have more technical expertise. Three days later, leading actress Nora Miao along with other members of cast and crew arrived in Rome, after spending nineteen hours on a plane routed by way of Thailand, India and Israel.

Bruce let the crew rest for a couple of days, but when actual shooting started on the 10th, he proved to be a demanding director who expected the same level of commitment from everyone else that he himself was prepared to invest. In the following days they buzzed around Rome, pausing to film illegally at the Colosseum. At the Trevi fountain, they stayed long enough for Bruce to throw a coin into the water and make a wish. It's not hard to imagine what it was.

Having shot the location set-ups, Bruce could now turn his attention to more important matters: the fight scenes. In contrast to the speed at which he'd hounded everyone around Rome, shooting over sixty scenes in one day alone, he now spent over forty-five hours on his fight scene with Chuck Norris. Bruce's choreographed directions for this scene took up nearly a quarter of the script itself. As with all the fight scenes, Bruce watched the daily rushes; any unconvincing moment of action meant the whole scene would be reshot. Knowing how it would look on camera, Bruce spent a lot of time teaching his co-actors how to react convincingly.

By the time the film was finished, Bruce had participated in yet another aspect of film-making: he played percussion on the music for the soundtrack.

In *Way of the Dragon*, Bruce Lee plays a country bumpkin named Tang Lung (China Dragon) who leaves Hong Kong and goes to Rome. While waiting to be met at the airport he goes into a restaurant, and having failed to communicate with the waitress, finds that he has ordered four plates of soup. Tang is later met by his cousin (played by Nora Miao) and as they drive to her apartment, she explains her problems. She has inherited a restaurant on some land wanted by the mob. But in the scene the story is more concerned with Tang's need to find a toilet, obviously something that had them rolling in the aisles in Hong Kong.

Way of the Dragon is played as a comedy. The film is cut with long pauses to accommodate the audience's reaction and the soundtrack is punctuated with comic 'wah-wah' sounds and 'boings' from the timpani. Yet for all that, with Bruce's direction the film features some outstanding fight scenes and even one or two excellent *kung fu* lessons.

All the waiters in the restaurant are learning karate in order to repel the thugs who are harassing them and driving away the restaurant's customers. Tang attends training sessions at the back of the premises where one of the waiters (Bruce's old friend Unicorn) is drilling the others (including Bruce's adopted brother Wu Ngan). An argument starts about the merits of the various fighting systems. 'It doesn't matter where it comes from,' says Tang, 'you can learn to use it.'

Later, when the thugs return to intimidate the customers, Tang does battle with them outside. The waiters are so impressed with what they see that they insist on a second lesson from him. In this lesson Bruce sidekicks an air bag and, just as he had done in *Longstreet*, sends the man who is holding it flying backwards. All the waiters vow to give up karate and learn Chinese fighting.

A further confrontation between Bruce and the thugs is played for laughs but contains some superb fight sequences, especially those featuring Bruce using the *nunchaku*.* The weapon's potential for being more dangerous to an inept user than to his opponent is a comic possibility seized on by Bruce. One of the Italian hoods manages to grab a weapon, and having seen Tang wielding it with nonchalant grace, now believes that he too is imbued with the supernatural power simply by possessing one. As he goes to strike Tang, he knocks himself out.

No matter how skilled a martial artist is, he can't beat a bullet. *Kung fu* movies were more credible in the East than in the United States and Europe because the martial arts tradition of places like Hong Kong and Singapore was intertwined with the British tradition of mainly unarmed police. There were no guns in the hands of most of the population because there was no access to them and most people could simply not afford them anyway. Men fought with their bodies, hand-to-hand, or used traditional and makeshift weapons.

In *Way of the Dragon*, Bruce had the gangsters carry guns

---

* In the UK version of *Way of the Dragon*, these scenes were so heavily censored that most of the action makes no sense at all.

and attempted to confront the problem by having Tang carve poison darts which he fires with unerring accuracy into the gangsters' gun hands, just as Kato had done in the first episode of *The Green Hornet*. These sequences do no more to overcome the major drawback of the martial arts genre than any other attempt and are the most unlikely scenes of the film. But the action that follows more than compensates.

Now that Tang has dispatched all of the local heavies, the godfather has to import hired fighters played by Wong In Sik, a Korean *hapkido* exponent, and karate stars Bob Wall and Chuck Norris. In the Western version of the film, Norris's character is named Colt. By offering a truce, the gang lures Tang into a trap. The first two opponents are dealt with, then, in a sudden shift of scene from the countryside to the centre of Rome, the final scene is fought out under the arches of the Colosseum. Tang and his ultimate Anglo-Saxon enemy, Colt, face each other with all the dignity and formality of two samurai warriors. The only spectator is a tiny kitten. Again there are comic moments, such as when Tang rips a handful of hair from Colt's chest, yet this fight scene is the best that Bruce Lee ever put on film. Although Bruce was anxious not to have the fight a completely one-sided affair, there was never any doubt as to what the eventual result would be.

In the first half of the screen fight, it is Colt who gets the upper hand, knocking Tang to the floor a couple of times and bloodying his mouth. The turning point comes when Tang speeds up his footwork and Colt follows him, not realizing that it is Tang who has gained the initiative and is now dictating the pace. Tang gets to his feet and bounces back, dancing and moving like Muhammad Ali, bewildering Colt who is accustomed only to the more rigid techniques of karate. The fight now follows a similar pattern to the one between Joe Lewis and Greg Baines. In the ensuing action, Tang delivers a devastatingly fast combination of strikes as he begins to over-whelm Colt, who sustains a broken arm and leg but struggles to his feet and continues the fight. Tang glances down at Colt's broken leg and shakes his head as if to tell him, 'Look, you've got nothing to prove. Stop this while you can.' But Colt's warrior code leaves him only two options: victory or death. Colt almost smiles in acceptance of his fate, then attacks with one last flurry of blows and in the final exchange, Tang breaks Colt's neck. At this moment that strange expression of remorse comes over Tang's face. He lowers Colt's body gently to the ground and respectfully places Colt's jacket and black belt over his body.

In beating Norris in the ruins of the Western world's greatest arena, Bruce Lee was again giving his audience exactly what they wanted to see. But he was also aware of the sentiments he was stirring and sought to include other lessons. The way he honours the opponent he has just killed is also in accordance with one of the tenets of the warrior's code: that a worthy opponent be treated with respect.

Bruce Lee told his friends that *Way of the Dragon* would be a hit on the Mandarin circuit but that he had no plans to release it in the West. Bruce's character is much softer and his haircut (brushed down with pointed sideburns) gives him an almost elfin look. The light humour, which had Eastern audiences convulsed with laughter, is perhaps a little corny. But Bruce's script was based on a real understanding of the Chinese psyche as he slowly strips his character Tang of his superficial naïveté, revealing the capable hero at heart.

To a chorus of disbelief from the Hong Kong press, Bruce predicted that the picture would earn $HK5 million. Shaking their heads in amazement, the journalists were also showing some irritation. They were no longer interested only in cele-brating the success of Bruce Lee but were now also looking for flaws. While dutifully reporting the new milestone in Bruce's career, the press also began speculating about who he might be sleeping with.

The Lee family had now moved from the small apartment on Man Wan Road into one of the few two-storey detached houses in Hong Kong, at 41 Cumberland Road in the Kowloon Tong area. Although the eleven-room house might have been considered average in Beverly Hills, in Hong Kong it was a palace. The large house had wrought-iron gates and an eight-foot stone wall enclosing a large Japanese garden where a stream wound through trees to a goldfish pond spanned by an ornamental bridge. All this could be viewed from the balcony of the main room in which Bruce had his hi-fi system set up. The house had enough space so that Bruce could have both a study for his thousands of books and a fully equipped gymnasium.

Bruce replaced the red Porsche that he'd had to give up in Los Angeles with a new red Mercedes 350 SL, most likely the same one seen in the closing shots of *Way of the Dragon*. And while he was again able to indulge his taste for silk suits, the press responded by voting him 'Worst-Dressed Actor of the Year'.

The new house had arrived just in time. It became Bruce's sanctuary – the only place he might enjoy some relative peace and privacy. A few years previously he used to put on impromptu displays of *kung fu* at dances, doing one-finger push-ups to attract an audience. Now he couldn't visit a restaurant without having to sit at a corner table with his back to everyone, hoping not to be noticed. But once the waiters began to hover, there would soon be a queue of people demanding autographs and asking familiar questions. By the time Bruce left the restaurant, he would have to face a jostling crowd of paparazzi. If he reacted badly to any of this, the next day's headlines would report on his arrogance and bad manners.

There was a double edge to all this. Bruce said that he now understood why stars like Steve McQueen avoided public places and regretted that he could no longer lead a normal life. Yet in recalling his earlier vow to be a bigger star than McQueen, Bruce couldn't resist revelling in his celebrity.

The pressure of sudden stardom is an entertainment business cliché, but it is real enough. While it drives some into becoming recluses or surrounding themselves with bodyguards, in Bruce's case yet another contradiction emerged. On the one hand, he fed off public response and the recognition that he had being trying for years to achieve. On the other hand, he could no longer pursue his art in the way that had made this all possible. The superficial social whirl of celebrity had no appeal for him. The paradox revealed itself at a party where a guest failed to recognize him: with a healthy dose of self-mockery he extended his hand and announced, 'Bruce Lee, movie star.'

The old money problems had eased but new problems were winding things up tighter than ever. Producers extended big offers, usually with the maximum of noise and the minimum of resources to back them up, simply as a way of increasing their own prestige and getting some free publicity. The *China Star*, a trashy Hong Kong daily, ran a series 'written' by Yip Chun, the son of Yip Man, who had at one time trained alongside Bruce. Yip Chun was quoted as saying that he had seen Bruce knocked down by an opponent during training. While no one could expect Bruce to have been invincible from the age of thirteen, the tone of the article upset Bruce enough to make him track down Yip Chun and ask him if he really had said what had been printed. Yip Chun denied it and claimed that it was an embellishment on the part of the article's ghostwriter. The *Star*'s boss, a hardbitten Australian named Graham Jenkins, duly reported that Bruce had threatened his paper's informant and Bruce began a legal action against the paper. Bruce found himself followed everywhere by photographers and reporters ready to hype up a sensation on the slightest pretext.

What the media didn't report were Bruce's simple acts of consideration towards others. Bob Wall offers an example:

> Both Bruce and I wore contact lenses and when we were fighting in the dust in the Roman countryside, we kept getting choked up. Bruce had some really good eye lotion and we were able to get through our fight scenes by using it. Later, as I was about to board the plane back to the USA, I saw a commotion outside the airport departure lounge – a crowd of people had gathered. Then I saw Bruce's red Mercedes and a few moments later he appeared in the lounge. He'd just driven out to the airport to give me a whole case of this eye lotion as a gift. Even with all the demands on his time, he'd taken the trouble to do that.

Bruce Lee had never been motivated purely by matters of wealth or status. Bombarded with invitations both to present or accept various awards and trophies, he elected instead to spend the time studying or training. Neither fame nor money were ends in themselves but the by-product of good work – things that arrived as the result of doing his work well. The biggest advantage of money was that it allowed him the autonomy to set his own standards.

As a martial arts teacher, Bruce had maintained standards which prevented him from over-commercializing his art. He sought to apply the same values to his films. It is doubtful whether the producers who were now hounding him understood the principles by which he was trying to operate; they simply tried to lure him onto their sets with promises of huge sums of money.

But just as fame was a side-effect of being the best, so wealth would be the natural outcome of work done with commitment and attention. For Bruce, what remained most important was the quality of one's work. A good studio carpenter earned his respect more than a hack director like Lo Wei.

In the slipstream of three successful films Bruce Lee planned a new film featuring some of the world's foremost martial artists, in part because he wanted to involve his friends and show his appreciation to them as both teachers and students. *Game of Death* was to be his crowning achievement.

19

GAME OF DEATH

WHEN BRUCE LEE was given the opportunity to meet the basketball giant 'Big Lew' Alcindor, he jumped at it. He was intrigued as to how he would solve the problem of fighting a man who was over seven feet tall. After their meeting in 1967, Big Lew became one of Bruce's star pupils. Alcindor is better known by the name Kareem Abdul Jabbar, taken when he converted to Islam. As the ace centre for the Milwaukee Bucks and later the Los Angeles Lakers, Jabbar became one of the top players in the game.

With *Way of the Dragon* finished, an exhausted Bruce planned to take a short rest. But when he heard that Jabbar was in Hong Kong, he swiftly arranged some action scenes that could be included in *Game of Death*. The two of them spent a week sparring and acting out fight scenes in front of the cameras. To make sure the action was convincing, Bruce practised one particular kick nearly 300 times. The result is some intriguing and strangely elegant footage of Bruce fighting a man who, two feet taller, towers over him.

There was no script for *Game of Death*, but Bruce had enough idea of the story to be able to take advantage of Jabbar's visit. The opening was clear in his mind:

As the film opens we see a wide expanse of snow. Then the camera closes in on a clump of trees while the sounds of a strong gale fill the screen. There is a huge tree in the centre of the screen, covered in thick snow. Suddenly there is a loud snap and a branch of the tree falls to the ground. It cannot yield to the force of the snow, so it breaks. Then the camera moves to a willow tree which is bending with the wind. Because it adapts to the environment, it survives. What I want to say is that a man has to be flexible and adaptable, otherwise he will be destroyed.

The rest of the story had been germinating in Bruce's imagination ever since he had stood on the northern border of India and seen the temples of Nepal. A national treasure is stolen and placed on the top floor of a pagoda on an island off the coast of Korea. As the hero, Bruce Lee is to recover the treasure. Outside, the pagoda is defended by a band of fighters led by a hulk of a man, while inside each floor is defended by a master of a particular martial art. The pagoda is, in fact, a training school for martial artists of different traditions; each floor is given over to students of different forms of combat. The first floor is ruled by a *karateka*, the second by a *hapkido* exponent, the third by a *kung fu* master, the fourth by an *escrima* master, and so on. The uppermost floor is guarded by a giant who fights unpredictably. This was the final spur of the plot where Lee, the master of anything that works, fights Jabbar, the master of no style. Here all the rulebooks were thrown out and each man relied entirely on his wits and his natural, native fighting skills. This, the final scene, entitled The Temple of the Unknown, was already in the can.

Bruce Lee was determined that expertise and quality would be the hallmarks of this film. He intended to assemble the most talented array of fighters available and had already called on Dan Inosanto to be the guardian of one of the floors. Dan

Inosanto studied *escrima*, together with its variants *kali* and *arnis*, the ancient Filipino art of stickfighting. The art was named by Spanish conquerors (*escrima* is Spanish for 'skirmish') who soon realized its effectiveness and banned it. In the northern Philippines, the movements were kept alive by practitioners who disguised it as a dance. In the south, where the native Muslims expelled the Europeans, the art still flourishes today.

Bruce forwarded a China Airlines ticket to Inosanto, who flew out as soon as he could make a break in his schedule. Linda met him at Kai Tak airport; Bruce could not have gone there without being mobbed. Within a couple of days they were working their moves using a video machine to immediately check the action, a technique Bruce pioneered in his *Green Hornet* days. Over several days they worked out the basis of the *escrima* bout, which was entitled The Temple of the Tiger.

Three weapons are used during this episode. First, the *escrima* uses the double sticks while Bruce uses a Chinese *bako*, a thin whip-like bamboo. As the two face off, Inosanto taps out a traditional challenge with his stick. Bruce's mocking response is the 'rat-tat-ta-tat-tat' knock of the postman. Using the *bako*, Bruce disarms the *escrima*. They then pick up *nunchaku* for a duel to the death. Dan Inosanto had originally introduced Bruce to the weapon; the footage of this scene shows that Bruce had mastered it perhaps better than his teacher.

Dan Inosanto recalls that shortly after he met Bruce in 1964, he had shown him a few basic *escrima* techniques. At the time Bruce had not been much impressed, and Inosanto had thought no more of it. On this visit to Hong Kong, when the subject came up, Bruce told Dan what he liked and what he didn't like about what he'd seen of *escrima*. Inosanto continues:

I was flabbergasted when he grabbed the sticks one day and said, 'Okay, now I'll show you what I would do.' I watched him closely, and with no previous background or training he ad-libbed a style of *escrima* he could never have known even existed. Shocked, I yelled out, 'Hey, that's *larga mano*!' Bruce said, 'I don't know what you call it, but this is my method.'

Dan Inosanto adds that *Game of Death* was intended to illustrate the same point – that the martial artist has to be better than the martial tradition. While Inosanto was dressed in a traditional Muslim costume and headband, Bruce wore a modern yellow and black catsuit. 'Bruce wanted to show imagination rising above tradition,' says Inosanto.

Bruce Lee had had a free hand in making *Way of the Dragon* and had revelled in it. In *Game of Death*, he reverted to improvising as he went along. He even took advantage of the fact that the sound would be dubbed later and, like silent film directors, sometimes shouted directions to his actors as the cameras were rolling for a take.

Bruce forgot about resting as he enthusiastically planned further duels. A third combat scene was filmed with Chi Hon Joi, a seventh-degree black belt in the Korean art of *hapkido* which, like *tae kwon do*, relies on high kicks. While filming their scene, the Korean had a rigorous enough time of it to comment that he did not want to act in any more movies with Bruce Lee. Bruce considered using an alternative *hapkido* exponent, Angela Mao.

Bruce made plans to hire the Shotokan karate champion, Yeung Sze, probably to play the hulking figure who first confronts his character outside the pagoda. He also planned to approach other martial artists, including Wong In Sik (from *Way of the Dragon*), James Tien (from *Fist of Fury*), the top *tae kwon do* practitioner Jhoon Rhee, as well as Hung Kam Po, Chuck Norris and Bob Wall.

Bruce was also planning to use actress Betty Ting Pei and the Australian actor George Lazenby. Neither Bruce nor his actors had any idea yet of what their roles were to be. Lazenby, like Bruce, had shot to fame overnight – from doing commercials to replacing Sean Connery as James Bond for the film *On Her Majesty's Secret Service*. But Lazenby had been less than a success as Bond and his career was in the doldrums. Fortunately the film had just opened in Hong Kong and Lazenby had chosen the right time to knock on Raymond Chow's door.

During this period, Bruce also contacted Taky Kimura. Says Taky:

> He sent me a plane ticket to go to Hong Kong and appear in *Game of Death*. I said to him, 'I've got three left feet and you know it. You don't need me. Do me a favour – I'm not looking for fame and fortune, I'm happy to see you doing well.' He said, 'I'm the director and producer; everyone looks good in my films.' I said, 'I guess I can't refuse.'

Becoming more serious, Taky adds, 'I recognized the feeling behind what he was doing. But in October the import business that I had started was just about to go and I wasn't able to go to Hong Kong. Then Linda called me and said don't bother, something else was breaking and *Game of Death* was being put on the back burner.'

Taky was also going through a severe personal crisis at the time, which left him emotionally devastated and haunted by the idea of suicide.

> I lost two brothers a month apart and then my wife left me. Bruce said, 'Taky, I haven't met your wife, but I've counselled you before. You must do everything in your power to solve the thing but, at

some point in time, you may just have to walk on.' I'd lost everything. When people tell you things like that, there's not always a lot of pith in it, but coming from him . . .

From wherever he happened to be in the world, Bruce would call to give support to his friend, saying, 'Walk on, Taky. Just walk on.'

When Bruce's old friend Doug Palmer was again in Hong Kong, this time with his wife, he eventually managed to track Bruce down via Golden Harvest, who passed on a message. Palmer's notes recall:

Five minutes later the phone in our hotel room rang. 'You son of a gun,' Bruce yelled when I answered. 'What are you doing in Hong Kong?'

He and Linda came and picked us up and took us back to the huge house he was having work done on, in an exclusive part of town called Kowloon Tong. The lot had a high wall around it with broken glass and spikes set in the top. He had made it, but fame had a price. His kids had to be escorted to and from school so they would not be kidnapped. My wife, Noriko, had to use the toilet; Bruce produced a bunch of keys to unlock the bathroom – apparently he had to keep every room in the house locked to guard against theft by the workmen.

While we were at his house, Bruce was looking through his mail and he read a letter from his old friend James Lee, in Oakland. I could see Bruce frowning as he read. Then I heard him whisper to Linda to send James 500 dollars. Bruce told me later that James was dying of cancer.

Later we went out to dinner. When we stopped at a light, people on the street or in adjacent cars would gawk in at him. The restaurant was full and we had no reservation, but they soon produced a table. I'm not sure if anyone else in the place got their dinner because every waiter was hovering near our table.

The next day we visited the movie studio where Bruce was filming *Game of Death*. He had recently brought Kareem Abdul Jabbar over to Hong Kong to shoot a fight scene, which had a very powerful David and Goliath quality about it. Bruce was very happy about the way the scene had turned out, in contrast to a more recent one where he had flown in a martial artist from Korea and was very disappointed with the caliber of the man's performance.

Bruce also had a few stories to tell about Kareem Abdul Jabbar. When he arrived in Hong Kong, Kareem let it be known that he was very interested in having 'a date'. Bruce tried to arrange something for him. When the girl showed up and was introduced to Kareem, she flat refused. No one had told her how big Kareem was. Kareem became very angry. 'He's very sensitive about his height, you know,' said Bruce, chuckling.

When Bruce had returned to Hong Kong in 1970, his childhood friend Unicorn had acted as a go-between when Bruce was sounding out a possible deal to make a film with Shaw Brothers. Now Unicorn asked Bruce if he would return the favour and help him with the fight choreography on a film he was making on a shoestring budget, to be called *The Unicorn Palm* (or *Fists of Unicorn*).

Bruce always tried to help his friends. He had already given Unicorn the role of head waiter in *Way of the Dragon* and now agreed to help his friend again.

In May 1972, at the request of the Sing Hoi Film Company, Unicorn met with its representative Tang Di at the Peninsular Hotel. With the sudden popularity of martial arts films, the company decided it wanted to get in on the act. As Tang discreetly put it to Unicorn, 'Frankly speaking, your name, of course, won't sell, but if you have "another" who can help you, the film will not only sell, it will earn a lot of money.' In short, Bruce Lee's involvement in the picture was the condition that would secure the starring role for Unicorn.

When Unicorn presented the idea to Bruce he wasn't expecting him to go for it, but Bruce replied that although he realized that he was being manipulated, he would help Unicorn out. When Bruce attended a publicity bash for the film at the Miramar Hotel in Kowloon, he got all the attention and had to ask the press photographers not to ignore Unicorn.

Filming started in August 1972. It soon became obvious that Unicorn was out of his depth as a leading actor and again Bruce had to back his friend. As well as supervising the fight action, Bruce came up with several script ideas, spending a day at the set while the cameras rolled.

When the film was released soon afterwards, Bruce Lee's name was given star billing and he was credited not only as the martial arts advisor but as a leading actor. Footage of Bruce arriving on the set and of him rehearsing the actors had been contrived to fit into a new storyline. Bruce could only issue a legal letter condemning the sorry project. Although Bruce continued to see Unicorn and to coach him on acting and training, he was angered and saddened by the incident, which had both betrayed his trust and increased his feelings of suspicion.

His superstar status left Bruce Lee open to exploitation. He now found his name used to endorse products of which he had never heard, much less used. Quotes attributed to him were used to hype films he had never seen. Producers advertised offers to Bruce Lee in the pages of the Hong Kong press, seeking only to generate publicity for themselves and to increase their prestige by association with Bruce, however tenuous. The situation in which he now found himself had changed so quickly that a normal life was no longer possible. He might wake up to find parts of a previous evening's conversation in a restaurant splashed across the newspapers. The press was becoming ever more ridiculous in its excesses.

In the United States, Kareem Abdul Jabbar owned a house whose occupants had recently been killed; a headline in Hong Kong read: 'BRUCE LEE LINKED TO MASS MURDER'.

In the 1960s, audiences tired of Shaw's musical epics and flocked to see samurai movies. Without missing a beat, Shaw switched production from the sentimental to the bloody. But soon samurai movies also came to a messy end, quickened by a series of speeches made by Chou En Lai attacking Japanese imperialism.

Shaw pulled another stroke. With no gunfighting or sword-fighting tradition to base his films on he set out to revive *kung fu* films, starting with *The Chinese Boxer*, an appealing combination of national feeling, secret societies and action. Soon after came *King Boxer* (US title: *Five Fingers of Death*) which grossed nearly $4 million in its first eleven weeks in the States. This film was quickly followed by *The Killer* and *The New One-Armed Swordsman* starring Wang Yu, which also broke out of the Oriental market to find success around the world. The Hong Kong press called Shaw 'Mr Kung Fu'.

Wang Yu was *kung fu*'s top star, having succeeded in beating Shaw's contract system by hiring himself out on a film-by-film basis. He became the first Chinese actor able to command a fee of $20,000. But audiences were quick to realize who was the genre's natural star. Ironically, Shaw had also opened the door for his most bitter rival. When *Newsweek* wrote about the emerging phenomenon, the story was head-lined: 'Bruce Lee – the Bright Star Rising in the East'. *Los Angeles Times* columnist Robert Elegant also wrote an article heralding Bruce. Raymond Chow lost no time in setting up distribution.

*

In his office at Golden Harvest, Bruce's only reminder of his past struggles was a pair of broken spectacles he kept to remind him of the time he couldn't afford to have them fixed. These were the same spectacles he had worn when he disguised himself as a telephone repairman in *Fist of Fury*. Now Bruce Lee was in an almost unprecedented position for any movie actor, let alone a Chinese one. He was potentially the highest-paid actor in the world; he could work in Europe, the United States or Asia, and he was a partner in his own production company. He was besieged with offers that continued to arrive daily. Film producer Carlo Ponti cabled Bruce from Italy with an offer of 'a large sum to be determined' to star in a film with Ponti's wife, Sophia Loren. He was offered $2 million to make two *kung fu* movies for a Hungarian producer. Bruce even turned down an offer from MGM to make a picture with Elvis Presley – the king of *kung fu* together with the king of rock 'n' roll.

The mind boggles at the thought of Bruce and Elvis working together; by this time the singer resembled a heavy training bag more than the martial artist he might have become. Elvis had picked up on karate while stationed in Germany with the US Army in 1958. Back in America he had continued training, first with Bob Wall and Chuck Norris and then with Ed Parker. Elvis had moved on because Wall and Norris would not promote him through the ranks and refused to train him when he was stoned. Ed Parker was more easily persuaded, promoting Elvis to an eighth-degree black belt, which so delighted the singer that in a spontaneous burst of generosity he gave Parker $50,000 and a new Cadillac. As he was the most famous celebrity to don a karate suit, karate circles knew what was good for business and were happy to give Elvis an inflated media profile to go with his own increasingly inflated physical one.

Bob Wall and Chuck Norris continued to train Elvis's wife Priscilla. 'We trained Priscilla – up to a green belt,' says Bob Wall. 'Although he was supposed to be a high-ranking black belt, Priscilla could kick the ass off Elvis.'

The authenticity of Elvis's *tae kwon do* ranking is equally questionable. Having given his Korean instructor a new car and $50,000 to start a new school (which the teacher promptly spent on a new house for himself) Elvis was promoted to a seventh-degree black belt. Soon the singer had advanced to the non-physical aspects of the fighting arts and, while others still sparred crudely, Elvis would keep a wise eye on them as he polished off another burger and meditated on the inner tranquility offered by Percodan and Demerol. By now, Priscilla had taken up with another karate champion, Mike Stone.

Meanwhile, back in Hollywood, Warner Brothers had at last decided it might actually be safe for them to commit to a Bruce Lee project. Further filming of *Game of Death* was interrupted by the offer that Bruce had worked for so many years to achieve: the starring role in a US-made feature film in which he would be given complete control over all the fight sequences.

At the time of Nixon's high-profile visit to China, interest in Asian culture was stirring in America. Warners' head of Asian distribution, Richard Ma, thought it might be time to expose a wider audience to *kung fu* films. Rather than give money to Run Run Shaw and take his films, Ma suggested an original project, saying that he knew a guy by the name of Bruce Lee. Richard Ma had a hard time trying to convince Warners' senior executives that this was a good idea, even though the budget of the proposed film was roughly equal to the kind of money the company was used to spending on a TV pilot episode. Fortunately, Warners' president, Ted Ashley, was convinced. Fred Weintraub and Paul Heller were appointed as co-producers and a subsidiary company named Sequoia was set up to manage the project.

Before becoming a film executive, Fred Weintraub had been the owner of the Bitter End, a folk music club in New York's Greenwich Village. For a time he had also managed Neil Diamond and Bill Cosby. In 1969 he joined Warner Brothers as a creative vice-president and had since overseen the production of many films, including *Woodstock* and *Klute*. Fred Weintraub had also been working for some years to give Bruce Lee a starring role.

'When I kept failing to get a feature going for Bruce,' says Weintraub, 'I told him to go to Hong Kong and make a film I could show people. He eventually sent me a print of *The Big Boss* and I went to Richard Ma with it because he was the only one who understood the genre. I also arranged a private showing for Ted Ashley and he said, "Try and get something going."'

When Bruce made *Fist of Fury*, Weintraub was again sent a print. Now, with the box-office figures from the Mandarin circuit, Warners realized that Fred Weintraub might be on to something, although he noted, 'There was still not a lot of enthusiasm for it. Nobody believed it would ever get done.'

Scriptwriter Michael Allin was commissioned to write a martial arts film to be called *Blood and Steel* and Weintraub set off for Hong Kong to do a deal whereby Sequoia and Concord would co-produce the picture. This proved not to be the simple formality which Weintraub had hoped for. After two weeks in Hong Kong he still didn't have Chow's signature on a contract. Although Weintraub found Bruce in favour of the project, he could never seem to get the two Concord partners together in the same room at the same time, and was about to call it a day, return home and ditch the project. But the evening before he was due to return to the United States he decided to give it one last shot.

That evening he managed to get Bruce and Raymond Chow to go to a restaurant. After dinner, Weintraub told Bruce that Raymond Chow was right to protect him, that the attempt to go international wasn't worth risking the successful career he had built up in Hong Kong. Weintraub said that it was all academic anyway, as he couldn't make a deal. Bruce looked over at Chow and said, 'Make the deal.' Chow could only smile and add that he thought it was a wonderful idea.

In October 1972, Bruce Lee and Raymond Chow flew to the States to finalize the contract and to meet the actors and director with whom Bruce was to work. Bruce had hardly unpacked his suitcase in his room at the Beverly Wilshire hotel before he called Steve McQueen to tell him the news that he was to star in his own US-made film. Bruce was not about to take the chance that McQueen might have ignored the interviews in which he had reminded McQueen that he was now just as famous.

Bruce Lee then called Stirling Silliphant. Part of a deal Silliphant had just done with Twentieth Century-Fox included the script of *The Silent Flute*. The writer thought that Bruce would be delighted, but Bruce had not forgotten his suffering in India and far from giving his blessing to the film at last being made, he told Silliphant that he was worth a million dollars now and they couldn't afford him any more. Bruce then suggested that if *The Silent Flute* were ever made, it would be Coburn who would have to accept second billing. Using the very same words that had burned into him so many years ago, he added, 'And why should I carry him on my shoulders?'

In the *Longstreet* episode that Silliphant had written for

Bruce two years earlier, Bruce's character had told the blind detective, 'Like most people you want to learn how to win. First, you must learn defeat.' Bruce knew all too well the taste of defeat. Even at the cost of alienating one of the few people who had genuinely helped him, Bruce wanted to savour his victory. Also having recently experienced a peculiar shift in his relationship with Unicorn, Bruce was now busy burning bridges back in Hong Kong.

All of Bruce's closest friends belonged to the period of his life when he was first and foremost a martial artist. But now they were either fading or being driven away. Perhaps Bruce's behaviour resulted from the blow he had taken when he realized that James Lee was dying of black lung, an occupational disease of the welding trade. James had only weeks to live and Bruce had invited him to Hong Kong for the premiere of *Way of the Dragon*, hoping that he would at least see the city before he died.

But James Lee wasn't able to share in Bruce's next success. He died on 28 December 1972, leaving Bruce emotionally ravaged and at a complete loss. Bruce knew that a good deal of his success was due to his friend's help with his conditioning and training. At times, James Lee had been more like a father to him than his own father.

Meanwhile, *Way of the Dragon* premiered and went on to surpass Bruce Lee's prediction that it would make $HK5 million: it grossed $HK5.5 million in the first three weeks of its opening run.

20
ENTER THE DRAGON

BY THE TIME pre-production on the new film began, Bruce had persuaded the studio to change the title: *Blood and Steel* now became *Enter the Dragon*. The $500,000 budget would hardly have covered one episode of a Hollywood TV show, but by Hong Kong standards it was sufficient for an epic.

Robert Clouse, who was hired to direct the picture, had begun his career as a stills photographer at CBS-TV. Two short films he composed from sequences of stills had received Academy nominations in that category, but Clouse had only made two features when he got a call from Fred Weintraub inviting him to meet Bruce Lee and Raymond Chow at the Warner Brothers offices in Burbank. Clouse wasn't the first person whose introduction to Bruce Lee began with a lightning-fast kick to within half an inch of his nose. According to Clouse, he was hired for *Enter the Dragon* because Bruce had been impressed by a fight scene in one of his films. According to Fred Weintraub, 'Nobody else wanted to direct the picture except him.'

Fees for the picture were not high, and so the world never came to hear of Rockne Tarkington, an actor who quit over the low pay three days before they were due to set off for Hong Kong; he was quickly replaced by karate champion Jim Kelly.

In early February 1973, just after Chinese New Year, the American party swiftly followed Bruce and Raymond Chow to Hong Kong. Clouse and Weintraub had been joined by leading lady Ahna Capri, Jim Kelly and Bob Wall, and scriptwriter Michael Allin, whose free trip to Hong Kong was a perk to compensate for his low fee.

On Robert Clouse's first night in Hong Kong, Bruce insisted that they go together to a cinema and watch one of his films. Bruce told Clouse that he wanted him to experience the atmosphere, but the real reason was that when they had first met, the director had not been aware of Bruce's reputation. Now Bruce wanted him to know just who he was working with. Although this outing was to impress Clouse, it was also for Bruce's benefit, to psych him up for the production that was soon to follow.

In *Enter the Dragon*, Bruce is Lee, an author and martial artist who is the top student of a Shaolin temple in the countryside near Hong Kong. In a plot that leans heavily on the James Bond film *Dr No*, Lee is met by an intelligence agent, Braithwaite (played by Geoffrey Weeks), who asks him to take part in a martial arts tournament to be held on a sinister private island in international waters off the coast of Hong Kong. Lee's mission is to flush out Han (Shih Kien), himself a former Shaolin student, who now runs a martial arts school on the island as a front for a drugs and prostitution racket. Braithwaite explains that Han is so fearful of assassination that he has a metal scanner covering the whole island to prevent any guns there. This is another attempt to get around the genre's main

Portrait of the artist as a young man.

Bruce Lee sitting in zazen on Malibu Beach.

Kato – kung fu chauffeur

Bruce with student Dan Lee

Bruce succumbs to the charms of Malalene in *The Big Boss*.

Bruce succumbs to the charms of Betty Ting Pei on the set of *Way of the Dragon*.

The Big Boss gets his come-uppance

Bruce behind the camera filming *Game of Death*.

Bruce with nunchaku in *Way of the Dragon*.

Bruce in his extensive library on the fighting and philosophical arts.
Note the *nunchaku* hanging from the centre of the bookcase.

The house in Kowloon Tong.　　　　　The bungalow in Bel Air.

A scene from *Enter the Dragon* – Bruce's peripheral awareness almost comes off the page.

In period costume for a screen test for Shaw Brothers Studio – a coded message to Raymond Chow.

Strength of spirit . . . just weeks before his death.

problem: that any *kung fu* film could be brought to a halt in a minute by 'any bloody fool who could pull a trigger'.

Also on their way to Han's island are Roper, Williams and Parsons. Roper (John Saxon) is taking part in the tournament in the hope of winning prize money to pay off gambling debts to mob members who have threatened to kill him. Williams (Jim Kelly) is on the run after fighting a couple of redneck policemen who have been harassing him. Lee meets Parsons (Peter Archer) at the boat for the island; Parsons challenges him, asking him about his style of fighting. When Parsons is tricked into boarding a smaller boat in which he is left stranded as it is towed along behind the junk, he realizes that Lee knows the art of 'winning without fighting'.

On arrival at the island, they are greeted by Han's mistress, Tania (Ahna Capri). After a banquet, Tania arranges women for any of the contestants who want them. Williams picks several, Roper chooses Tania herself and Lee sends for Mei Ling (Betty Chung), one of Braithwaite's female agents who is already in place.

That night, against Han's orders, both Lee and Williams take a stroll on the island. Lee discovers the massive underground operation where Han processes opium and keeps his prisoners, including young women who have been kidnapped and hooked on drugs, ready to be dispatched to a life of prostitution.

The following morning the tournament starts when Roper and Williams, despite their night of indulgence, find they still have enough *ch'i* left to win their contests, while Han has his huge bodyguard Bolo (Yeung Sze) beat to death the guards who had allowed someone access to the underground caverns.

Now it is Lee's turn to fight; his opponent is Oharra (Bob Wall), the man who caused the death of Lee's sister. Seen in flashback, Lee's sister, Su Lin (Angela Mao), while taking part in a similar martial arts tournament on the island, was attacked by five of Han's men led by Oharra. Trapped, she stabbed herself to death with a shard of broken glass to avoid being raped.

Although Oharra is a powerful fighter, Lee gets the upper hand. Sensing his own defeat, Oharra attacks Lee with two broken bottles but Lee finally kills him with a stamping kick. Han then fights Williams, believing him to be the one who stumbled on his operations and fought with his guards the previous night. Han wins the fight, killing Williams using a powerful artificial hand with steel fingers he had been concealing. Later, Han tries to coerce Roper into becoming his organization's US contact by making him witness Williams's body, impaled on a hook, being lowered into a vat of acid.

That night, after capturing a cobra left to guard against further intruders, Lee goes back into the caverns. He penetrates to the heart of the plant and fights his way to the radio room, where he calls Braithwaite. Eventually he is overpowered and captured by Han.

The next morning, Roper fights and kills the bodyguard, Bolo. Han's ambition to have Lee and Roper fight to the death is thwarted when Roper becomes Lee's ally. Han sends his men to kill the pair while agent Mei Ling releases the prisoners who rush the tournament ground to battle with Han's men. Han slips away from the battle and is pursued by Lee, who corners him in a maze of mirrors. They fight to the death and Han is left impaled on one of his own spears. Han's army is defeated as helicopters with soldiers, sent by Braithwaite, descend to the island.

Bruce Lee was genuinely concerned about the character he was portraying in *Enter the Dragon*. He was unsure whether the West would accept a Chinese hero and, at the same time, whether the Chinese would accept his new approach. While his earlier films also show him battling against gangsters involved in drugs, prostitution and protection rackets, the Chinese films all involve crime at the level of the factory floor, the sweatshop or the restaurant, crime with which the overworked and underpaid worker of Hong Kong could identify. But now Bruce could no longer simply play the naïve country boy for his fellow Chinese; he had to look and act like a man of the world, at home in both East and West. Yet neither could he be seen to favour the Western element at the expense of his own people, nor could he act in a way that would make him appear foolish to his countrymen.

According to Robert Clouse, scriptwriter Michael Allin made flippant remarks to the effect that Bruce needn't worry himself about such things, claiming that the only reason the film was getting made was that it was cheap, and Bruce Lee's name would guarantee enough of a success for the studio to recoup costs. Allin added that the film wasn't being made because it was a fine piece of literature. Bruce tried to brush aside this unfortunate start to their collaboration, but Allin persisted in his attitude and made script alterations. Knowing Bruce found certain sounds difficult to pronounce, he contrived to include as many 'r's in Bruce's dialogue as he could.

Things got no better and in the end Bruce said that he couldn't and wouldn't work with Allin and demanded a new script. The producer suggested Allin lay low for a few days. Later, while Bruce was out wearing his customary public disguise of beard and dark glasses, he happened to get on the same ferry as Allin. Of all the millions of people in Hong Kong, they had to meet. Bruce was angry at this deception; he was under the impression that the writer had been sent home. The blow to Bruce's pride was doubled because he was Chinese, for whom loss of face is one of the worst things that can happen.

*

From the first day of filming, nothing went right. Major difficulties arose from using American and Chinese crews. Even a simple instruction would have to find its way through an agonizingly slow route of misinterpretation to the person for whom it was intended. There was a shortage of translators and often no adequate Chinese words for some of the English jargon and technical terms, and vice versa. Matters were further complicated because people who made mistakes would often simply disappear from the set rather than lose face.

Hong Kong's methods were not Hollywood's. There were no power tools for set construction; some of the sets were literally built from chicken wire and mud. The 'steel bars' of the prison cells were made by shaving down pieces of scrap wood because here hours of manual labour came cheaper than round lengths of wood. Five hundred Chinese workmen built everything from scratch.

Bruce walked off the set almost as soon as he arrived, after an argument with Raymond Chow. Bruce felt that Chow was trying to assert himself as mastermind of the project, a situation he found intolerable knowing it was his own creative efforts and abilities that would make or break the film and it was his career that was on the line. There were daily arguments between the two because Bruce felt he wasn't being kept informed of everything going on in the partnership. Chow thought that business was his side of the partnership and he didn't have to consult Bruce on every decision, and told Bruce to get on with the acting.

The whole project was coming closer and closer to being cancelled and there was growing anxiety that Bruce was about to withdraw from the film. As the days passed, he continued to be absent from the set. Warners kept sending revised versions of the script, alternating them with telegrams asking where the hell Bruce was.

On 28 February Bruce was in fact back at his old school, St

Francis Xavier, as guest of honour to present the sports day prizes. On the platform, Bruce stripped to the waist to flex his muscles for his young admirers, laughing and joking for an hour or two, happy to be away from all the problems.

Meanwhile, actor John Saxon had arrived in Hong Kong thinking (and acting as if) he was the real star of the film. He had said earlier that he was being hired to give the film some class, but there was never any argument about who was the real star of *Enter the Dragon*. The week production began, Bruce Lee's face was on the cover of no less than twenty-seven different magazines, adding to the many pressures and tensions he was feeling. During the years that he managed Neil Diamond and Bill Cosby, Fred Weintraub had seen how, as their ambitions were realized, they had changed – indeed, how they had *had* to change. 'But Bruce had got so big, so fast,' added Weintraub, 'it had scared him.'

Bruce Lee was only too aware that *Enter the Dragon* was the big chance he'd worked his whole life for. But he had yet to prove to himself (and to Jim Coburn and Steve McQueen) that he could pull it off. Bruce kept telling the producer that he would only be happy if *Enter the Dragon* out-grossed the film that McQueen was currently making. But beyond this goal, Bruce's first wish was to give his family a good life. Hard times weren't so far behind; the money from the first two pictures had been spent as soon as it arrived, while revenue from *Way of the Dragon* was not yet coming in.

In just two furious years, Bruce had made three hit action films and started a fourth, doing virtually everything on the latter two films and much of the work of writer, fight arranger and director on the first two. Now, it was as if all his incredible energy, self-belief and motivation had suddenly deserted him. He even began to talk about what should be done 'if anything happened' to him. Despite the deep inroads he'd made into writing, acting and directing – despite his new-found fame and massive potential wealth – Bruce was painfully aware that his family's future depended more than anything on his supreme physical fitness and incomparable abilities. Suddenly, every-thing seemed very fragile.

Meanwhile, Warners sent another new script. 'It was a piece of shit,' says Fred Weintraub, 'all philosophy and no action.'

Filming had to start without Bruce, as Linda continually assured everyone that he would eventually show up. But even the simplest of things would not go smoothly: a brief scene was attempted in which seven praying mantises (specially flown in from Hawaii) were to fight to the death, but they too refused to fight. Meanwhile, on the set, real fights were breaking out between stuntmen and extras hired from rival 'families' of Triads, the Chinese crime syndicates.

The Triads have their roots in Shaolin religious and martial traditions; the word 'triad' comes from a symbol that repre-sents the linking of heaven, man and earth. But Triads had long since lost their way, just as freemasonry fell from its original purpose in the West.

Around 1900, there was a rebellion in China against the dominance of Western influence and exploitation. Many *kung fu* fighters (members of secret organizations linked with the Triads) were trained to a level of fanaticism by instructors who told them that they had developed enough *ch'i* to be immune to the bullets of the invaders. These instructors then proved this with convincing demonstrations in which a gun loaded with blanks was fired at them and they emerged unscathed. After these unarmed fighters, the conflict came to be known as the Boxer Rebellion. Of course, when these boxers went into battle against armed British soldiers firing real bullets, they were massacred. As a result, the Triads lost their power base in China and gradually moved into Hong Kong, New York, San

Francisco, London and other cities, engaging in Mafia-like criminal activities such as drugs, prostitution and protection rackets. The Triads had a finger in any pie with money in it, including many areas of the Hong Kong movie business.

Run Run Shaw, who had informants at every level of the production of *Enter the Dragon*, was well aware of what was happening in the enemy camp. While he said publicly that the film would never be made, privately he might well have hoped that it would bring ruin to Raymond Chow. Perhaps seizing an opportunity to make mischief, Shaw invited Robert Clouse and Fred Weintraub to dinner at his opulent house in his studio grounds.

Shaw's guests were met at the high gates and escorted up the long sweeping drive by his armed uniformed guards. At the long dinner table, Shaw sat next to his associate, the wily Mona Fong. Other guests included actor William Holden, there to pitch a film version of the book *Tai Pan*, and a British film censor who moralized as pompously as his colleagues who would later remove the *nunchaku* scenes from the British version of *Enter the Dragon*. While they dined on snake soup (something approaching cannibalism for the host), Shaw praised Bruce Lee, showed his concern for the picture, and asked questions to which his spies had already told him the answers.

Nearly two weeks into the shooting schedule, there was still nothing of Bruce Lee on film. While Fred Weintraub continued to assure Warners that everything was going well, in reality he was asking Linda what on earth they could do. Linda made one last attempt to calm Bruce and restore his confidence, then called Weintraub and promised him that things were going to be all right.

The first scene that Bruce filmed was shot in a room with a girl, but right away there was a problem: his face had developed a nervous twitch that was only too apparent in close-ups. Nothing was said about it while long shots and various angles were improvised. The ploy worked; after lunch the twitching nerve had settled down, never to reappear.

On top of the tremendous psychological stress Bruce was feeling, enormous demands were made on his physical energy. In just one take, Bruce might have to fight ten or twelve attackers in rapid succession – leaping to the side, to the front, twisting behind, spinning, striking, kicking, blocking with inch-perfect accuracy and split-second timing, all with the right expressions and reactions – in a way that was totally convincing. Bruce couldn't even use a stand-in to rehearse the other stuntmen because as the choreographer he had worked out and timed all the moves and he needed to fine-tune them himself. And besides, who could match his abilities? Bruce Lee was the only person in the world who could do what he did. If only one man missed his cue or miscalculated, the whole sequence would have to be run again. Sometimes the fight scenes required fifteen or twenty takes.

'No director could ask more from a performer,' solemnly wrote Robert Clouse in his book *The Making of Enter the Dragon*. But Bob Wall remembers it differently:

> The walls of the dressing rooms were paper-thin and Bruce over-heard Bob Clouse talking about him, saying how it was ridiculous making a film with an actor who couldn't even speak properly. It was Clouse himself who asked Michael Allin to change the name of the British agent in the script – to fuck Bruce up. Clouse changed the character's name to Braithwaite because he knew Bruce would have trouble with 'Yes, Mr Bwaithwaite; no, Mr Bwaithwaite.' It made him sound like Donald Duck. How Bruce kept from punching out Robert Clouse, I'll never know . . . Bruce was not greatly secure

in his acting ability, but he knew how to direct action – something which Clouse had no idea about. While Clouse got at Bruce through Michael Allin, Bruce insisted that Clouse be barred from the set during the fight scenes. Bruce said that if he couldn't direct the action then he wouldn't go out. *That's* why he spent so many days not showing up; he refused to show up until Clouse was off the set.

Fred Weintraub comments:

There wasn't really any animosity, just a lot of tension. Bruce was so nervous – he'd wanted this so much – that *his* tension was the tension of the film. He argued with everyone, played everyone off each other; sometimes I kept out of the way and sometimes I stepped in to help. At different times, Bob Wall, Bob Clouse or myself took our turn to give him some support. But any time I had a real problem I would go to Linda; she was the only one who had the sensibilities to be able to deal with Bruce. *Enter the Dragon* would not have been made without Linda's help.

The intense demands on Bruce's physical and nervous energies, the heat and humidity, the draining, ever-present back pain all dug deeper and deeper into his internal resources. He was suffering from dehydration and losing weight at an alarming rate. At night he could not sleep and, unable even to rest, spent most of the night working out fight scenes and drawing complex diagrams of the action. People who had known Bruce for years said that his skin tone had changed completely and that he didn't look well. Even so, on the set Bruce declined the privilege of special meals, electing to eat with the rest of the crew.

Along with challenges in front of the camera, Bruce also had to face other problems off-camera when he should have been able to snatch a moment's respite and a cup of his favourite chrysanthemum tea. Bruce got on well with the stuntmen; they had become a team and Bruce had earned their respect just as they had earned his. They too were taking risks; unlike the way stunts were arranged in Hollywood, there were no air bags or mattresses out of shot to break their falls; there were no fake glass bottles or balsa wood chairs. Usually, one or two of the stuntmen were injured. Bruce did what he could to help and would even lend them money or arrange a bonus.

There were also hundreds of extras – sometimes between three and four hundred – most of them street kids much like Bruce had been many years before. Every so often one of these kids would walk up to Bruce and openly question the genuineness of his performances. The usual way was to tap one's foot three times in front of him, a reference to the nickname Bruce had been given by the stuntmen, who called him Bruce Three-Legs, or Three-Kicks Bruce because he could deliver three consecutive kicks very rapidly.

For the most part, Bruce would ignore this. As he knew only too well, most of these kids had little to look forward to and had seen the opportunity for a moment of glory. They might even get in a lucky punch – then who knew what opportunities might follow for 'the man who beat Bruce Lee'? Bruce himself would never actually initiate any such fight but if the challenger kept insisting or insulting him he might ask what his challenger knew about fighting, anticipating the reply, 'As much as I need to.'

It was in these brief confrontations that one could witness the vast difference between Bruce Lee's movie fighting style and his real fighting method. The movie style used a lot of visually spectacular spinning and flying kicks from northern Shaolin *kung fu* (whose original purpose was to unseat people attacking on horseback). But when Bruce Lee fought for real, there were no fancy moves and no wild noises: only simple, direct and efficient strikes with no facial expression except for the look in his eyes – a fierce and unflinching gaze that he himself called 'controlled cruelty'. He did just enough to let the kid know that the game was over.

During the making of *Enter the Dragon*, cameraman Henry Wong shot five hours' worth of 16 mm film to be edited down to a ten-minute behind-the-scenes documentary which was to be used to promote the film prior to its release. Some of this footage featured Bruce's unscripted fights. On completion of the promotional film and with the studio's approval, the New York editing company that had assembled it destroyed all the remaining film. Nobody realized then that they might well have destroyed the most valuable Bruce Lee film of all.

Contrary to the usual production methods in Hong Kong, sound was recorded while filming but it was impossible to keep both the hundreds of extras and crew quiet during shooting. A feast scene was scheduled, but there was no food. Someone misinterpreted an order and instead of doves, frogs would arrive. Props that had been there the day before weren't there the next. Lighting set-ups were changed overnight, meaning that scenes had to be shot all over again. Extras who arrived for an exciting day in the movie business found themselves sitting around for hours, and would fail to show up the next day.

Robert Clouse reports that when cameraman Gil Hubbs arrived at Golden Harvest Studios he found most of the camera equipment in a bad state of repair and with none of the lenses he wanted to use. Hubbs took the initiative of hiring the equipment he needed from another supplier, upsetting the producers and Golden Harvest who were presented with additional costs. Even so, the entire picture was shot using just two cameras and three lenses. The second cameraman, Charles Lowe, was presented with similar problems in the lighting department, where equipment was so badly rusted it was, he said, now only good for one last stand in India.

To add to the difficulties there were voltage fluctuations in the electricity supply. The Golden Harvest studios were originally a textile mill and the daily rushes would usually be covered in tiny white specks. As sumo wrestlers ate their way through tons of food, there was an occasional flutter of feathers as an exotic bird tumbled from its perch, half-roasted by the heat of an arc lamp. Each morning the sound stages had to be cleared of dogs and squatters who had spent the night sleeping on the couches or on the floor. The hundreds of extras needed to play the derelict prisoners were real derelicts recruited from the streets of Hong Kong. There was a problem getting actresses to play prostitutes, so real prostitutes were hired. Actress and martial arts champion Angela Mao got only $100 for two days' work, while chief cameraman Gil Hubbs was making only $250 a week; at $150 a day, the prostitutes were the highest earners on *Enter the Dragon*, resulting in a lot of ill feeling on the set.

Actor Peter Archer almost drowned during the filming of the scene where Lee tricks Parsons onto the boat being towed along behind the junk taking them to Han's island. In the movie itself, we can see that the boat is rapidly shipping water; seconds after the scene was cut, the boat capsized, dumping the actor into the churning waters of the China Sea. There were several further accidents, two of which involved Bruce Lee.

In the early part of Bruce's fight with Bob Wall, he kicks Wall over a row of chairs and through a line of Han's men. Wall picks up two bottles (there to provide water for the tournament contestants), smashes their ends together, and confronts Bruce with a broken bottle in each hand. This being Hong Kong, these were real bottles, not the fake bottles made of sugar that would normally be used for a stunt like this. So far everything had gone precisely as rehearsed, but as Bob Wall moved in, Bruce kicked and then whipped round to punch, hitting the edge of the broken bottle with his hand. The assistant director, Chaplin Chang, had to rush Bruce by car to hospital where twelve stitches were required to close a deep gash on his finger. He was unable to resume work for several days.

The stuntmen took a dark view of this, convinced that it was no accident. Bruce's deeply superstitious countrymen grew more and more restless until there was a meeting at which he got entangled in their accusations.

Robert Clouse writes that meanwhile he had received a call from Raymond Chow saying that Bruce, in order to save face, would have to get his revenge on Wall and that it was up to the director to find a way out of the problem. Clouse says he had to tell Bruce that Wall was needed for further filming and that Wall had to stay healthy for the good of the picture. In his account of the incident Clouse states that Bruce intended 'to kill' Bob Wall. But the account of Clouse's dramatic intervention smacks more of fanciful and dramatic invention.

Bob Wall is now a real-estate broker and entrepreneur based in Tarzana, California. Behind his desk in his 'Victorian' penthouse office, he recalls the incident: 'Clouse's account is bullshit. We'd already shot that scene seven times before the accident. Not only that, I was breaking real bottles and then having to fall to the ground like a slain ox without being able to look down and see where all the glass had landed.'

Wall springs up from behind his desk to show how the fight was choreographed. He was to lunge at Bruce's chest with a broken bottle. Bruce would block it with a kick to Wall's forearm and then turn quickly to deliver a spinning back kick. On the eighth take, Bruce's first kick landed fractionally high so that he hadn't deflected Wall's arm far enough, so when he spun into his kick there was not enough clearance, resulting in his hand striking the broken glass.

'I called Bruce at home,' continued Wall, 'and asked him if he had heard the rumours. He said that he had. I asked him if he intended to kill me; he replied that he had said no such thing. We could never prove it, but we were convinced that Clouse made up the whole story and spread the rumour. Sure, Bruce got cut, but it was an accident. If Bruce had wanted to kill me he got several opportunities. We retook that scene about ten times; all he needed to do was to kick me a bit higher or a bit lower than he did.'

Yet, on one of those takes, Bruce did kick Wall so hard that an extra positioned to catch him sustained a broken arm from the impact. 'Bruce knew I could take a good shot,' says Wall. 'He wanted emotional content and power, not fake reactions.' Wall took several good shots and emerged covered in red welts, bringing at least some satisfaction to the complaining stuntmen.

A second accident happened while preparing to shoot the scene in which Bruce Lee re-enters the underground cavern, now guarded by a cobra. Before each take, Bruce would rap the snake across the nose a few times in order to get the hood around the cobra's head to flare out. Finally the cobra struck back. Fortunately, the snake had previously been drained of all its venom but Bruce was left wounded and shaken. 'Bruce had already beaten the snake nine times before it beat him,' adds Bob Wall.

Both Bruce Lee and Bob Wall were skilled martial artists. The fact that there was only one accident of timing between them shows not their imperfection, but highlights the phenomenal level of control at which Bruce and his 'opponents' would work. If anything did go wrong with one of the fight routines, Bruce would usually take responsibility himself, saying that he would have to check the rushes to see what he'd done wrong.

The film's editor, Kurt Hirshler, had the perfect opportunity to study Bruce: stopping the film, slowing it down and running it back and forth, just as Bruce had done when studying the actions of boxing champions. Viewing Bruce's stand-off with the vile Oharra, he was intrigued to see (or rather to *not* see) the 'untelegraphed' punch that Bruce had perfected in sticking hands training, where his fist would shoot out without warning.

Robert Clouse wrote, 'I have been asked many times if Bruce was really as fast as people claimed. All I can say is he had the fastest reflexes I've ever seen. In one shot, Bruce was in a stand off with Bob Wall. In order to see his hand lash out and hit Bob, we had to speed the camera up to thirty frames [a second]. At normal speed it didn't show on film.'

Even after a day's filming, Bruce would often remove his shirt on the way from the car to the house, going straight through the kitchen to his exercise room to work out and experiment. Having mastered every physical technique of fighting, Bruce was now looking into psychological, almost supernatural ways of continuing to develop his skills. He had tried many methods and had even devised what was in effect his own self-hypnosis audio system.

In *Longstreet* Bruce's character had asked, 'From your thought to your fist, how much time is lost?' He wished to bypass altogether the physical mechanisms of fighting, to be able to strike instantly with his eyes and his intent. On the film set, he offered $100 to anyone who could catch his hand before he jabbed them; Gil Hubbs took up the challenge. Hubbs told Robert Clouse, 'He would establish eye contact and control you so that you knew he was about to jab at you.

You would be ready to catch his hand. But all of a sudden it had happened. He could control you with his eyes.'

What is more likely is that Bruce's real power of seeing, his general level of attention, was much more highly developed than that of most people. He would simply keep his attention focused and jab instinctively at the moment he sensed a fluctuation in the concentration of his opponent.

Legend has it that when great martial artists used to meet they would often not actually fight, but would stand opposite each other and maintain eye contact. After a few minutes, one of the two would concede to the other recognizing that his spirit was not as strong as that of his partner.

The final scenes of *Enter the Dragon* were shot hurriedly while the dungeon scenery began to crack and crumble around them. The fight scene in the dungeon ranks as another of Bruce Lee's most stunning sequences on film. Eliminating Han's guards first in ones and twos, he is soon dealing with them in increasing numbers, now using a series of weapons: the pole, the *kali* sticks and *nunchaku*. To describe the complex fluidity and flow would be a long and futile exercise. It is enough to say that as a movie martial artist, Bruce Lee's ability had become almost luminous.

'In the end, it was all worth it,' wrote Robert Clouse. 'You couldn't have recreated that Oriental atmosphere in Holly-wood for a million dollars. The sights and sounds – even the smells – combined to create a feeling of intense realism for everyone involved in the production and I believed that quality would come over on the screen.'

The atmosphere in Han's dungeons must have been pretty realistic; there were hundreds of hookers and tramps pressed together for hours in claustrophobic conditions with no ventilation or air conditioning. As filming continued some of the mud-and-chicken-wire sets literally fell to bits during takes and everyone had to be careful not to hit any walls during fight scenes. In the climactic mass fight on the tournament field, the rehearsed encounter rapidly turned into a free-for-all between rival families of Triads who took the opportunity to settle old scores. The fights continued long after the cameras had stopped filming.

During the last two weeks Bruce Lee stayed on with the director while they filmed the fight sequence between Lee and Han in the mirrored maze. This sequence was not in the original script (which ended with Han impaled on his own metal claw) but was improvised. At one time or another almost everyone except Bruce Lee has taken credit for this idea.

A box about six feet square faced in mirror glass was placed in the centre of a room lined with mirrors. From any position in the room there were multiple reflections. Against one wall three mirrored booths were constructed that further fragmented the images. A glass hide was built to cover the camera.

When the sequence was shot, Shih Kien was forced to call out, 'Take it easy, son. This is only a movie!' The actor (who had played the villain in the Master Kwan films Bruce had watched as a boy) was a veteran of some 800 martial arts films and had spent over fifty years in daily *kung fu* training. Now over sixty, Shih Kien was a lot older than he looked.

The sequence in the Shaolin temple in which Lee teaches a young monk how to kick with feeling and without thinking was not in the original script and was added at Bruce's insistence. But what was left out of *Enter the Dragon* is also of some importance. Lee's discussion with the head monk had been much longer before the following exchange was cut.

As Lee pays his respects to his teacher, the head monk remarks that Lee's skill has gone beyond mere technique and is now one of spiritual insight. The monk asks Lee the same question that Lee has just asked the young monk: what was his immediate feeling towards his opponent while they were sparring?

Lee replies that he experienced no separate opponent. There was only one fluid spontaneous interplay of energy so that, 'when the opponent expands, I contract, and when he contracts, I expand. And when there is an opportunity I do not hit, it hits by itself.'

Joe Hyams once asked Bruce Lee, 'What if someone were to attack you and seriously meant to do you in? What then?'

Bruce answered, 'I would probably hurt him. If I did and I were on trial, I would plead not guilty; that I did not do it, it did it.'

At first, Hyams didn't understand. Bruce explained further. 'I throw a ball and you catch it. You walk into a dark room and without conscious thought you turn on the light switch. A child runs in front of your car and you jam on the brakes. You don't think about these things, it just happens. If someone tried to hit me, I wouldn't think about it, it would happen. I would do whatever was called upon to be done without conscious thought.'

Anticipating that *Enter the Dragon* would be his biggest movie to date, Bruce ordered a gold Rolls-Royce Corniche. He was now beginning to think about returning to California, saying that soon he would only come to Hong Kong to make the occasional picture.

21
COLLAPSE

A HEAVINESS PRESSED down on the back of Bruce Lee's neck like a giant hand in a wet glove – another typhoon was approaching. On 10 May 1973, Bruce was in a dubbing room at Golden Harvest, looping dialogue for *Enter the Dragon*. He repeatedly recorded his voice over a loop of film until the new voice matched the original speech movement as closely as possible. The air conditioning unit had been shut down to avoid its noise also being recorded. Inside the tiny room it was sweltering.

Still drained from the gruelling weeks of filming, Bruce had spent many days under these conditions. No one was surprised when he said he felt a little faint and had to get out for a minute. He went to a lavatory in the next building and splashed his face with cold water to clear his head. But suddenly he was falling; the scene faded and dissolved to black.

Out of the darkness he heard footsteps approaching. As he slowly came round he pretended that he was looking for his glasses which had fallen to the floor. Twenty minutes had passed and the studio assistant who had come looking for Bruce now helped him to his feet. Bruce was pale and sweating sheets of water. He had to be helped as he walked unsteadily back to the dubbing room. Suddenly, he collapsed again as his body was wrenched into a vomiting fit and he couldn't breathe properly.

Bruce was rushed to the nearby Baptist Hospital where an American physician, Dr Charles 'Don' Langford, saw that Bruce was running a fever of 105° and wouldn't respond to any stimuli. Langford immediately summoned neurosurgeon Dr Peter Wu and anaesthesiologist Dr Cecilia Wong. Now and again Bruce's eyes would open, though they could not focus, and every breath seemed like his last gasp; his body was lathered in sweat. An anaesthesia machine was employed as a respirator via a breathing tube into Bruce's throat and an intravenous glucose drip was set up. Various suggestions about the cause of the collapse were considered in rapid succession: exhaustion, kidney failure, epilepsy; the appropriate action was discussed. When a swelling of fluid pressing on the brain was discovered most credence was given to a diagnosis of cerebral edema. When Bruce lapsed again into complete unconsciousness, it was decided to give him Manitol (a dehydrating agent) to reduce the swelling detected by Dr Wu, and a catheter was set up to drain the flow of urine, a side-effect caused by the Manitol.

'From being semi-comatose,' says Don Langford, 'he suddenly became very agitated, with almost seizure-like behaviour. He could have injured himself so we had to tape his arms and legs down – even four of us had trouble controlling him. Then we got ready to perform brain surgery should there be no improvement.'

During an anxious wait of two hours, it was obvious to everyone present that Bruce was fighting for his life. When he showed signs of pulling back from the brink, he opened his eyes and stared out in confusion.

'By the time we got him into the ambulance to take him to St Theresa's, where there were beds available, he was still out of it and couldn't speak coherently,' continues Dr Langford. 'Both Dr Wu and I knew that he'd been very close to death.'

When Bruce had recovered enough to be able to travel, he and Linda flew to Los Angeles and went to the University of California Medical Center, where a team led by Dr David Reisbord did a complete physical examination, including exhaustive brain tests.

Eventually they accepted the diagnosis of the doctors in Hong Kong: that Bruce had suffered an accumulation of excess fluid around the brain, followed by a convulsion of no identifiable cause. Dr Reisbord prescribed Dilantin, a drug used to calm the brain activity of epileptics. In the end, the bewildered doctors could only give Bruce a clean bill of health, remarking that his body was in superb condition.

Bob Wall reports:

Bruce and Linda checked into the Beverly Hills Hotel for a week, and I saw him several times during that week. He was miserable. He looked chalky white and thin, nervous and upset. I tried to get him to join me in training but he didn't go out running once in that whole week. That just wasn't Bruce Lee. He said, 'I'm getting cheques poked at me from everywhere; people are making up stories about me. Fame isn't what I thought it was. I haven't got time to train.' Bruce was always so clear in his intentions and direction but now he seemed jumbled, unsure and just plain worn out. Occasionally he would repeat himself in conversation. He told me that his collapse had really scared him and he really thought he was going to die. I told him to take a couple of months off. He said, 'But I've got to promote the film, there's the *Johnny Carson Show* . . .' He knew it was all finally happening for him and he didn't want to lose it; he was scared that everything he'd worked so hard for was suddenly going to be taken away; at the same time he wondered if it was all worth it. Bruce was putting a lot of pressure on himself.

While in Los Angeles, Bruce finished off the final lines of dialogue for *Enter the Dragon* and then attended an early screening of the film at Warners. At this point the music soundtrack and sound effects were yet to be added along with the fades, dissolves and other optical effects. Even so, when the house lights came on at the end of the screening, Bruce punched the air and exclaimed, 'This is the one!'

Warner executives also knew it was a winner, and even though they had already gone over budget they immediately authorized an extra $50,000 to upgrade the music soundtrack. Warners also began stepping up publicity for the film's release, and the premiere at Graumann's Chinese Theater in Hollywood was scheduled for 24 August. Bruce had already confirmed plans to return to the States in August to appear on several TV shows, including the *Johnny Carson Show* in New York.

The buzz about *Enter the Dragon* travelled fast on the industry grapevine. Bruce was happy to let it, now that he was free to accept any new offer he wanted. Suddenly every studio and producer in the world had a project that was absolutely perfect for him. Warners had already asked Bruce to sign for five more features, offering to pay him $150,000 per film, per year.

Perhaps in his heart the film that Bruce still wanted to make was *The Silent Flute*. But when Coburn and Silliphant travelled to talk with Bruce, who was now back in Hong Kong, he could only remind them that he was now worth a million dollars a picture even though it was mainly Silliphant who had helped him to reach that status. Their talks were to no avail. Silliphant said that more than anything, Bruce was annoyed with him for having gone back to practising karate.

There were other conflicts. When Warners decided they wanted to change the title of *Enter the Dragon* back to the original *Blood and Steel*, Bruce fiercely disputed it. The studio responded by conceiving a new title that was staggering in its awfulness. Bruce had to make them back off by threatening never to work for them again. And so a week later, *Han's Island* had once again become *Enter the Dragon*.

When Bruce went back to Hong Kong to resume work on *Game of Death* he also resumed his running battle with the Hong Kong press over his rumoured relationship with Taiwanese actress Betty Ting Pei. Betty was used to the attention of the scandal press and had a reputation for fooling around and taking drugs. Golden Harvest alleged that many of the rumours circulating about Bruce were transparent lies planted in the press by unknown persons at Shaw Brothers Studios.

Yet Bruce's relationship with Raymond Chow was now beginning to turn a little sour. He began to put pressure on him by asking Run Run Shaw for $HK2 million to do a film for him. Bruce had gone as far as shooting some test footage for a film in which he would act in traditional Mandarin warrior roles, although this would seem to be a contradiction of his earlier rejection of the classical arts. In truth, Bruce had no intention of signing any contract with Shaw or of going through with the project: it was simply a ploy to deliver a message to Chow. But Shaw lost no time in trumpeting the news of the project from the headlines of the Hong Kong newspapers.

Bruce was pressurizing Chow because he was concerned about whether he was providing accurate accounting information over *Way of the Dragon*. Bruce was also angry that Chow had gone ahead on foreign release deals while he had wanted to hold out for better offers. He was upset by a story that had appeared in Golden Harvest's in-house magazine, which claimed that Raymond Chow had not only discovered

Bruce Lee but was 'like a babysitter' to him. Bruce retorted, 'The article puts forth the notion that I am like a stupid child who relies solely on Raymond.'

On 10 July 1973, Bruce Lee was at Golden Harvest studios when he heard that one of the many others who claimed credit for discovering or making him was also in the building – none other than Lo Wei, the man who had proclaimed himself Hong Kong's first millionaire director and the man who 'had taught Bruce Lee how to fight'. Now it would seem that Lo Wei's genius had suddenly deserted him. While Bruce Lee had gone on to make *Enter the Dragon*, Lo Wei had completed what was originally intended as Bruce's third film, *Yellow-Faced Tiger* (US title: *Slaughter in San Francisco*) starring Chuck Norris. The movie had not made Lo Wei his next million dollars.

Rather than letting the obvious speak for itself, Bruce could not resist confronting Lo Wei and telling him once more what he thought of him. Bruce burst into the screening room where the director was viewing a film called *Snake Girl* along with Mrs Lo Wei and Chow's partner, Leonard Ho. Bruce yelled at Lo Wei, who did not react, knowing it would have been futile to fight with Bruce Lee. Bruce then returned to Chow's office.

Minutes later, Mrs Lo Wei appeared in Chow's office to tell Bruce that he should behave with more decorum. This had quite the opposite effect. Tempers flared and a small crowd gathered. Bruce charged back to the screening room and berated Lo Wei even more. The police were called after Lo Wei claimed that Bruce had pulled out a short knife concealed in his belt buckle and threatened to stab him. The police could find no such knife and attempted to smooth out the situation rather than make arrests and involve lawyers.

Lo Wei insisted that Bruce sign a hastily improvised 'cease and desist' letter promising simply, 'I, Bruce Lee, will leave Lo

Wei alone.' The whole studio was in uproar and in order to get the police out and reporters away, Bruce signed the letter. Later he became annoyed when he realized that this had given Lo Wei's version of the events more substance.

That evening, when Bruce appeared on *Enjoy Yourself Tonight*, the incident was raised by the show's host, Ho Sho Sin. Without mentioning Lo Wei by name, Bruce made his dislike of the director more than obvious. Bruce had explained earlier that if he really wanted to kill anyone, he would not need to use a knife but could simply strike with his fingers. But on the TV show and at the host's insistence, Bruce offered to give a slightly less drastic demonstration of his skills. Although it was only a simple shoulder push, Ho was sent sprawling across the floor. To viewers who, like Ho, were unused to the rigours of martial arts training, it looked severe – as if Bruce had slammed into the host very hard. This resulted in yet another wave of critical headlines. Worse still, the articles all tended to sympathize with Lo Wei and the day's events were cited as further evidence of Bruce's growing arrogance.

'Just after his collapse,' recalls Taky Kimura, 'Bruce called me from LA and said, "You never write, you never call me." I said, "I'm enjoying what you're doing; you don't need me." He said, "If I can help you, Taky, you're still my number one friend and don't you forget that. Let me know what you need. Anything you want. I haven't changed. I'm still the same guy." He never forgot that I had helped him out in the past and that I never asked for anything. He told me to send the old plane ticket that he'd given me – to go to Hong Kong to start work on *Game of Death* – and he'd replace it.'

Certainly, Taky was happy to see Bruce Lee doing well. But maybe he was wrong when he said that Bruce didn't need him.

22
GOALS

WHEN BRUCE LEE was twenty-two and had been in America just over three years, he began applying the principles of positive thinking to his life. He visualized his aim of *kung fu* becoming as well known as karate, with a chain of his schools across the country. He saw an affluent lifestyle and a family to share it with. And he saw himself overcoming all obstacles to achieve his ultimate goal, peace of mind. But this vital force within him had both carried and driven Bruce to the point at which life seemed to offer him both the best and the worst that it could.

Bruce had once signed a photograph for James Lee, adding the message, 'Circumstances? Hell, I make circumstances!' But now circumstances were no longer being made by him; they had become ugly intrusions into the simple and private life to which he wished he could return. He saw success as something to be avoided, now that he'd experienced the damage it could do and the painful realization that it was not what he'd anticipated.

*

Bruce was continually being pestered by people who claimed to be friends of friends or long-lost relatives, before presenting some deal or asking to borrow money – all of them wearing the same stuck-on smile that he had come to detest. There were few people Bruce could talk to without a deal being offered.

Bruce was unable to go anywhere in Hong Kong without being mobbed. He could eat only in restaurants with private dining rooms and even then all the waiters would want autographs. Bruce had started to drink, and at one dinner drank his way through twenty pots of sake. Where once Bruce had supplemented his natural vitality with ginseng and royal jelly, vitamins and herbal teas, he was now drinking liquidized steaks for strength and chewing cannabis to help him relax. His complexion had become pale and dull.

Bruce was spending nights away from home. Suffering from insomnia, he would sometimes head for the studio where he worked through another restless night on ideas for *Game of Death*. Other times, he would head elsewhere.

Just as life now offered Bruce Lee its best and its worst, so was Bruce Lee now showing life the best and worst aspects of himself. His mood swings became more pronounced; one moment he declared that he still wanted to act but not make any more martial arts films, adding that the public would only be interested in *kung fu* movies for about three years. At other times he reaffirmed his aim of wanting to educate audiences through the medium of film so that they would understand that there was more to martial arts than mere fighting.

One minute Bruce could see no end to his possibilities; in the next he had no idea if he could maintain the effort needed to realize them. The more he did, the more he felt the need to stretch himself further. He would cut people short, telling them that 'trying to relax' is a contradiction. Bruce's friends perceived him pulled in opposing directions: he was either pressed down by a great burden, or just spiralling away aimlessly. Bruce recalled Yip Man's advice given twenty years before – that nobody can oppose a problem head-on, one has to flow with it. Attempting to apply this wisdom to his fast-paced life, Bruce decided that the answer was to match the speed of the changes happening around him. Even Linda's mother expressed her concern for Bruce. She told Taky, 'He's losing weight. Tell him to rest; he'll listen to you.' But Bruce could not let up.

Saddest of all for Bruce was that his relationships had become riddled with suspicion. Bruce told Thomas Chan, an actor who had appeared in *Fist of Fury*, that he had a mountain of money in front of him if he wanted it, but the people who offered the money thought that it would buy Bruce; they believed they would own him. 'I must be very, very careful,' Bruce told Chan. Yet while there were mountains of money in front of him, Bruce was also concerned that someone in Hong Kong had cheated him.

Friends could only witness Bruce's growing isolation. Fred Weintraub says that Bruce was now a different person to the one he had been only weeks previously in Los Angeles, adding that he was no longer so friendly and kept others at a distance.

'Bruce Lee felt lonely in the few months before his death,' says Nora Miao. 'He was a changed man. He used to phone me and tell me that he felt lonely. I told him, "No one dares get close to you!" Confused, he said, "Why? Why do I feel that I don't have a real friend when there are so many people around me?" I said, "It's not so strange. You've become an idol. People only flatter you. Then, when they do this, you despise them. On the other hand, if they criticize you, you resent it. You are a victim of fame."'

Perhaps Bruce Lee now had occasion to recall what his

mother had told him when he was ten years old. When he had told her of his ambitions, she had replied, 'The life of a famous film star is not so comfortable as you imagine. Their lives are abnormal.'

Grace Lee says:

Following his increasing fame, he became thinner and thinner. When he returned to Los Angeles after finishing *Way of the Dragon*, he had lost a lot of weight. I told him, 'Have a good rest and relax a little.' I was really worried about his health. Later, he started filming *Enter the Dragon*. When I saw him in May 1973, I couldn't believe the person in front of me was my son, he had changed so much. He told me that he wouldn't live much longer because doctors in Hong Kong had told him that there was a serious problem inside his head. He said, 'Mom, don't worry about your future, there will be no money problems.' I reproached him at once and told him not to talk like that.

Maria Yi had also noticed a worrying trait:

Before he died, he developed amnesia. Some time after filming *The Big Boss* – when I visited him at the studio – he often took out a picture of his car and asked me to admire it. He repeated this action several times a day without knowing that he had done it before. It was very unsettling.

On 16 July 1973, as a fierce typhoon approached Hong Kong, Bruce made a rambling $200 phone call to Unicorn, who was in a hotel in Manila while working on location. Bruce told his friend that he was worried about the headaches he was experiencing.

After his collapse, when he returned to Hong Kong from Los Angeles, Bruce told his brother Peter that he hoped to live to be a hundred. He had even made drawings of himself as a wise old Taoist priest. He told Chuck Norris that he planned to retire at thirty-five, spend ten years with his growing family, and then re-emerge to see what he could do for society, adding that he hoped people would not expect too much of him.

But all that was years away on the morning of 20 July 1973, as Bruce sat down to type a letter to his lawyer in Los Angeles. There were possibly some big changes ahead. Bruce talked first about meeting Raymond Chow to 'hear him out'. He listed five deals to be considered and anticipated spending the whole weekend looking at these offers, working out a tax plan and endorsement deals for books and clothes. There were details of a hectic promotional tour for *Enter the Dragon*, including the trip to New York for the *Johnny Carson Show*. Bruce added that by 24 August he would be ready to come back to Hong Kong, 'hopefully in one piece'.

Says Taky Kimura:

> Every week there would be a new rumour. Someone would say, 'I see that Bruce was killed in a tournament last week.' I would hear stuff like that from all over. One day, one of my packers told me, 'Bruce Lee is dead – it's in all the papers.' I didn't even bother to check. Then Linda's mother rang and told me . . .

23
20 July 1973

TYPHOON DOROTHY LASHED warm rain hard against the windows of the Hotel Miramar where Raymond Chow and George Lazenby sat in the opulent restaurant. They ordered another aperitif and made small talk as they waited patiently for Bruce Lee and Betty Ting Pei to show up for dinner. It was to be an informal meeting to discuss ideas for *Game of Death*. But at that moment in Betty's apartment over on Beacon Hill Road the actress was desperately trying to rouse Bruce Lee from sleep, shaking him and then slapping him across the face. Earlier in the day, Bruce and Raymond Chow had met Betty at her apartment before Chow had left alone. Shortly after, Bruce had complained of a headache; after being given a pill by Betty, he had gone to lie down on the bed.

Now, at just after nine o'clock in the evening, Chow received a call from Betty. He left the hotel and drove straight over to her apartment, which took some thirty or forty minutes due to bad traffic. When he too could get no response from Bruce, Betty's doctor was summoned and then, after a further delay, an ambulance was finally called. The ambulance arrived at the same time as Betty's mother and brother, who tried to calm the distressed actress. Raymond Chow phoned Linda Lee, telling her to get over to the Queen Elizabeth Hospital, where Bruce was being taken.

Linda rushed to the hospital and arrived before the ambulance. There was an agonizing wait until the doors burst open and Bruce was rushed in, unconscious on a stretcher and surrounded by a swarm of paramedics; one was thumping Bruce's chest, trying to keep his heart going. Events blurred – emergency room, stimulant injections, electric shock pads – but despite the frantic activity, Bruce lay still. Now there was an eternity for the truth to hit home.

As the momentum of events picked up, Raymond Chow's wife arrived to collect her husband and take Linda home. There was a long slow walk down a calm white hospital corridor and suddenly they were confronted by the starburst of flashbulbs and the babble of reporters.

Grace Lee didn't believe the news of her son's death. For months stories had been appearing in the Hong Kong press saying that he was dead. She would immediately call up the paper or magazine to see if it was true; it never was. When she told Bruce how much the stories upset her, he would explain the obvious: that they were simply lies to sell magazines. He told her the next time she heard or read such a story, not to believe it. When one of Grace Lee's friends called her, crying, with the news that Bruce was dead she told her friend that it was a lie. But her friend said that she hadn't read it in a magazine but had seen it on TV. When Grace Lee found out it was true, she said simply, 'Too much work.'

Like Grace Lee, nobody could believe that the fittest man in the world had died at thirty-two. One popular rumour to surface was that it was all a publicity stunt to promote *Game of Death*. People were laying bets on whether or not it was true.

Five days later, Bruce Lee's symbolic funeral was the largest Hong Kong had ever witnessed. Three hundred police were on duty outside the Kowloon Funeral Parlour where the body lay in an open bronze coffin. Thirty thousand mourners gathered to fill Maple Street, crowding balconies and lining the roofs as far as the eye could see. Inevitably, people fainted and were injured in the pushing and shoving. Emotions ran high.

Whenever the crowd spotted a celebrity arriving at the funeral parlour they broke into clapping and cheering, prompting the *South China Morning Post* to describe the scene as 'a carnival'. Nora Miao arrived, then Lo Wei and George Lazenby along with a gaggle of minor local stars. Some had come to pay their respects; others recognized a photo opportunity when they saw one. Two people not seen were Run Run Shaw and Betty Ting Pei.

Inside, the midsummer air was stifling and thick with the aroma of flowers and incense. On arrival, each mourner would pay his or her respects at an altar; small bunches of flowers from tearful children lay next to expensive wreaths. Candles and incense burned before a photograph of Bruce surrounded by decorations – long silk ribbons and flowers – above which hung a banner that read in Chinese, 'A Star Sinks in the Sea of Art.' Each mourner would bow three times at the altar and then take their place in the hall.

Then came the arrival of Linda, helped by Raymond Chow, almost buried in the folds of her traditional mourning clothes, a white burlap robe and headdress, red-eyed behind her dark glasses. The children, Brandon and Shannon, each dressed in a little white robe, seemed blissfully unaware of what was happening. They took their places; to their side sat Bruce's mother Grace, his brother Peter, and Unicorn, who had returned from

Manila. The band struck up the traditional funeral song. Now Bruce's coffin was brought in and placed near the altar for the mourners to file past. His body lay swathed to the chin in white silk; his face looked grey and somehow distorted under heavy make-up. In the pocket of his suit were his broken spectacles.

Long after the funeral was over, police with megaphones were still patrolling the streets, urging people to go home.

Raymond Chow's account of events on the night of Bruce Lee's death implied that Bruce died at home with his family. Perhaps Chow was simply trying to spare Linda's embarrassment, knowing full well what the press would make of the actual situation. In any case, the first reports to be sent around the world said that Bruce had died at home. One paper typically romanticized the story even further, saying that Bruce had died while walking in his garden with Linda.

But Henry Parwani, a reporter from the *China Star* (the paper that was still the subject of Bruce's legal action) went to the hospital to look over the ambulance call-out records and found that the call had not come from Bruce's home but, as he had suspected, from the apartment of Betty Ting Pei. And so, on the day before the funeral, the *Star*'s headline blazed 'DRAGON KILLED IN BETTY TING PEI'S FRAGRANT CHAMBER'. It was a particularly bitter irony that Bruce Lee, who had spent his whole life endeavouring to make known the Chinese art of *kung fu*, was referred to as a 'karate star'.

Raymond Chow, for once, swiftly ducked out of the spotlight and left the actress to face the press alone. Bewildered and on the defensive she made things worse by lying. 'On the night he died I was not at home. I had gone out with my mother. I last saw him several months ago, when we met by chance in the street.'

Bruce's friends and family supported this version of events in the belief that the press was taking revenge on Bruce for his treatment of them in the past. But journalists spoke to Betty Ting Pei's neighbours who confirmed that Bruce had been a regular visitor to her apartment for months prior to his death.

The day after the funeral Linda left for Seattle with Bruce's body. At Kai Tak airport Linda, now dressed in black, her face strained with sorrow, read a press statement in an attempt to stop the controversy surrounding Bruce's death. The tickets that were to have been used to travel to New York for Bruce's appearance on the *Johnny Carson Show* had been traded in for tickets to return his body to the United States. The funeral in Hong Kong had been for family, friends and fans there, but because Bruce's happiest times had been in Seattle it was decided to bury him in the peace of Lake View Cemetery, where he used to enjoy walking alone in the rain.

On 31 July, a small crowd of twenty people gathered outside the Butterworth Funeral Home on East Pine Street to watch colleagues and friends arrive for Bruce's funeral. During the journey, Bruce's coffin had been damaged. This was taken by some to be an omen that Bruce's soul was not at peace, and with all the controversy, it is hard to see how it could have been. The new coffin was covered with red, yellow and white flowers making up the *yin/yang* sign he had first adopted as an emblem for his *gung fu* institutes.

The pall-bearers were Robert Lee, Taky Kimura, Dan Inosanto, Steve McQueen, James Coburn and family friend and actor Peter Chin. As Bruce had wished, there was no traditional music. The music played was Frank Sinatra's 'My Way', Tom Jones singing 'The Impossible Dream', Sergio Mendes' 'Look Around', and the Blood, Sweat and Tears song 'And When I Die'. Though all of these songs have since become cliché standards of mawkish bar singers the world over, Bruce Lee, more than most, could rightfully claim to have lived life his way in attempting to achieve an almost impossible dream.

'He lived every day as a day of discovery,' Linda Lee eulogized. 'His thirty-two years were full of living. Bruce believed that the individual represents the whole of mankind, whether he lives in the Orient or elsewhere. He believed that man struggles to find a life outside himself, not realizing that the life he seeks is within him.'

Taky Kimura said, simply, that Bruce had inspired good in others.

Ted Ashley expressed a more businesslike philosophy: 'It could be viewed as a pity that Bruce passed on right at the beginning of his realization that he would make it big. I have a sense of sadness mingled with the knowledge that, while he may not have gotten up the ladder, he at least got his foot on it.'

Finally, at the graveside, James Coburn made the last short speech, 'Farewell, my brother. It has been an honour to share this space and time with you. As a friend and as a teacher, you have given to me and have brought my physical, spiritual and psychological selves together. Thank you. May peace be with you.'

The coffin was lowered into the grave along with the pall-bearers' white gloves.

Even as Bruce Lee was being laid to rest in Seattle, the press in Hong Kong were whipping up new headlines, most of which were a combination of malice and fantasy. In the end, the Hong Kong government ordered a full-scale official enquiry into the circumstances of Bruce's death.

*

On 3 September, the inquest opened in Tsunwan under coroner Egbert Tung. It had assumed enough importance for the official autopsy to have been carried out by British government forensic laboratories.

With reports that the autopsy had found traces of cannabis in Bruce's stomach, some headlines suggested that he had died a drug addict, others that he had taken drugs to accomplish his extraordinary physical feats. In Hong Kong, cannabis is seen as worse than heroin or opium. Bruce's father and even his *wing chun* master Yip Man were no strangers to the opium pipe, but cannabis was associated with the 'hippie-tourist foreign devils'.

The cannabis question had also become important because of the attendance at the inquest of David Yapp from the American International Insurance Company. The company had seen a way out of paying on Bruce's life insurance policy. If it could be shown that Bruce had taken cannabis before he had filled out the application form, he had answered untruthfully the question of whether he had ever used narcotics.

Various tests for evidence of poisoning, made at the request of detectives, all proved negative. The only further finding was that Bruce had taken the equivalent of one tablet of an aspirin compound, Equagesic.

Dr R. R. Lycette, the clinical pathologist at Queen Elizabeth Hospital, told the coroner's hearing that death could not have been caused by cannabis but was due to hypersensitivity to one or more of the ingredients of Equagesic. While the doctor had found no injuries to the skull or evidence of a brain haemorrhage, the brain had swollen very rapidly from its normal weight of 1,400 grams to 1,575 grams.

Ronald Teare, a professor of forensic medicine at the University of London, was flown in as the inquest's heavy-weight – in thirty-five years Teare had supervised nearly 100,000 autopsies and provided evidence for almost 20,000 inquests. The professor said that the presence of cannabis was a mere coincidence, adding that it would be both 'irresponsible and irrational' to say that it might have triggered either the events of Bruce's collapse on 10 May or his death on 20 July. Although it was a rare and unusual case, he said, the only conclusion that could be reached was that death was caused by an acute cerebral oedema due to a reaction to compounds present in the prescription painkiller Equagesic.

At the start of the inquest, police barricades had been set up to deal with the crowds who had come to get a glimpse of Betty Ting Pei. But once the medical testimony had begun the crowds drifted away. By the end of the inquest, on 24 September, only a handful of reporters approached Linda Lee for her comment on the verdict. She could only ask them what difference it made.

PART TWO

LEGEND . . . AND REALITY

24

WOMEN

WITHOUT LINDA, BRUCE Lee would not have achieved everything he did. Early in their relationship it must certainly have occurred to the young Linda Emery that Bruce Lee was no ordinary man and that there was a choice to be made. Bruce Lee needed a woman to share his vision, just as he did when he asked his first girlfriend, Amy Sanbo, to live her life through his, and just as he did when he wrote a long letter explaining his dreams to his dancing partner, Pearl Cho.

Linda Lee was Bruce's greatest strength during the two most intense crises of his short life. When he injured his back and could hardly move, she would spend a full day looking after the family and then go out to work in the evening to earn money. Not only did she keep the family together throughout this period, but she agreed to do it secretly so that Bruce's pride didn't suffer. Again, when Bruce faced his most important test – just prior to the filming of *Enter the Dragon* – it was Linda who brought the stability and support that allowed him to succeed. Both director Robert Clouse and producer Fred Weintraub have said that without Linda Lee there would have been no *Enter the Dragon*.

The director's wife, Ann Clouse, was once talking to Bruce

when she happened to look over at Linda who, with an air of total devotion, was silently repeating his words, 'as if she was trying to memorize his life'.

In August 1972, Miss Pang Cheng Lian, a reporter on *New Nation* (an English-language newspaper in Singapore), went to Hong Kong for a week to write four features based on interviews with Bruce Lee. She spent time with Bruce at Golden Harvest studios where he was dubbing *Way of the Dragon* and where they had lunch together, after which Bruce made his customary call home. When he returned, Miss Pang brought up the subject of female martial artists.

Bruce told her that a woman could never match a man for strength and her best bet was to use her powers of seduction and persuasion to gain an opportunity to jab her assailant in the eyes or kick his groin, before running like hell. With talk of seduction and 'vital parts', the questions turned to Bruce's relationship with 'a certain actress'. This brought his response that the people of Hong Kong had too much time to invent stories that would upset the girl in question.

Betty Ting Pei had stayed away from Bruce's funeral. When questioned about their relationship she either spoke evasively or implied that she and Bruce did have a special relationship. 'Silence is the best answer to scandalous rumours. Because I treasure his friendship, I put up with the gossip.'

The actress then threatened to sue the press if they persisted with stories of an affair. 'It seems people want me to die,' she told the *Star*. 'Bruce is dead. Why don't you leave it at that?'

One paper retorted with the headline: 'BETTY TING, SUE US!' and printed a fresh list of disclosures. The beleaguered actress eventually went into hiding and spent her time watching television.

After Bruce's death, one of the first people to speak to Betty Ting Pei was Felix Dennis (then publisher of the underground magazines *International Times* and *Oz*). Dennis had already begun work with Don Atyeo on the book *Bruce Lee: King of Kung Fu*, published in 1974.

According to Dennis, Betty told him that she and Bruce had been having an affair. Friends openly confirmed it had been going on for about a year. At one point Bruce attempted to end the affair, resuming it only after Betty had broken down and been admitted to hospital. The general feeling was that Bruce was still fairly naïve when it came to sex. Betty had been around a bit and Bruce was simply getting an education, though the relationship was obviously more than a brief affair.

Dennis adds:

> Although Betty Ting Pei initially admitted that she and Bruce had been having an affair she changed her account because she 'felt responsible'. If Betty had picked up the phone the moment Bruce collapsed, then he could have been saved. But she panicked, hoping that he would recover, then waited too long before calling Raymond Chow on the other side of Hong Kong. By the time Chow had got through the traffic jams it was too late. Bruce Lee was not dead on arrival at the hospital, and the doctors were astonished that he'd lasted as long as he did.

Betty Ting Pei changed her story one last time and has stuck to it resolutely for the past two decades. She denied that she and Bruce ever had any sexual relationship and insisted that her relationship with Bruce was 'spiritual'. She was even filmed performing religious devotions for Canadian TV. In more recent years the actress has not been seen publicly and cannot be traced.

In his early career as a child actor, Bruce Lee often played the the problem child, sometimes portraying scenes that were not much different from his actual life. The obvious question is: how much did these roles influence his real life and how much did his life influence his acting? The answer is that they each reflected the other, just as Bruce's roles in *The Big Boss* and *Way of the Dragon* championed exploited workers and so reflected the everyday concerns of his audience.

In the same way – although we should be careful not to blur the distinction between Bruce's roles and his actual life – it is true to say that women were portrayed in his films in the same way they were viewed in Chinese society. In his films there are only good girls or bad girls; they tend either to be virgins who smile bashfully and serve food, or whores who pour drinks and remove their clothes at the first opportunity – 'part of the perks', said Bruce.

In *Enter the Dragon*, all the tournament contestants take up the offer of having women brought to their rooms. Lee also has a woman in his room, but she is a female agent, a colleague with whom he must exchange information. When the film was first shown in Hong Kong, the scene in which Lee passes up the offer of a beautiful woman for the night provoked the audience into howls of derision and hoots of laughter.

As far as the majority of Chinese people were concerned, *any* film actress was a whore. Moral standards were as closely defined as those in Britain or the United States a century earlier. There were good girls and bad girls; and bad girls were actresses of any description. Even so, to his co-star Maria Yi, he was simply Uncle Bruce.

Nora Miao said, 'He was like my brother or my teacher. He kept on teaching me. He said, "Everyone must create their own future. Even though I may someday die without fulfilling my ambitions, I will have no regrets, because I made sincere efforts."'

*

Bill Ryusaki is a movie fight arranger who worked with Bruce on *The Wrecking Crew*. He says, 'Around the time that Bruce was playing bit parts, he didn't spend so much time at home; things were a bit strained. He used to spend a lot of time hanging around my school. I had an all-girls' class, and, y' know, Bruce liked the ladies.' Even so, Bruce invariably spent the rest of the evening in a restaurant with Ryusaki, talking martial arts.

When younger, Bruce carried a joke visiting card to give to women, with a message suggesting that if she would like to sleep with him then she should smile. In later life, when introduced to a woman he would ask her to feel his abdominal muscles or his thigh. In fact, Bruce would ask anyone, male or female, to admire some new improvement to his physique, and would remove his shirt at the drop of a hat. If the woman was unmarried, then she might be encouraged to feel his thigh, as he guided her hand towards the muscle in question and grinned charmingly. Married women were asked to feel his biceps. Ann Clouse said that it was like feeling warm marble. Bruce even asked his mother to feel his muscles. 'When he lived in the States,' she said, 'he practised *kung fu* day and night. Sometimes he would put his hands out in front of me and ask me to try his muscles. They were like iron bars.'

After Bruce's death the rumours continued, including one that he had died of an overdose of the aphrodisiac Spanish fly. Journalists went back through the photo files for every shot of him with a woman. One paper printed five pages of him with different women, smiling with his arm around them, with the implication that every single one had been his lover.

It is true that Bruce Lee was seen and photographed with many glamorous women, but then what international movie star isn't? He even played it up and, being a natural show-off, he enjoyed being seen with beautiful young women. Although he took things a lot further with Betty Ting Pei, I believe that at heart Bruce was neither fickle nor promiscuous.

It was a big risk for a young girl from a narrow-minded middle-class family to marry someone who at the time had no money or prospects. Not many women would have taken it. Linda Lee lived very much in Bruce's shadow and had to devote herself to his needs. No doubt he was grateful for that, but for both of them the happiest years were probably the early ones, before he became a star.

25

FOUL PLAY?

EVEN ON THE night of Bruce Lee's death the rumours and exaggerations were already sweeping through Hong Kong on a tide of high emotion. Word at the Press Club was that Bruce had been involved in a fight with ten or twenty men who had beaten him to death.

With his sudden death, one could almost hear the anguished echoes from the opening scenes of *Fist of Fury* when Chen Chen discovers the death of his master: 'How can a healthy man die!'

As with John Lennon, there were probably many people with whom Bruce Lee had no connection at all who nonetheless wished him dead.

Some speculation ludicrously imagined the hand of Run Run Shaw or even Raymond Chow behind Bruce's death. Further extravagant suggestions were that Bruce Lee had been murdered by members of the Triads whom he had crossed or offended, or that he perished at the hands of Japanese martial artists who were tired of his dismissive attitude to karate.

Others suggested that *kung fu* masters had killed Bruce with a secret 'death-touch' technique because he had exploited the art, and in his dealings with Hollywood had gone too far and brought the martial arts into disrepute. In reality, Bruce Lee had already paid a heavy price driving himself to perfect his art while striving to bring it to a mass audience.

Almost overnight a cult sprang up around Bruce Lee. *Kung fu* fanzines looked in desperation for any angle. Astrologers were hired to say why everyone should have seen it coming and to speculate on what Bruce would be doing if he were alive. Some believed that Bruce was not dead at all and had retreated to the mountains to make a messianic reappearance at a later date.

The theories became more and more extravagant. Bruce had died from taking steroids (even though his weight had fallen alarmingly); or he had died from having his sweat glands removed so that he looked good on camera! The silliness spread until months later Golden Harvest's Andre Morgan received a letter from a woman in Goose Bay, Labrador, saying that her family had just seen one of Bruce's films and they understood he was now dead. Could Golden Harvest please confirm that the mafia had shot Bruce because he was too big to control any more?

There are bound to be many theories about the premature death of one of the world's fittest men. Bruce had suffered a serious brain trauma only two months before he died, so a weakness was already present. Whether that weakness had been present from birth or whether it had been brought about by injury should be the first point to consider. At the coroner's enquiry, Raymond Chow testified that during the course of making his films Bruce had taken many blows not included in the scripts; Chow added that some of these accidental blows had been 'quite severe'.

*

Much was made of the signs and omens surrounding Bruce's death. Journalist Mel Tobias observed that Kowloon Tong, where Bruce's house was situated, means, Nine Dragon Pond and speculated that the big dragons did not like having the Little Dragon in their midst and devoured him. Another Chinese superstition has it that one should never put the word 'death' in the title of a book or film. On 20 July Bruce was making plans to resume the filming of *Game of Death*.

We have all experienced strolling along a beach looking for the right spot to sunbathe, or waiting for the right place to stop for a picnic. At its highest level of expression, this intuitive faculty, known in the West as geomancy, is in the East called *feng shui*. The art/science of *feng shui* allows one to live more in harmony with the environment. When building a house, the Chinese give a great deal of consideration to its relation to the natural features and forces of the area, so that it may relate to the local environment and resonate with it like an organ in a healthy body. The site of the house must take into account the lie of the land, where water runs, the direction of the prevailing wind and so on. The principles of *feng shui* extend even further, to the layout and colour of room furnishings, the position of lamps, and so forth.

The *feng shui* advisor who had been called in to look over the house that Bruce bought in Kowloon Tong was not happy. The area had a reputation for bringing down wealthy families, symbolized by its situation at the lowest point of a depression in the land. The two previous owners of Bruce's house had both suffered financial reversals. Additionally, the house was on the landing approach to Kai Tak airport, meaning that the natural wind currents were disturbed; while the house itself was facing the wrong way. The *feng shui* man devised a solution: a mirrored figure was placed on the roof of the building to reflect away the bad influences. Two days before Bruce died, this figure had been blown off the roof in a typhoon.

Events and situations like these should certainly not be considered the cause of Bruce Lee's death, nor were they the result. These events simply happened at the same time. These coincidences, or as Jung terms them, synchronicities, were neither cause nor effect but resonate with the same quality and reflect the nature of each other. 'Coincidences,' said the writer G. K. Chesterton, 'are spiritual puns.'

Doug Palmer made notes on his own opinions concerning Bruce's death:

His broad-mindedness made him impervious to any restrictions, whether on martial arts techniques or the conventions surrounding them. He was the first to teach *gung fu* to non-Chinese, at a time when he risked criticism and even ostracism from the Chinese community. Ultimately, coupled with the jealousies of his over-whelming skill and popularity, was the effect of his impatience (some called it arrogance) with those who relied on cant and tradition instead of merit and ability. All this, I believe, led to his death.

The mutual dislike between him and some of the more trad-itional *gung fu* masters in Hong Kong grew as fast as Bruce's reputation. Several masters from other schools were with Bruce on a TV show, a benefit show for charity, as I recall. At any rate, one of the other masters was bragging about his inner power, goading Bruce and challenging him to strike him in the stomach. The master stood in the ready stance, one arm at his side and the other pointing at his stomach, insisting that Bruce hit him there, adding that it was impossible to hurt him. Bruce approached and struck him right on the nose. The master jumped back, startled, then incensed, and demanded to know what Bruce was doing. 'Anyone can learn to resist a blow if he is prepared for it,' Bruce said. 'A *gung fu* man must be prepared for the unexpected.'*

'The last time I saw Bruce,' Palmer adds, 'was while he was filming *Game of Death*. Sure he was thin, but he was very fit. I don't believe he was working himself to death. Bruce made many enemies in Hong Kong for openly flouting tradition and causing loss of face; that TV show was seen by three million people. Nobody could openly challenge Bruce; no one could beat him one to one, so the only way to get rid of him without leaving any evidence, would be to poison him.'

Another of Bruce's early students, James DeMile, was so convinced that foul play was involved in Bruce's death that he mounted his own investigation. DeMile's first suspicion was that the Chinese *wing chun* clans were unhappy about Bruce Westernizing the art. In Hong Kong, people took up a fighting style as part of a deeply ingrained family tradition. Unless you are privy to that tradition it is difficult to understand the depth of feeling that might be involved, just as it is probably impossible for Asians to comprehend that violent deaths result from the rivalry of fans from competing soccer teams.

Later DeMile revised his thinking, saying that he believed Bruce had been poisoned by people he had antagonized in the Hong Kong film industry because Bruce's independent attitude had stirred up too many ambitions in an exploitative industry that had previously run like clockwork.

In *Bruce Lee: King of Kung Fu*, Don Atyeo wrote:

---

* In August 1972, Bruce Lee appeared on Hong Kong's TVB channel as part of a benefit programme that raised over $HK5 million on behalf of the victims of a recent typhoon. An alternative account of the day's events was that Bruce told the traditional *kung fu* master, 'It's easy to defend, if you dictate how you are going to be attacked.'

Bruce Lee destroyed face like a leprous aftershave . . . To many of those beaten by Lee, in business or in the ring, his superman self-confidence was unbearable, his blunt candidness an insult. Then again, Lee cost many of his rivals large amounts of money. Besides siphoning off much audience support from the established studios, there were numerous complaints that, under competition from the Lee films, smaller production companies floundered and were squeezed out of the race.

Lee irrevocably altered not only the products of the Mandarin film industry, but also the structure of the industry itself. As the first Mandarin actor to take control of his own career, he showed the way to a more equitable share of the profits for his fellow performers. Certainly, in Hong Kong, in the early months of 1973, there were many people who would have been more than happy to ring down the curtain on the meteoric rise of Lee's star.

Immediately after Bruce Lee's death, Alex Ben Block, then the entertainment editor of the *Miami News*, wrote *The Legend of Bruce Lee*. Despite the fact that Block had no experience at all of the martial arts, it is from his book that all the tales of clandestine assassination squads and jealous *kung fu* masters arose.

Block made many suggestions: Bruce Lee was murdered by those who had not wanted *kung fu* made public, or by people jealous of his fame, or by those angry that he didn't endorse their products. Block leaves it for us to decide whether the assassination itself was done by 'one talented enemy with the knowledge and the will', or 'by *ninja* poisoners using cannabis', or by Malaysian martial artists using a ' "vibrating palm" technique', or by Shaolin monks who were 'upset' with Bruce and who used the delayed death-touch known as *dim mak*, and so on. Such wild speculation from Block's book was soon being quoted as 'authoritative' and 'well-researched' fact. *Popster* magazine promised to reveal that Bruce was killed by a

secret death-touch by unknown assassins, while on the following page it attempted to answer the rather more fundamental
question, 'What is *Kung Fu?*'

This is not to suggest that subtle ways of using energy to injure
and kill do not exist. Indeed, Bruce Lee himself knew the art,
as did my own teacher Derek Jones. *Dim mak* (death-touch)
is perhaps the ultimate expression of *bil jee* (stabbing fingers),
whereby massive amounts of energy may be transferred to an
opponent, sometimes with only a minimum of actual contact.
The technique itself extends far beyond the physical realm. It
may be likened to a kind of reverse acupuncture in which
energy circuits are broken and disrupted rather than harmon-
ized and balanced. The success of *dim mak* requires knowledge
as to which areas are more vulnerable to attack at specific
times; like the art of *feng shui*, it requires an intuitive understanding of energy and the ability to find the right spot at the
right time. The success of *dim mak* further depends on meditating on the desired results. It might even be considered more
akin to an occult art than a straightforward fighting technique.
In a sense, *dim mak* operates as a kind of reverse spiritual
healing. The use of energy depends on how it is channelled by
the combination of intention, desire and action into a unified
force. That any inappropriate use of this energy will also have
its consequences must be understood.

Alex Ben Block is now the executive editor of the entertainment trade paper the *Hollywood Reporter*. 'Have I revised any
of my opinions? To a certain extent I have, though personally
I always believed Bruce Lee died of natural causes. I wrote that
book in a matter of weeks, when nobody really knew what was
happening. I just threw out everything I could that might offer
some explanation. I don't, for example, believe any of that
stuff that Goldman wrote in *Penthouse*.'

Block is referring to Albert Goldman's two-part article that appeared in the January and February 1983 issues of *Penthouse*. In this article Goldman asserts that Bruce Lee showed all the classic signs of the coward/bully, also calling him an overrated 'show biz brat', a 'fortune-cookie philosopher' and a control freak who had become addicted to a powerful Nepalese hash resin that eventually killed him. The core of Goldman's thesis was extrapolated from two phone conversations, one with Bob Wall and one with Bruce's doctor, Don Langford.

Says Bob Wall:

Goldman talked to me once on the phone, and then misquoted everything I'd said from the most negative point of view.

The last time I was at Bruce's little Japanese house in Kowloon Tong, we had a spirited disagreement about the relative merits of wine and hash. I was encouraging him to drink wine to relax. I told him that a couple of glasses of wine with a meal is considered beneficial, that he didn't have to get drunk and that he could use it without misusing it. Bruce was enthusing about this article which he'd read in *Playboy* about the relaxing effects of hash. Because Bruce neither drank nor smoked, he liked the idea of putting hash in cookies. I told him that there was no way you could know the source or the quality of hash, whereas with a bottle of wine, there was a label with the name of the vineyard.

Bruce countered that he only bought the best quality and, as Wall sipped his wine, ate a hash cookie. As the evening wore on the spirited debate turned to conversation on the martial arts and philosophy, with Bruce becoming 'mellow, relaxed and charming'.

Some weeks later, Bruce suffered the collapse in the dubbing rooms of Golden Harvest, and after his treatment by doctors in Hong Kong had gone for further tests at UCLA Medical Center. During that time, Bruce stayed in a bungalow at the Beverly Hills Hotel and met Bob Wall several times.

Bruce told Wall that he had almost died and that when he recovered, the doctors said that something strange had happened and, along with other information, they wanted to know everything that Bruce had eaten around the time of the collapse. When it came to light that one of the things he'd eaten was a hash cookie, it was suggested that he may have had a bad reaction to the drug. He was advised not to eat it any more. Clearly, he didn't follow this advice.

Don Langford left Hong Kong in 1989, at the invitation of the medical faculty he now heads in Lafayette in his native Louisiana. Also a Baptist minister, he speaks in the measured tones of a Southern gentleman:

> My first contact with the Lee family was when Brandon was brought to me because he had injured his hand when he trapped it in a folding chair. I didn't know who Bruce was; I simply remembered Brandon's father as being a muscular and intelligent man. Then a nurse said to me, 'Don't you know who that is?' When I realized that the family lived nearby I would notice Bruce jogging every morning. After that, I treated Bruce whenever he'd been injured on the set.

Don Langford recalled the Goldman article in which he is quoted as calling Bruce a 'hysteric' and in which Bruce supposedly presented both Dr Langford and his colleague, Dr Peter Wu, with a sample of cannabis while exclaiming, 'It's the only thing that stops time!'

Dr Langford continues:

> That article caused me some embarrassment. I remember with some disappointment that Albert Goldman's data was incorrect. Bruce was certainly made to look like less than he really was. Bruce was theatrical rather than hysterical – he was a dramatic person, an actor – and he used to act out the events of his injuries. Bruce and I

talked about it, and he said that, when he was acting, he *became* the part, and I guess that was what he was doing when he was in the surgery. But he was always in control. I think that the other account was overdramatized.

Neither Dr Wu nor myself ever saw Bruce with cannabis but he told us that he used to chew the root. He did say that it made time slow down for a little while. I can see why it had appeal for Bruce; cannabis would induce a sense of timelessness that might relieve some of the pressure from deadlines that he was under. Bruce was in touch with reality in every way; he had a very realistic self-view. He didn't think that he was more than he was.

Bruce Lee was a man of unusual ability, but the opportunities, his importance and his fame all arrived in such a deluge that he literally didn't have time to cope with it. From being a minor TV star he suddenly leaped to being the biggest thing in the world. If he hadn't had to deal with all the phoniness of that world, I think he could have coped. But what he was given to deal with was more than any mortal could have coped with.

Even up until the time that I left Hong Kong, I would stop every day at my local news stand and scan the covers of the papers and magazines. There wasn't one single day when Bruce's face wasn't on at least one cover, even sixteen years after his death.

Dr Peter Wu now runs his own clinic in Hong Kong. When I contacted him, he clearly had no knowledge of Albert Goldman and asked to be sent a copy of the infamous article. In his recommendation to the coroner, Dr Wu was of the opinion that the verdict should be that the cause of death was due to hypersensitivity to Equagesic or cannabis. As the cause of death was not clear and cannabis was present, realistically, this conclusion couldn't be denied. The official verdict, however, named only Equagesic as the presumed cause.

Dr Wu adds, 'Professor Teare was a forensic scientist recommended by Scotland Yard; he was brought in as the expert on cannabis and we can't contradict his testimony. The dosage of cannabis is neither precise nor predictable, but I've never known of anyone dying simply from taking it.'

Again, the negative light in which cannabis is viewed in Hong Kong cannot be overestimated; the situation between East and West is reversed. While the Chinese view opium liberally, cannabis is considered a foreign drug with sinister overtones. The official verdict reflected some cultural or even political pressure.

Don Langford cites other reasons for the verdict eventually reached by the inquest:

> There was a great deal of concern because of Bruce's life insurance policy. For a long time I believed that if I said anything the case might be reopened. I even took Bruce's notes out of the file at the Baptist Hospital in case someone might attempt to get to it.
>
> Cannabis has a known chemical alkaloid that can produce seizures: it can be extracted and administered to produce that effect. Equagesic was not at all involved in Bruce's first collapse. Thousands of people take Equagesic with no adverse effects, whereas people can be adversely affected by cannabis. It doesn't even need a hypersensitivity to it, simply exposure, and it's impossible to determine the dosage. There's not a question in my mind that cannabis should have been named as the presumptive cause of death. I would like to have seen a truer verdict rendered. But the whole world was watching this inquest to see if a precedent would be set. If cannabis had been ruled as the cause of death it would have opened up a real can of worms, because no one had ever before said that it had that potential. Hong Kong didn't want to set that precedent particularly in view of the fact that the coroner was a layman.

The coroner Egbert Tung was a lawyer with no scientific background. By all accounts the inquest was something of a shambles and not without its comic moments. Langford continues:

He would stop us and make us spell medical terms for him, which he would then write out in longhand. It was ludicrous.

Does all this make Bruce Lee out to be some raving drug fiend? Of course not! He had the money and access to anything he wanted. Opium was more plentiful; and drugs would certainly have not been frowned on in entertainment circles. In my opinion, Bruce had simply taken very practical steps at seeking out something that would alleviate some of the great pressure he was under.

As with Albert Goldman's cynical biographies of Elvis Presley and John Lennon, his account of the life of Bruce Lee revealed less about its subject than it did about the writer's own strange psyche. In Goldman's world, Bruce Lee worked out with 'grimy' punch bags and 'bizarre' dummies – even martial arts training could be imbued with a sleazy atmosphere. The writer appeared to quite literally hate his work, despising those popular heroes he wrote about while resenting having to feed off their achievements to make his living. Behind Goldman's portrait of Bruce Lee – behind the loaded questions and the stretched quotes – one could always sense the writer's own heartless and unfulfilled self. Just as the truth is that foul play did not kill Bruce Lee, so Goldman's own brand of foul play was always a failed attempt to kill the truth.

Given the pressure and the outpouring of energy in the last two years of Bruce Lee's life, something had to give. There was the sheer physical effort of fighting in stupefying heat and humidity, doing take after take, while sometimes writing and directing at the same time. There were the constantly turning thoughts over what direction he should take next and the strains created by his instant celebrity and press intrusion.

It was not only producers and advertisers who were exploiting him but old friends and long-lost relatives looking to turn a quick buck. Too many people were looking at Bruce Lee and seeing only a pile of dollar bills. While he tried to swim with what was happening to him, it was all too much, too fast. Not only had he stopped training, in the end he had even stopped laughing.

26

BEYOND THE LIMITS

AS AN ATHLETE, Bruce Lee always drove himself higher, further and faster, but toward the end he was trying to do so while chained to the heavy load of stardom. He never seemed to have the inclination to rest, even if he had the opportunity. Only once did he ever speak on the subject of rest, seeing it not as a desirable state but as somehow being static, frozen and dead. Bruce broke through his own limits time after time.

When people talk about Bruce Lee, the word used most often is 'intense'.

'He built himself,' says Bob Wall. 'He took this skinny weakling body and turned it into something incredible. He put in hours of training, very intense, very complete. I don't know what motivated him to do it.'

Golden Harvest's Russell Cawthorne said:

I think the first impression you'd get from Bruce would be the incredible aura of energy that surrounded him, like an energy field. In fact, he seemed much bigger than he physically was. You almost got the impression that his feet never really touched the ground; he seemed to be standing about six inches above it. It was quite a remarkable experience just meeting him. The intensity you see in his films is just a watered-down version of what he always had in real life. Bruce always stays in my mind as someone of incredible intensity, force and power, and so motivated and so forward-driven you'd almost believe he could fly!

Another Golden Harvest executive, Andre Morgan, says:

He spent a whole morning doing one fight sequence, something like a dozen takes. We viewed the rushes; the third, fourth and fifth takes were all good, and yet he went on and did the sixth, seventh and eighth, and so on, because all the time he didn't feel comfortable about them. As a person he was very intense. That was part of the problem. He was always going off in too many directions at once, to find out about everything as quickly as possible, always in a hurry.

There are 'channels' through which life's energies flow. The Chinese recognize this in the interlocking of their religion, medicine and philosophy. Acupuncture and *kung fu* both demonstrate that these energies are not secondary to life but are fundamental to existence. The flow of energy is the very basis of life itself. It is as if our very bodies and personalities are formed from ripples and patterns of energy. These channels extend far beyond everyday physical reality; they move within the nervous system, within the psychic realm and throughout everything that exists.

Occasionally, someone with a phenomenal concentration of will power, emotional intensity or physical determination strives to go beyond the normal uses of the body or mind or beyond normal human needs, which are usually concerned only with comfort. Such a person begins to open up to the higher, more universal energies. This happens through intense spiritual work or creative effort done with great motivation or intent. To different degrees, this process can be seen in the lives of many of the great composers, writers and artists, and in the lives of both spiritual teachers and powerful dictators. A partial connection with this energy is evident in the addiction of the workaholic or in obsessional behaviour and hyper-activity.

Anyone who makes a connection to this energy also opens up a super-sensory awareness, as he or she begins to experience a wider world. Some people may get to the point eventually where they can no longer channel the energy into expression. For example, the painter Vincent van Gogh made courageous attempts to transfer to colour and canvas the intense world that blazed before his eyes – before it all became too much. There is a Greek myth describing this process: Prometheus steals the fire of the gods from heaven to bring back to earth but ends up being consumed by this fire.

Did Bruce Lee simply burn himself out? Had the 'unlimited expression of his being' that Bruce found in his martial art turned inside out so that it was now these powerful forces that were moving *him*? Was the boy who could 'never sit still' unable to stop, so that at a very deep level his body could no longer handle what was taking place? As it came under increasing stress and demand, was his body pushed beyond its limits? I believe that there is more to it than this.

To use Western terminology for a moment, Bruce Lee was able to channel the archetypal energies that exist beyond the energy bound up in our own personality structure. He accessed levels of extraordinary, supernatural energy. These energies can only be experienced by the one who has accessed them. Even so, this process has been described by many different traditions in many different ways.

A shaman is someone who is skilled in accessing dimensions

of reality outside the commonly perceived norm. Plains Indians medicine men would use various disciplines, rituals and meditations to carry out 'vision quests' in order to acquire knowledge and power. In a similar way, the Chinese warrior-priests found that lessons and techniques in martial arts could be passed on by allies and spirits in other dimensions of consciousness. In both traditions, these teachers would be experienced directly as energy in the body but might later be described as the spirit of an animal or as some other supernatural force or being, perhaps even as a 'demon'.

Bruce Lee accessed energy that came out of the depths of his unconscious as he linked with these archetypal forces, the fundamental energies that hold all things together. Others get a spurious taste of this energy in the presence of those who have accessed it. It is this energy that makes us feel so good when we watch Bruce Lee on film. We get a kind of secondary charge from him that has a curiously uplifting quality.

Fred Weintraub recounted a telling incident: at the premiere of *Enter the Dragon*, a friend of his was so charged up by the end of the film that he asked his wife to drive back alone to Beverly Hills, because he wanted to *run* back.

In the end, perhaps the best explanation as to what killed Bruce Lee is provided by Bruce himself. Once he was accompanying Stirling Silliphant on a three-mile run. Towards the end, Bruce said that they were now going to 'shift gears' and do a couple of extra miles. The writer protested that he was forty-five and couldn't do it. After an extra five minutes' running, Silliphant's head was pounding.

'If I run any more, I'll have a heart attack and die,' he gasped. 'Then die!' said Bruce.

This made Silliphant so mad that he went the extra miles. Later, while showering, Bruce explained:

254

If you always put limits on yourself and what you can do, physical or anything, you might as well be dead. It will spread over into your work, your morality, your entire being. There are no limits, only plateaux. But you must not stay there, you must go beyond them. If it kills you, it kills you.

27

A NEW BRUCE LEE?

ON 8 AUGUST 1972, due to public demand, the *Kung Fu* pilot was shown again, following which thousands of letters flooded the production office. It became a weekly series in January 1973 and quickly rose to being the number one TV show in the United States. In the week ending 6 May 1973 (around the time *Enter the Dragon* was being completed), *Kung Fu* was attracting an audience of 28 million viewers.

The series had a tremendous impact. It was the first time most of us in the West had seen a Chinese martial art or any depiction of the way of life in a Shaolin temple – characterized by the relationship between Master Po and the student Caine, who is addressed as Grasshopper.

Perhaps the most memorable part of the *Kung Fu* series was the title sequence showing the initiation of a Shaolin warrior-monk, whose supreme test was to pick up a huge bronze ritual urn embossed with the designs of a dragon and a tiger. Filled with red-hot coals, the urn was effectively a branding iron. The monk was required to grip the urn between his forearms and lift it aside; as a result, his left forearm was branded with the emblem of a dragon, and the right with that of the tiger. This brand was the badge of Shaolin martial arts mastery and while a master would never openly display it, this mark was honoured and respected.

Before taking the role of Caine, David Carradine openly admitted that he had only heard the expression *kung fu* twice and had certainly never practised the art. Astonishingly, in *The Spirit of Shaolin*, a pretentious autobiography published in 1991, he confidently asserted that 'no one on the planet was more prepared on as many levels to play the role of Caine as I was'.

In this book, Carradine also claims that 'many of Bruce's moves were done by doubles'. In fact, in his entire career Bruce Lee was only doubled on three shots. In the opening sequence of *Enter the Dragon* a gymnast did the somersault; this same gymnast later did the backflip in Bruce's controversial fight scene with Bob Wall. Bruce's backflip in *Fist of Fury* was also doubled.

Not long after Bruce's death, Carradine paid him a dubious tribute: 'That Bruce Lee, man, he's just too good. I must take over from him and carry on his work.'

And so he tried. In 1978, Carradine acquired the rights to *The Silent Flute*. Just as Carradine knew he was 'the most prepared person on the planet to play Caine', so he considered himself perfect for the role of Cord the Seeker, adding, 'with my reputation I was sure I could get the picture made'. But in the end he modestly opted to take the four roles that Bruce would have played.

According to *The Silent Flute*'s director, Richard Moore, the script was unfilmable. Moore had further difficulties when Carradine insisted on using his old buddy Jeff Cooper in the role of Cord. According to the director, Cooper couldn't act his way out of a paper bag. Faced with trying to get a performance out of Cooper and going way over budget, Moore elected instead to bring the film in on time even though he knew most people would find Cooper's performance hard to swallow.

Before the part of Cord was offered to Jeff Cooper it had been offered to Joe Lewis, who had turned it down because he was unwilling to work with Carradine. Lewis says, 'I didn't want to be associated with a lousy martial artist. They shot the film anyway, in Israel, and it came back a piece of junk!'

Lewis ended up having to supervise the reshooting of several of the fight scenes and had to hire martial artists to double for the actors used in some of the earlier sequences. Lewis hired Mike Stone to double for Carradine, who considered it an insult and, according to Lewis, some screaming and shouting and damage to the film set ensued. Joe Lewis ended up showing Carradine some slick easy moves which he used in the film; Lewis also doubled some of Jeff Cooper's flying kicks at the end of the film.

The film was released initially as *Circle of Iron*. Bruce Lee's name appears no less than five times in the credits, although the film was far removed from anything for which he had hoped. To this day, James Coburn refuses to see the film and has retained his copy of the original script.

Of course, in an ideal world, Bruce Lee would have acted the leading role in *Kung Fu* at the height of his powers, working with quality scripts and direction. Had *The Silent Flute* been made with Bruce, not only would it have been vastly superior, but it would have been a better film than some of those he eventually did make. Instead we ended up with *Kung Fu* and *The Silent Flute* being mangled into a vehicle for 'a lousy martial artist' and with such ridiculous claims as Bruce being 'taught to fight' by the millionaire director Lo Wei.

In 1986, a second *Kung Fu* TV movie was made featuring a youthful Brandon Lee. In 1993, Warner Brothers aired a new TV series, *Kung Fu: The Legend Continues*, set in a present-day US city, where Carradine's character is the grandson of Caine. Now a tranquil and philosophical father, he leaves the fighting mainly to his detective sons – one with a flute and one with a gun.

In more recent years, Carradine has marketed himself as something of a Jane Fonda of the martial arts, releasing a *Kung Fu Workout* video. More recently Carradine has appeared as Grasshopper in a TV ad for Lipton's tea – a spoof on the original *Kung Fu* series. Despite the altruistic 'wisdom' expounded in his autobiography, we may safely assume that there is nothing closer to Carradine's heart than his wallet.

Chuck Norris went on to become an action star in his own right, but his acting is somewhat pedestrian; he is not blessed with great powers of expression. As Norris himself graciously admitted, 'David Carradine is about as good a martial artist as I am an actor.'

Along with Norris, there are several other martial arts-based actors, like *aikidoist* Steven Seagal and the Belgian karate exponent Jean-Claude van Damme. There are women stars too; the best known is Cynthia Rothrock. At the start of the 1990s Steven Seagal was setting box-office records, although his films are really action adventures with only a passing reference to the martial arts. Yet the actor poised to eclipse them all was Brandon Lee.

In the early hours of 1 April 1993, I received a phone call from a friend in Los Angeles, telling me that Brandon Lee had been killed on the set of a new film he was working on called *The Crow*. TV news bulletins confirmed the astonishing news that Brandon Lee was dead at the age of twenty-eight.

After his father's death, nine-year-old Brandon Lee became angry and withdrawn for a while. When the Lee family moved to the upmarket Rolling Hills Estates in California, Brandon had trouble re-adapting to the American way of life. His heritage meant that he was constantly challenged at every school he attended and he ended up attending nearly all the schools in the South Bay area. Not surprisingly, he rebelled against his image as Bruce's son and wanted his own identity. Brandon got involved in teenage crime, joyriding in a stolen car and once impersonating a driving-test examiner. He spent a couple of years on the road exploring the West Coast. Four months before graduation, he was expelled from college.

When he was fifteen, Brandon spent a year training with Dan Inosanto and Ted Wong:

> I had a bit of a love–hate relationship with the martial arts. There was a year where I was very involved, then a period where I said, 'Hey, I don't have to do this.' About the only constant through the whole thing was acting. My dad never told me to get into acting, and neither did my mother, but from a little boy, it's all I wanted to do. I never thought about anything else.

In the 1980s, Brandon moved to Boston to study acting at Emerson College with the aim of being an actor who could do realistic fighting, rather than being a martial artist who could act. But his name opened no doors and he wound up as a script reader until a casting agent finally got him his debut in *Kung Fu*. But further roles did not follow. Like Bruce, Brandon broke into films in Hong Kong, where he made the low-budget film *Legacy of Rage*, followed by *Laser Mission*, made in Germany. He made his first US feature, *Showdown in Little Tokyo*, with Dolph Lundgren in 1991. Inevitably, Brandon's work was compared with his father's.

> In a perfect world, I'd rather that comparisons to my dad didn't happen, but I'm lucky; he's somebody that people admire a lot. I've met a lot of people who've been really positively affected by his film work, people who say, 'It changed my life after I saw one of your

dad's films.' So long as people are respectful about my dad, I try to be respectful to them as well.

Brandon Lee's second feature, the martial arts action movie *Rapid Fire*, showed him more willing to embrace his heritage. While the film's props master listed fifty-six guns (in a weapons count that ran to six typed pages) there are no shortage of hand-to-hand fights choreographed by Brandon and Jeff Imada, whom he met at Dan Inosanto's academy.

Like his father, Brandon Lee was also given to showing off and tearing down Mulholland Drive, not in a Porsche but on his motorcycle. Comparing Brandon with his father, producer Robert Lawrence said, 'His father had a burning intensity; Brandon is more fun. He's freewheeling, hip and more tongue-in-cheek.' Little did anyone know that Brandon was to share his father's tragic fate.

Filming of *The Crow* began in Wilmington, North Carolina, on Brandon's twenty-eighth birthday: 1 February 1993. The story was of a murdered rock star who returns in the form of a crow to exact retribution. From the very start, the production was plagued by mishaps and the crew began to speak openly about the 'curse of *The Crow*'. On the first day's shooting a carpenter had to be hospitalized with burns over 90 per cent of his body after his crane fouled a live power cable. A construction worker slipped and drove a screwdriver through his hand. Then a disgruntled set sculptor went berserk and drove a car through the props room, destroying it. On 13 March a storm wrecked most of the set.

Just before the incident that resulted in his death, Brandon expressed concern over the levels of fatigue among the crew. Shortly after midnight on 31 March, the crew had just finished a gruelling day. The next scene to be filmed was Brandon's death scene in which he was to be shot, with special effects used to simulate the bullets hitting him. As the cameras turned and a fellow actor fifteen feet away fired blanks from a Magnum 44, Brandon slumped to the ground. So convincing was the performance that the crew broke into spontaneous applause. Then, slowly, the onlookers realized the true situation.

Brandon was rushed to Wilmington Medical Center. Doctors gave him fourteen pints of blood as they fought for twelve hours to save him. Just as she had done twenty years earlier, Linda Lee heard herself asking for an autopsy to be done.

The cause of death was later established: a dummy bullet, which had been loaded for a close-up scene, had become lodged in the gun. Subsequently, a blank charge used to simulate gunfire had shot the fake bullet with enough force to cause the tragedy that resulted.

But, just as happened immediately after Bruce's death, the tabloid press had a field day. Early stories told of Brandon being killed by *yakuza* (Japanese Mafia) assassins or jealous lovers. It was speculated that he had been killed by the same 'black demon' that had pursued his father; such a theory sounded suspiciously like the product of a publicity machine. On 3 April, Brandon was buried in Seattle's Lake View Cemetery alongside his father.

In May 1994, *The Crow* went on general release and straight to number one at the box office, earning nearly $12 million on its opening weekend. It is a visually stunning film in the same vein as *Blade Runner*. Despite the external baggage that goes with the film, it avoids being exploitative. But this does not make the death scene any easier to watch. With the burden of hindsight it is impossible to separate Brandon from his role in the film, and the tale from the truth.

Brandon received widespread posthumous acclaim for his performance. *Rolling Stone*'s Peter Travers described Brandon's acting as having 'a probing intelligence and a passionate heart'. He added, 'Lee is sensational on all counts in a final performance that brims over with athleticism and ardor.'

In the *LA Weekly*, Manohla Dargis wrote, 'If Brandon Lee hadn't died, it's likely that *The Crow* would have been a great movie; as it is, it's implausibly great. Inevitably, Lee will be folded into the same history as his father, Bruce. But Brandon Lee deserves to be remembered for himself.'

Although Bruce Lee will always be the unparalleled genius of martial arts on screen, Brandon Lee had become a confident, compelling and convincing actor and martial artist in his own right. His father would have been very proud of him.

Brandon's enduring memory of his father was of a hard-working man: 'I rarely met anyone who put so much into everything he did. He always impressed upon me that there isn't an endless amount of time. I've always remembered his words and try, consciously, not to waste any time.' His words echo sadly.

Jackie Chan, a star in Asia and Europe, has never quite managed to break into the United States. Born in 1954, Chan spent his youth in a Peking Opera school where he studied gymnastics, acrobatics and martial arts. Like Bruce Lee, he was also a child movie actor in Hong Kong.

Chan then spent years as a stuntman (appearing in both *Fist of Fury* and *Enter the Dragon*) before he came to the attention of Lo Wei, who was still looking for a new Bruce Lee and another million-dollar payday. Lo Wei cast Chan in his 1976 movie *New Fist of Fury*, which takes up where the original leaves off: with the survivors of the Chinese *kung fu* school fleeing from the Japanese. Bruce's co-star, Nora Miao, has a continuation of her role and eventually meets Chan's character, who then returns with her to take vengeance.

Lo Wei used Jackie Chan as the 'new Bruce Lee' for eight movies until Chan discovered and developed his own screen personality. By this time, Lo Wei's lack of resources to make a serious *kung fu* film had resulted in a send-up of the genre: Chan would play a bumbling fool who dreams of being a real martial artist. Here, his fighting style owes as much to Buster Keaton and Benny Hill as it does to Bruce Lee. Chan's real successes began when he started to write his own scripts for films like the slick, action-filled *kung fu* comedy *Drunken Master* (US title).

For a time Chan teamed up with Fred Weintraub and Robert Clouse in an attempt to break internationally with *The Big Brawl* (1980) and *The Cannonball Run* (1981). But eventually he returned to Golden Harvest to write, direct and star in further successes like *Armour of God*, *Police Story* and others.

Though Jackie Chan's fights have an element of slapstick to them, there is also a satisfying level of skill. He works closely with a regular team of highly trained stuntmen to create an immaculately choreographed and slickly edited blend of comedy, fighting, and stunt work. Chan, who insists on doing all his own stunts, has nearly killed himself three times, once in a fall of over forty feet broken only by a single sheet of canvas. The audience's knowledge that Chan is risking his life brings them to his films and each film features an epilogue of out-takes showing the stunts that went wrong, with Chan limping away and wincing in agony.

For every good *kung fu* movie that has ever been made there are a hundred with bad plots, bad acting, bad production and titles like *Kung Fu Exorcist*, *Kung Fu Zombies*, or even *Kung Fu-ry*. When the honeymoon with *kung fu* was over, there was a similar spate of *ninja*-oriented films, depicting the exploits of the black-hooded martial artists who were a cross between secret agents and guerrillas. The *ninja*, like mixtures of Spider-man and James Bond, were also equipped with all manner of weapons and devices. They first came to the attention of audiences in the West through the 1967 James Bond film *You Only Live Twice*, in which Sean Connery stays at a *ninjutsu* training camp prior to an attack on an enemy stronghold with machine guns and samurai swords.

In 1979, Fred Weintraub made *Jaguar Lives* with Joe Lewis, followed by *Force: Five* in 1981. Then, in 1982, Mike Stone, another of Bruce Lee's karate students, tried to crack the movie business with his own script for *Enter the Ninja*. There followed a series of largely exploitative *ninja* films; the genre caught on enough for a *ninja* film to be made in Swedish! For the studios, the greatest appeal of these films was that masked actors didn't have to be paid as much as famous faces.

The 1981 film, *The Shaolin Temple*, marked the entry of Communist China into martial arts film-making. Three years in production, the film uses real martial artists in all the major roles. The attention to detail and camerawork more than compensate for the weaknesses of the standard plot about a boy who, seeking revenge for the murder of his father, learns the martial arts from a group of Shaolin monks. The film's leading actor, eighteen-year-old Li Lin Jei, became a star and changed his name to Jet Lee. Meanwhile, the movie inspired thousands from the West to make the trip to the Shaolin temple itself.

In 1982, one of the quintessential *kung fu* movies was made: *Legendary Weapons of China* (US title: *Legendary Weapons of Kung Fu*), directed by Liu Chia Liang. Neither a thriller, a western, nor a comedy with *kung fu* thrown in, but a pure martial arts film dealing with the genre's greatest enemy, the gun, the film climaxes in a weapons sequence that has never been equalled.

Billy Jack (1971) is an old film worth seeking out. Tom

Laughlin plays a mixed-race American Indian who also happens to be an ex-Green Beret and karate expert, battling on the side of hippies against various redneck oppressors. The follow-up films were a series of increasingly extravagant miscalculations.

Also worthy of mention are the three *Karate Kid* films, which show very well the relationship between the master and his student. For the purpose of moving the storyline along, the 'Kid' unrealistically masters a technique in three lessons and then uses it to win a tournament at the climax.

One of the best of the more recent martial arts movies is *Iron and Silk* (1989), based on the book by Mark Salzman concerning his experiences as a language teacher in China. Salzman was a childhood devotee of Bruce Lee's films and other *kung fu* classics like *The Shaolin Temple*. While in China, he sought and trained with one of his heroes, Pan Qingfu, the weapons master from *Five Fingers of Death*. This is a film in which a genuine *kung fu* star and martial arts master plays himself.

Finally, honourable mentions must go to Tsui Hark's two-part *Once Upon a Time in China*, whose impact comes from explosive visuals rather than explosive devices; and to *By The Sword* and *The Princess Bride*, both of which feature superlative swordsmanship.

In the West the history of martial arts movies is very simple. There is no 'before Bruce Lee' and there certainly hasn't been anyone to follow him. *Enter the Dragon* is accepted as the classic of the genre and it regularly features at film festivals alongside classic movies directed by the likes of Federico Fellini and Ingmar Bergman. Yet despite these accolades, in dealing with the legacy of Bruce Lee we are still bound to consider what might have been: Bruce's original vision for *The Silent Flute*, a starring role in *Kung Fu*, or his own completed version of *Game of Death*.

Bruce Lee was right: *kung fu* pictures only captured mass public imagination for three years, and are part of a long tradition of action movies: war films, historical epics, spaghetti westerns and James Bond. They gave way to the post-apocalyptic, cybernetic world of *Robocop* and *Terminator*, and the menace of Freddie Krueger and Hannibal Lector. It is part of our modern disease that the new movie hero is not the warrior but the serial killer, and that the inspired skills of men are made out to be no match for the ruthless efficiency of a new breed of machine.

While martial arts films are still being made both in the East and West, they are no longer important in world cinema. Bruce Lee's meteoric rise and sudden death marked both the beginning and the end of the genre on a world scale. Many modern so-called martial arts films are simply formula action thrillers with plenty of violence and gunplay. Any martial arts content is there simply because, after Bruce Lee, directors can no longer get away with characters lumbering through balsa wood furniture and slugging it out with good ol' Minnesota haymakers.

Yet Bruce Lee transcended the martial arts genre and his star is again on the rise as the decades reveal the extent of his abilities. Put quite simply: he has not been and will never be replaced. It seems odd now that Bruce Lee was ever concerned that he would one day be as big a star as Steve McQueen.

Bruce Lee once told a Hong Kong TV interviewer:

> When I look around I always learn something, and that is to be yourself always, express yourself, and have faith in yourself. Do not go out and look for a successful personality and duplicate it. Now

that seems to be the prevalent thing happening in Hong Kong, like they always copy mannerisms but they never start from the root of being and ask, 'How can I be me?'

Yet a multitude of imitators did emerge: Bruce Le, several Bruce Lis, Bruce Leong, Bruce Rhe, and Myron Bruce Lee, not to mention Tarzen Li and Tarzen Lee; Kowloon Li and Hong Kong Lee; Rocky Lee, Jet Lee, Bronson Lee, Dragon Lee, Conan Lee, Clint Lee and Gypsy Lee. Those few, like Billy Chong and Alex Kwon, who didn't actually change their names, were usually billed as 'the new Bruce Lee'.

In 1974, one of the first attempts at creating a new inter-national martial arts star was the British production *The Man from Hong Kong*. Director Brian Trenchard Smith brought in Wang Yu, changed his name to Jimmy Wang Yu and hired George Lazenby to play the villain. During the previous few years, Wang Yu had carved out a career in a series of successful films in which heroism was superseded by superheroism and then farce. Each film had to outdo the previous one, with Wang Yu eventually playing a one-armed fighter. But Jimmy was soon heading back to Hong Kong. This is not meant dismissively; unlike the imposter Carradine, Jimmy Wang Yu was in fact a good martial artist, as were others, like Jet Lee and David Chiang. But none of them could come close to Bruce Lee.

Dozens of films worked the name of Bruce Lee into their titles and used deceptive promotional material. Other films managed to use every possible combination of 'Fist', 'Fury', 'Game', 'Dragon' and 'Enter' in their titles. There was even a rumour of a full-length animated feature starring a fighting cartoon version of Bruce Lee, but thankfully this failed to materialize.

The very qualities that make a good fighter make a poor screen fighter – speed, the ability to hide emotions and disguise the effect of blows received, not telegraphing moves – and all these attributes have to be reversed so that audiences can see what is happening. Bruce Lee also set screen fighting standards with his many innovations, his technical mastery, inventive chore-ography, dramatic pauses and humour. These innovations created another form of martial art in itself.

Once, when someone was asked, 'Who is the next Bruce Lee?' the reply was, 'Why? Wasn't the first one good enough for you?'

28

LEGEND . . .

IMMEDIATELY AFTER BRUCE Lee's death, as grief and controversy raged across the world, the line between being the film industry's hottest property and becoming a legend was quietly crossed. Cinema crowds worldwide flocked to his films in greater numbers than ever before. The Bruce Lee cult had arrived. Fans even packed into showings of the B-feature *Marlowe*. The movie had flopped when first released, but MGM reissued it with Bruce Lee's name now given top billing.

A month after Bruce's death *Enter the Dragon* was released. During its first seven weeks in the United States it grossed $3 million. In London it monopolized three West End cinemas for five weeks before becoming a sell-out throughout Britain and the rest of Europe. The film went on to gross over $200 million, the ratio of cost to profit making it perhaps the most commercially successful film ever made.

The box-office takings were also augmented when Raymond Chow decided to raise his admission prices by more than 50 per cent after Bruce Lee's death. The Warners publicity department took a similarly pragmatic view of circumstances; as one executive put it, Bruce's death was worth a two-million-dollar publicity campaign.

Although *Enter the Dragon* was Bruce's biggest film world-wide, it was not his greatest success in the East. The box office revenue on the Hong Kong circuit was about the same as it had been for *The Big Boss*. In the East the bad publicity surrounding Bruce's death went against him. The Chinese audience was also upset that *Enter the Dragon* had been released in the West first, adding to the feeling that Bruce Lee had suddenly gone from being a Chinese hero to just another Oriental heavy in a Western thriller. The Chinese preferred Bruce as the country bumpkin or the underdog who wins against the odds. It is true that there is little of Bruce's natural charm in this film. The Chinese, who had come to look on Bruce as a national hero, perhaps even something of a messiah, now felt that they had been abandoned and left without a representative.

In Japan, on the other hand, people had no trouble with the style of *Enter the Dragon* and the film was an enormous hit there. Raymond Chow had not bothered to release Bruce's earlier films in Japan, thinking that they would never accept a Chinese star. *Enter the Dragon* turned out to be an even bigger hit in Japan than it was in the States, prompting Chow to release all of Bruce's films there, further increasing Golden Harvest's earnings.

Although reviews in the West were that Bruce Lee had played in little more than a James Bond-style pastiche, the film worked to Bruce's advantage. It is solely his appearance on screen that lifts *Enter the Dragon* out of the ordinary and makes it the genre's classic movie.

After Bruce Lee's death, opportunistic attempts to cash in on his legend lurched between the tasteless and the ridiculous.

Twentieth Century-Fox did not simply re-release the

twenty-six *Green Hornet* episodes. If they'd been aired on a daily basis, like *M*A*S*H** or *I Love Lucy*, they would have lasted less than a month. So in late 1974 the studio instead released a movie called *The Green Hornet*, which was simply an inept and sloppy compilation thrown together from three of the TV episodes, so poorly edited that it made no sense at all. To add to the confusion, random fight scenes from other episodes were patched in to lengthen the action sequences. It was billed as a 'Kato and the Green Hornet film' and stills from other Bruce Lee films were used to promote it. Ambiguous newspaper ads implied that it was a new Bruce Lee *kung fu* movie.

In 1975, Betty Ting Pei starred in the Shaw Brothers' production, *I Love You, Bruce Lee* (US title: *Bruce Lee: His Last Days, His Last Nights*). This piece of soft-porn sleaze had Betty romping semi-nude while 'Bruce' clutches his head in agony to give a subtle clue as to later events! After Bruce's death, Betty tells a barman that she is having to leave town because of the hate being directed at her from his fans. The barman beats up some thugs and tells them to respect Bruce Lee's memory. If respect for Bruce's memory was the issue, then this film would never have been made. Not only did Betty get the writer's credit but she also persuaded Run Run Shaw to shell out $20,000 for twenty dresses, ten times as much as Shaw had originally offered Bruce to star in one of his films.

It is hard to believe that it is the same woman who protested, 'I did not gain anything because of him, be it in name or profit. Each day I confined myself to my room, blaming myself, cursing myself, my feelings numb.'

After making the film for Shaw, Betty Ting Pei married a wealthy Taiwanese businessman, ran two clothes shops, drove a Mercedes sports car similar to Bruce's, got divorced and became a nightclub singer and then a vegetarian. In a further ironic twist, for a while she fled to a convent and became a

Buddhist nun, just like Yim Wing Chun, the woman who had devised the original martial art of *wing chun*.

Super Dragon followed, an even more ludicrous biopic. In this film Linda Lee is portrayed as an evil hag while 'Bruce', dressed in a yellow tracksuit, battles a giant basketball player to rescue a Betty Ting Pei lookalike who is being held at the top of a pagoda!

In 1976, Ng See Yuen directed *Bruce Lee: The True Story* (US title: *Bruce Lee: The Man, The Myth*). The film starred Ho Tsung Tao, one of the better Bruces of the time, and also features Unicorn as himself. With a set that must have cost at least a hundred dollars, the most bizarre scene of *The Myth* shows Bruce Lee as some latter-day Frankenstein, wiring himself up to electronic devices to develop his phenomenal energy. The grain of truth from which this scene derives concerns a prototype muscle-stimulating machine that was then used by the UCLA football team. This type of machine can now be found in health clubs all over the world, but back then it was the only one. Bruce, who was always on the cutting edge of training methods, just had to buy it.

For a while, Linda Lee and Robert Clouse tried to put together a biopic starring Alex Kwon, but the project never came to fruition. But considering the talent and the money involved, the worst was yet to come.

Raymond Chow heralded *Game of Death* as 'Bruce Lee's Greatest Film', and scheduled it for release in 1978. According to Chow, there were over a hundred minutes of film already in the can; Robert Clouse was brought in simply to shoot a couple of bridging sequences using Bruce lookalikes. But from the twenty-eight minutes of fight footage that Bruce had *actually* completed, only fifteen minutes were usable and a script had to be written to exploit them. Bruce's intended storyline concerns a martial artist nobly attempting to retrieve a treasure belonging to his people. This was replaced with a formula plot in which an actor struggles against a criminal agent who is manipulating his career.

Even so, this was by far the most expensive film Golden Harvest had yet undertaken to make. Chow claimed that eventually $HK4.5 million was spent. At one point during the planning of *Game of Death*, Golden Harvest approached both Steve McQueen and James Coburn to appear and later contacted both Muhammad Ali and the Brazilian football star Pelé! In the promotional material for the film, Robert Clouse is quoted as saying:

> This electrically charged film contains the most spectacular footage of the Chinese-American superstar ever filmed. It is, we feel, a fitting memorial to Bruce Lee.

The film's beginning is deceptively classy: John Christopher Strong's opening titles are excellent and might lead an unprepared viewer to think that he is about to enjoy an equally high-quality film. The Bond-style opening titles are accompanied by theme music from John Barry, who actually wrote the music for many of the Bond films. But the reality soon becomes apparent, and as dim shots of doubles are mismatched with shots of the real Bruce Lee in action, a feeling of sadness descends on the viewer. It brings to mind the 'worst film of all time', Edward Wood's *Plan 9 from Outer Space*, in which a laughably unconvincing double for Bela Lugosi completed the film by holding a cape in front of his face, after Lugosi's death halfway through the project.

Despite the simplistic story, *Game of Death* is tortuously contrived to include several Bruce Lee stand-ins along with footage from *Fist of Fury* and *Way of the Dragon*, and employs the plot device of plastic surgery which allows 'Bruce' to change his face halfway through. The film's most revolting image occurs early on, when actor Hugh O'Brien talks to a cardboard cutout of Bruce's head with someone else standing behind it! Yet even Bruce's cardboard figure has more life and spirit than the pitiful affair that follows. Soon the sense of betrayal and exploitation is complete as footage of Bruce Lee's actual corpse is worked into the story. It is a devastating irony that 'Bruce' is shown playing an actor who is killed on a film set when somebody substitutes real bullets for the fake bullets in a stage prop gun.

The redeeming moments are of course in the footage that Bruce shot before his death, the fight with *hapkido*ist Chi Hon Joi and the unique confrontation with Kareem Abdul Jabbar. The British version of the film removes all trace of the great *nunchaku* duel between Bruce and Dan Inosanto. In these scenes there is a quantum leap in the quality of the action. But these brief moments of pleasure soon give way to some particularly inept and ham-fisted slugging involving Hugh O'Brien, who is so unskilled that he makes John Wayne look like Bruce Lee!

Laying the blame squarely at Robert Clouse's feet, Bob Wall comments:

> *Game of Death* was hindered by having the man I consider to be one of the worst action directors of all time. I told Raymond Chow that Clouse would ruin it because this time he didn't have Bruce to save him. Under the circumstances, I think we did the best possible job.

In his own biography of Bruce Lee, Clouse comments:

> Several people close to Raymond Chow suggested, even pleaded, that the project be buried forever. But Chow argued that the film had already been pre-sold to the Japanese market, which had paid a great deal for the privilege. The final cut, with an attempt to use two lookalikes, was disappointing at best. There were even some embarrassing moments such as the scene where a head shot, taken

from a previous Lee film, was optically attached to the body of one of the doubles, the head turning quite strangely and eerily. Yet the film was quite successful, as was almost anything about Bruce Lee, no matter how tasteless or fraudulent.

While one can hardly blame him for trying to dodge the bullet, Robert Clouse writes about *Game of Death* as if he had nothing to do with it!

Although the story of *Game of Death* is no better or worse than that of any of Bruce Lee's other films, the final version falls way below the intentions he had for it. As he had hoped to do with *The Silent Flute*, Bruce Lee had intended *Game of Death* to be a quality film starring the foremost martial artists of the day. It would surely have surpassed all of his previous work.

But by the late 1970s audiences were so desperate to see any 'new' Bruce Lee footage that *Game of Death* equalled the revenue generated by *Enter the Dragon*.

The sage Lao Tzu said, 'Wine may become so dilute that few will drink of it.' Yet with *Game of Death II* a further attempt was made to perform the same trick, though it would be hard to be more tasteless than Clouse's version. When the real Bruce Lee 'dies' halfway through, the film quickly turns into a fist-and-pillow movie with macho posturing, feats of strength and speeded-up fights leading to a sci-fi, Bond-style climax that goes on for ever.

In 1983, Raymond Chow redeemed himself a little and over-saw what is perhaps his only worthwhile tribute, despite the fact that he also found it necessary to include several irrelevant minutes showing himself going about his daily business. *Bruce Lee: The Legend* includes some valuable, previously unseen footage, including Bruce's screen test which led to his role in *The Green Hornet*, along with excerpts from *Longstreet*.

In 1992 and 1993, ATV–Hong Kong aired *The Young Bruce Lee*, a series of one-hour shows supposedly dealing with Bruce's life before he became famous. The stories were put together with a great deal of dramatic licence; in one episode, Bruce saves a boy from a kidnap attempt. The series was shot in Toronto because the locations there most resembled both San Francisco and Seattle.

In May 1993, Universal released its Bruce Lee biopic *Dragon*. Made for $15.5 million, the film grossed $8 million and went to number one at the box office in its first weekend. The director, Rob Cohen, had bought the option on Linda Lee's biography of her first husband (written with her second husband, Tom Bleecker) and threw the script together in one month flat. He was certainly accurate when he said that he was doing a 'fictional version of a nonfiction story – neither a true story nor a documentary'.

The story of *Dragon* centres around Bruce and Linda's highly romanticized relationship. Not only does it take far too many liberties with the characters, but it stretches artistic licence with the facts way beyond breaking point. To list the absurdities in the story would amount to a virtual reprint of the entire script.

It is difficult to excuse such exploitation. Recent films on the lives of Malcolm X, Jim Morrison, Tina Turner and Geronimo all stretch the facts quite a bit. Even so, they treat their subjects with a great deal more accuracy and respect. Bruce Lee deserves far better than this. Even more appalling is Michael Jahn's 'novelization' of *Dragon* (Warner Books) which is not even worthy of further comment.

If the film *Dragon* has any merit, it is in the performance of its leading actor, Jason Scott Lee (no relation), who brings an emotional intensity to the role that a mere martial artist could not. Lee has been equally impressive in his other film roles.

By the usual criterion – the generation of large numbers of

dollars – *Dragon* was a success. In reality, the film does no one much credit; *Dragon* is nothing more than an expensive version of the earlier Hong Kong-made biopics.

In 1993, Warner Brothers released *The Curse of the Dragon*. Produced by Bob Wall, Fred Weintraub and Tom Kuhn, this film features Wall and Weintraub as themselves. Interviews involve James Coburn, Brandon Lee, Kareem Abdul Jabbar and Chuck Norris. While there are all-too-brief contributions from Jesse Glover, there are unnecessary ones from Alex Ben Block and the dreadful Albert Goldman. It is disappointing that Bruce's colleagues used an easy and sensationalized title. The only 'curse' hanging over Bruce Lee is that he will forever be associated with fantasized accounts of his life. The *reality* of his life is far more remarkable.

Also in 1993, Lumière released the video, *Bruce Lee: Martial Arts Master*, featuring interviews with Bruce's co-stars, minor crew members and journalists. It includes some of Henry Wong's documentary shot on the set of *Enter the Dragon*. Later, the same company released the video of Bruce Lee's 1971 interview with Pierre Berton for Canadian TV.

There is a history of some ill feeling between Linda Lee (now Linda Lee Cadwell) and Bruce's siblings. Linda has never shared any of the revenue from Bruce's estate with the rest of the family. The main rankle concerns Bruce's mother, Grace, who now suffers from Alzheimer's disease and lives in a publicly funded nursing home in Monterey Park, California.

But on 28 April 1993, the family kept the peace long enough to gather and celebrate Bruce's award of a star on Hollywood Boulevard's Walk of Fame. Rob Cohen, along with Linda and Mayor Tom Bradley, spoke before the assembled guests at a VIP dinner.

Unfortunately, in recent years Hollywood Boulevard, like London's Piccadilly Circus, has become a sleazy area frequented mostly by tourists and losers. Many of the gold stars there belong to names that no one now remembers. Those that are worth remembering are often littered with half-eaten slices of pizza. Bruce Lee's contribution to film-making certainly demands recognition, but as he himself told Pierre Berton, 'I don't believe in the word "star". To me that's just an illusion.'

On 7 August 1993, Linda Lee held an auction of Bruce's possessions that she had originally provided to add what was the only note of authenticity in the *Dragon* film. At one point the idea of opening a Bruce Lee museum had been considered, but in the end 140 of his personal items were sold off. Bruce's Hong Kong driving licence fetched $7,200. His Kato cap and braces went for $8,600, only a little short of what he netted for the entire *Green Hornet* series. At $29,000, by far the biggest moneymaker was Bruce's written affirmation 'My Definite Chief Aim', in which he vowed to achieve world fame as the highest-paid Oriental superstar by making $10 million between 1970 and 1980. Handwritten on a single sheet of paper in 1969 – the year before his back injury and just two years before his affirmation started to become a reality – this item was bought for the Planet Hollywood burger bar jointly owned by Sylvester Stallone, Arnold Schwarzenegger and Bruce Willis. All the auctioned items were accompanied by a letter of authenticity from Linda Lee, who grossed nearly $334,000 from the sale.

In view of the many dubious tributes and accolades that Bruce Lee's memory has suffered over the years, Bruce himself would almost certainly have been most touched by the simple recognition that came from his childhood hero, Master Kwan, China's first martial arts screen actor.

When journalist Bey Logan asked Master Kwan what he thought of Lee Little Dragon, Master Kwan walked off towards his inner sanctum. Even though he was in his eighties he still had a clear gaze and walked with a straight posture. When he returned he had a book on Chinese movies in which both he and Bruce appeared. 'Maybe you can get this book in the library,' he said, modestly acknowledging the acclaim that they had both enjoyed.

29

. . . AND REALITY

NO MATTER WHO you see fighting on screen, instinctively you compare them to Bruce Lee. He is one of the giants of the business. Like a handful of others, Bruce Lee has become larger in death than in life. James Dean represents the restlessness and rebellion of youth. Marilyn Monroe is the goddess of Hollywood. Despite everything, Elvis Presley will always be the king of rock 'n' roll. John Lennon epitomizes the optimism of the 1960s. All have become both fantasy images and symbols of an ideal. While most people know Bruce Lee as a screen fighter who was unstoppable, many also recognize that he is the most important figure in the martial arts of modern times.

In real life, the best martial artists do not always make the best martial arts film performers. Nobody can question the fighting abilities of Mike Stone or Joe Lewis, yet their movie careers sank as rapidly as they began. As fighters, neither van Damme nor Jackie Chan would be a match for them. Yet because they work well on screen, the latter have become two of the foremost martial arts stars of East and West.

While Bruce Lee often said that acting was his career and martial arts his real love, for brief, glorious moments he found a resonance between his ambition and his vocation and they became one and the same thing.

Bruce Lee was unique as a screen fighter because he was real. John Wayne was big and slow; he won fights because he was the good guy in the script. Charlton Heston rode a chariot against a barely convincing back projection. The exploits and gadgetry of the Bond films are pure escapist schoolboy fun. But to see Bruce Lee on film is to see a human body brought to a level of supreme ability through a combination of almost supernatural talent and a lifetime of hard work. Like seeing a brilliant goal by Pelé or hearing a blistering guitar solo by Jimi Hendrix, the human imagination doesn't need to be captured when what it witnesses is *real*.

Bruce Lee had abilities and a screen presence with which only a handful of others have ever been blessed. But he became imprisoned by his own success and the compulsion to be what everyone wanted him to be. There is no doubt that the stresses of international celebrity affected Bruce Lee deeply. Having achieved almost everything he had set out to do, he was faced with the question of what he might do next.

As 'Lee' told Longstreet, one can't just move for the sake of moving; it has to relate to something. Bruce felt that it was wrong simply to wish without acting on that wish; yet he also felt that it was wrong to act without having a clear intention. He guessed rightly that *kung fu* films would have mass appeal for only a few years. He was aware that too much philosophy in his films wouldn't appeal to mainstream fans. He was also beginning to suspect that he might not be able to maintain the level of physical performance needed. Yet he couldn't resist the urge to keep forging ahead. He refused to step back, rest and recharge himself. There were pressing decisions over career direction. Would he play roles outside the martial arts? Would he consider parts that showed some vulnerability or that denied his athletic abilities? Would working with better quality scripts and actors, directing, or doing non-martial art dramatic roles have been the challenge he needed? Might such roles have revealed that his acting was too 'unrealistic' for Western audiences?

Brandon Lee believed that his father would have met these challenges:

> When I see his films, I can see that he acted sincerely. He put over what he really felt, neither more nor less. When he was filming, I remember that he never overacted to make an effect, it would have rung false. He was a very intense man and that's why he only did what he believed he had to do. His performances were a pure expression of something he had deep within himself. He never tried to portray something he didn't feel, and even less to imitate someone else. I hate that bunch of Chinese actors who try to act like my father did. He was naturally great. If he had lived, I am sure he would have made other films, without restricting himself to *kung fu* films. In any case, he would have made other films.
>
> Honestly, you have to admit that apart from *Enter the Dragon* the others are not particularly good films. I mean by that, that the stories were very poor. The actors couldn't act and even *Enter the Dragon* was, all in all, let us say a rather simple film. Were it not for his presence these productions would not have made a cent; they would be nothing today. My father would certainly have made films that could stand on their own, by the story and by their acting. The problem is, my father disappeared at the moment when he could have done great things.

As Brandon continues, he gets closer to the essential Bruce Lee:

> Like everyone, I was real respectful towards my dad. He was quite a hero. But he wasn't superhuman, just a guy. One of my biggest regrets is that I never got to spar with my dad after I was bigger

than him . . . The impression I have retained of my father is of a very hard-working man. I have rarely met anyone who put so much into everything he did. The vivid memory I have of him is that of a man training all the time in the yard of our house.

After Bruce's death the Lee house became the focus for 'disciples'. Some merely wanted an old article of clothing, while others offered fortunes for his Mercedes. Later, fans who made the pilgrimage to Bruce's house in Hong Kong were disillusioned to find that it was now the Kam Wah Gardens, a 'hotel' used by businessmen to entertain their lady friends. Magazine advertisements offered Bruce Lee puppets alongside those lovable creatures the Wombles, or invited readers to join the 'Bruce Lee Secret Society'.

Today, the name of Bruce Lee sells more magazines than ever. One can even join a Bruce Lee fan club with the motto: 'Toward Personal Liberation'. There are regular seminars and memorial days where devotees can buy Bruce Lee T-shirts, posters and coffee mugs, watch a few minutes' faded footage of Bruce dancing the cha-cha, or listen to a crackling recording of one of his phone calls.

Bruce Lee expressed regret that after he died people would probably hang pictures of him in their schools and then bow to him. Hoping to prevent this, he advised them to think of him as nothing special. One can understand the deep regard that might prompt genuine students to pay their respects to Bruce Lee. As for the trivia collectors, we can almost hear Bruce's laughter from here!

Every celebrity attracts devotees, sad people who have no inkling that what they are really looking for is within them-selves. Even the musical group of which I am a member attracted a strange cult, known as the Information Society, who published entire books of lists of songs we had played at every single concert we had ever done. Did this give them any greater insight?

Bruce Lee attracts more than his fair share of neurotics. There are those who treasure unpublished photographs which, of course, they won't let anyone else see. There are collectors whose files are crammed with every last detail about Bruce Lee, as if accumulating facts has anything to do with understanding. These pursuits are as obsessive as they are joyless and pointless. The Bruce Lee cult has been called, quite rightly, the 'geek *kune do*' fraternity.

Just as the products of Vincent van Gogh's genius are locked away as investments in some corporate concrete mono-lith in Japan, so there are those Bruce Lee fans and Bruce Lee experts who would try and imprison his spirit in their mauso-leums of fact and hero-worship. I have no intention of serving their cause.

Bruce Lee decried the false sense of self-esteem based on a contrived image, on the illusions of stardom or possessions, or from being a cog in some religious or political machine – on something that is not an *essential* part of ourselves. He might well have spoken of the futility of trying to find self-worth by identifying with celebrities or of expecting to be liberated through joining a fan club!

In May 1994 I was working in Seattle. While there, I took the opportunity to visit Lake View Cemetery. I found Bruce and Brandon's graves situated beneath a pine tree at the crest of a hill. The area around the graves had been cordoned off so that no one could walk on the recently seeded lawn. I sat a short distance away. The azaleas were in full bloom and there was a warm gentle breeze.

After a short while, a minibus entered the cemetery gates

and wound its way up the hill to stop a few yards away from where I sat. Ten people got out, babbling excitedly, and soon began taking photographs of each other. Each of them took their turn to climb over the cordon and pose for the cameras, standing on flowers that had recently been placed there. A few minutes later they were all back on the bus and making their way to the next stop on their itinerary. When the photographs were viewed later, all would doubtless recall that they had been to Bruce Lee's grave. It is hard to believe that any of them had experienced actually *being* there.

The inscription on Bruce's grave reads: 'May Your Inspiration Guide Us Toward Our Personal Liberation'. I reflected that in trying to wake people up to their real nature, Bruce Lee had created the hardest of all his goals.

Doubtless the Bruce Lee cult will continue to pursue its daydreams. But those who really want to understand Bruce Lee, or any other aspect of life for that matter, will do so only to the degree that they understand themselves.

Shanlon Wu grew up in suburban New York in the 1960s. He had no Asian heroes to use as role models until he saw his first Bruce Lee movie. He described his subsequent experience of dawning self-awareness in a 1990 article for the *New York Times*:

> I was born in 1959, an Asian-American in Westchester County, New York. During my childhood there were no Asian sports stars. On television I can recall only that most pathetic of Asian characters, Hop Sing, the Cartwright family houseboy on *Bonanza*. But in my adolescence there was Bruce.
>
> I was fourteen years old when I first saw *Enter the Dragon*, the granddaddy of all martial arts movies. Between the ages of fourteen and seventeen, I saw *Enter the Dragon* twenty-two times before I stopped counting. During those years, I collected Bruce Lee posters,

putting them up at all angles in my bedroom. I took up the Chinese martial arts and spent hours comparing my physique with his. I learned all I could about Bruce.

My parents, who immigrated to America and had become professors at Hunter College, tolerated my behavior, but seemed puzzled at my admiration of an 'entertainer'. My father jokingly tried to compare my obsession with Bruce to his boyhood worship of Chinese folk-tale heroes. But my father's heroes could not be mine; they came from an ancient literary tradition.

After college, I competed as an amateur boxer in an attempt to find my self-image in the ring. It didn't work. My fighting was only an attempt to copy Bruce's movies. What I needed was instruction on how to live. I quit boxing after a year and went to law school.

One grey morning many years later, Shanlon Wu visited Bruce Lee's grave.

The headstone is red granite with a small picture etched into it. The picture is very Hollywood – Bruce wears dark glasses – and I think the calligraphy looks a bit sloppy. Two tourists stop but leave quickly after glancing at me.

I realize I am crying. Bruce's grave seems so small compared to his place in my boyhood. So small in comparison to my need for heroes. Seeing his grave, I understand how large the hole in my life has been, and how desperately I'd sought to fill it.

I had sought an Asian hero to emulate. But none of my choices quite fit me. Their lives were defined through heroic tasks – they had villains to defeat and battles to fight – while my life seemed merely a struggle to define myself.

But now I see that the very struggle has defined me. I must be my own hero even as I learn to treasure those who have gone before. Their lives beckon like fireflies on a moonless night, and I know that they – like me – may have been flawed. Still, their lives were real. They were not houseboys on *Bonanza*.

Understanding can arise only out of a strong sense of self-awareness. Anyone who looks for Bruce Lee in the details and events of his life, while ignoring his pleas to actively work on self-awareness, will not only miss the essence and purpose of this book, they will also miss the essence and purpose of Bruce Lee's thirty-two years on earth.

It is not the 'fans' or the 'experts' who truly honour Bruce Lee's spirit; they merely keep his name and reputation going. Neither is his spirit served by those who would turn his life into some cheesy Hollywood fabrication. There are already more than enough 'heroes' and daydreamers in the world. What is needed now is something far more extraordinary. We need to share in the same insights and understandings that lie at the heart of Bruce Lee's *experience*.

The truth of that experience can be understood not only by the genuine martial artist who would reach the same kind of understanding for himself, but by anyone seeking to realize his or her own fullest potential. Those of us who would now discover the real Bruce Lee need to delve deeper into the concepts of his art, not in order to accumulate more information but to invoke a shift to a new level of awareness where everything is much simpler.

Bruce Lee was both an exceptional fighting star and an exceptional martial artist. But, to put things in perspective, we should remember that he spent five years training in *wing chun*, and a further twelve years teaching and developing his own fighting method and philosophy. Only the last two years of his life were given over to film-making.

Even amid all the action and excitement, Bruce maintained that he hoped gradually to educate people through films with both a surface story and a deeper message. He was never able to realize his ambition to educate people about the inner aspects of his art. The thousands who streamed into the cinemas were not going to Bruce Lee movies to learn about awareness or to discover freedom. But the lessons *are* there in the films: the teaching sequence at the beginning of *Enter the Dragon* was added to the script on Bruce's initiative and is unlike any other part of the film. It is a significant addition for those who are able to make use of it.

While people will continue to enjoy Bruce Lee's screen performances, there is a rich teaching in his life's work from which we can all learn something and which illuminates the real purpose of his life.

PART THREE

FIGHTING SPIRIT: THE ESSENTIAL BRUCE LEE

30
FIGHTING SPIRIT

AFTER EMIGRATING TO the United States, while living and working in Seattle, Bruce Lee taught his early students a *wing chun*-based fighting method that came to be know as *jun fan*, after his birth name. Even so, Bruce Lee always acknowledged his debt to *wing chun* and honoured his teacher, Yip Man.

The two died within months of each other. The last time they met, Bruce asked Yip Man, 'Do you still regard me as your student?'

He replied, 'Do you still regard me as your teacher?'

They both laughed.

There is no doubt that Bruce Lee's fighting methods emerged from having first embodied *wing chun* principles. These roots are obvious in his comment that *jeet kune do* simply follows a straight line to the objective. Even with his later depth of knowledge and experience, Bruce would often encourage his students to use the simple technique he had found effective in the many battles he had taken part in as a youth. Bruce knew that in many situations a flurry of centreline punches would do the job. 'If in doubt, straight blast,' he told them.

Jun fan gung fu witnessed the gradual assimilation of techniques drawn from various other styles of *kung fu*, along with those of Western boxing, Thai boxing, ju jitsu and fencing. Modifications were never made for the sake of themselves but only where a genuine improvement could be demonstrated. Although he borrowed techniques from other systems, Bruce still used them to conform to *wing chun* principles such as awareness of the centreline and non-telegraphic, economical movement.

'I learned the fundamentals of what he started,' says Taky Kimura, 'but he was on a quest, going by steps himself. As he came up to Seattle he would keep me abreast of what was going on. He had to change his fighting method because he was no longer dealing with little Chinese guys who were his size.'

This explains the first principle departure in Bruce Lee's fighting method. Where *wing chun* maintains an ambidextrous approach, Bruce adopted an attacking stance like that of a boxer or fencer by keeping his more powerful right side forward all the time.

Howard Williams was only fifteen when he began training with Bruce Lee and James Lee at their Oakland school. He recalls that the actual transition from *jun fan* to *jeet kune do* was not a gradual one but happened almost overnight:

> Bruce was coming up to Oakland every other weekend with his family, between *Green Hornet* shoots. One day he said, 'Listen, this is not *jun fan*: it is now *jeet kune do*.' Bruce showed us this new stance. We thought it was boxing; it looked more like kickboxing at first but he still used the trapping from his old art.

Tim Tackett, a schoolteacher by profession, teaches small classes in *jeet kune do* concepts at his home in Redlands, California. In attempting to define *jeet kune do* he says:

There are different aspects to it – sensitivity, trapping, grappling, boxing, kicking, kickboxing – and putting all those together. Once you have experienced it all, and can do it, then you have a core. This core is the thing that is going to come out of you when the guy steps out of a truck because you had an accident with him, or you accidentally ran him off the road, and he's just had twelve beers, and he's 260 pounds and couldn't care less if you're a black belt when he comes out of the truck after you! Whatever comes out of you then has to be *automatic*.

Again, we should bear in mind that Bruce Lee's screen fighting and street fighting were two entirely different affairs. He would never have used a spinning heel hook on the street.

In a real confrontation two things are vital. First, through training, one must have already *experienced* some of the severe emotions that are stirred up in order to be able to draw strength from them. Second, one must have practised often enough so that one can act despite oneself in an *automatic* and *spontaneous* flow of action that overrides any other consideration. The 'freeze or flail' response has to change into the 'no-mind' fighting state of reflex action.

Dan Inosanto told martial arts writer Jerry Beasley:

When a fight closes in, there's no referee to separate you. A match in the ring is not a fight. To this day, you can get an outstanding boxer and he might lose out on the street. But get in the ring and it's within his confines. A fight is really hard. A lot of times it might be rolling around on the floor, you can't say whether it's *choy li fut* or *wing chun*. A fight is terrible: it's smashing faces on concrete, it's knifing. You don't know if your art will save you. Nobody knows. Everything changes once you put a weapon in a guy's hand. What worked for an empty-hand system doesn't now. A guy could have ten years' kickboxing experience, but now, the circumstances are totally different.

Bruce had plenty of fights in the streets of Hong Kong. He was in his own words, 'a punk who travelled around in a fight.' I've seen him in what I don't even call fights. I've seen guys who wanted to punch his nose out, or break his bones, or whatever. But they could never do it, so it turned into a lesson. They found out that he could just, literally, play. Bruce could change in midstream. One minute he could favor a kicking system, then at middle range he could explode like a savage streetfighter or a Western boxer. When it got in tight, it would look like *wing chun*. When he got to the ground it was like ju jitsu. Bruce knew how to integrate styles. If there is a common thread, then it's an understanding of range.*

The inner aspect of the martial arts as a vehicle for spiritual growth dates back to Bodhidharma and the Shaolin temple. But it was in the teachings of Krishnamurti, in particular, that Bruce Lee found the philosophical underpinnings of *jeet kune do*.

Jiddu Krishnamurti was born in 1895 to an impoverished family in Southern India. His spirituality was recognized early and at the age of ten he was adopted by an esoteric organization, the Theosophical Society, to be groomed as their future figurehead and was sent to be educated in England and France. In 1929 he renounced his role of 'messiah', saying that religious sects and organizations stand in the way of Truth. Though he continued to teach and lecture throughout the world, he remained unwilling to offer any ready-made system for approaching this Truth.

Bruce Lee took many of Krishnamurti's sayings on self-realization and applied them directly to his own way. Speaking of the traditional religions, Krishnamurti wrote, 'If you deny

* Dan Inosanto, quoted by Jerry Beasley, *In Search of the Ultimate Martial Art* (Boulder, CO: Paladin Press, 1989).

the traditional approach, as a reaction, you will have created another pattern in which you will be trapped.'* Referring to the classical martial arts, a sign on the wall of Bruce's school read, 'Do not deny the classical approach, simply as a reaction, or you will have created another pattern and trapped yourself there.'

People take up a martial art for many reasons: for self-defence, to compete, to get fit, for self-discipline, for culture and philosophy. All of these are good reasons. While there are many benefits to be derived from practising a martial art, surely the primary reason that one takes up a fighting discipline (as Bruce Lee did at the age of thirteen) is in order to learn to fight.

'*Jeet kune do*,' says Tim Tackett, 'is concerned with being able to walk away, using any means at all to win. You can have all the technique in the world, but if you don't have the attitude then it won't do you any good at all. Bruce taught all this without people realizing. In the *Longstreet* episode, Bruce has got the blind detective in a chokehold which he can't get out of. Bruce says, "Well, gouge my eyes out." And Longstreet says, "I can't." Bruce replies, "Then you will not win."'

One aspect of combat that the anti-violent seem never to comprehend is that learning how to fight and being prepared to fight somehow create a state of being which lessens the need for ever having to fight. In learning to fight an opponent, one also has to meet all kinds of inner opposition and resistance. By the time that one has come a little nearer to mastering a fighting art, one has come a lot closer to mastering oneself. As a consequence, one is more prepared to meet and master an opponent.

As Krishnamurti put it:

* J. Krishnamurti, *Freedom from the Known* (New York: Harper and Row, 1969).

Man is violent and the ideal of non-violence is only an immature approach to violence. What is important is to face the violence, understand it and go beyond it, and not invent an escape, an ideal called 'non-violence' which has no reality whatsoever.*

Perhaps no one has been associated with the concept of non-violence more than Gandhi. Those who imagine the frail Indian to be a simple pacifist will be surprised at his words here:

Non-violence is infinitely superior to violence. But the message of non-violence is for those who know how to die, not for those who are afraid of death. If one has not that courage, I want him to cultivate the art of killing and being killed, rather than in a cowardly manner to flee from danger.

Bruce Lee once said:

Whenever some big guy attacks you, instead of reacting to his ego, teach him to react to yours. You must think to yourself, 'How grateful I am that this wonderful target of opportunity is presenting itself to me at this moment.' Think not that your assailant is going to harm you, but take joy in the havoc you're going to lay on him after he's been so obliging. Right now, I'm trying to teach the spirit of what I'm talking about – *fighting spirit*.

* J. Krishnamurti, *Freedom from the Known* (New York: Harper and Row, 1969).

31

THE ROOTS
OF COMBAT

'ALTHOUGH BRUCE LEE was grounded in the school of *wing chun*,' wrote Doug Palmer, 'every time I met him he had expanded the style to include not only the corpus of what had gone before but a whole new dimension that magnified the effectiveness and universality of his own 'school'. This was not mere technique, *jeet kune do* transcended style. Style was too limiting, a straitjacket, in Bruce's view. *Jeet kune do* was an approach, a philosophy, a Way.'

This way was summarized in the words of a sign which hung on the wall of Bruce's school. It read, 'The truth in combat is different for each individual. Research your own experiences for the truth. Absorb what is useful. Reject what is useless. Add what is specifically your own. Man, the creating individual, is more important than any style or system.'

During the 1970s a lot of martial artists, believing they were following Bruce Lee's philosophy, cast aside their systems only to discover that with no structure they were virtually useless. They had moved away from being blindly traditional only to become blindly non-traditional.

The philosophy of *jeet kune do* also prompted many martial

artists to take a more eclectic approach. But again, if the individual is not grounded in one form to begin with, then this approach will fall well short of what Bruce Lee intended. To absorb what is useful does not mean simply to select, assemble and accumulate techniques from many different styles, thinking that your new hybrid will have the best of everything. To absorb what is useful first requires a 'body feel' that you can work from.

'Bruce thought you could teach a discipline without discipline,' said William Cheung. 'This is not possible. However much people venerate Bruce Lee, this part of his thinking is mistaken. You *do* need forms; otherwise, how can you break away when you have nothing to break away from? What is *jeet kune do* but an amalgam of styles which is claiming to be free of styles? I told Bruce this. I say that we are born without knowledge. We have to acquire it first before we can be free of it.'

These remarks are echoed by Dan Inosanto: 'Bruce didn't like anything organized and, according to him, *jeet kune do* was not to have a blueprint; that was his whole philosophy at the time. I said, "Well, you've got to start from someplace; even a child has to be taught something before he can express freedom." '

Despite William Cheung and Dan Inosanto's assertions, we should remind ourselves that Bruce practised the *wing chun* forms regularly long after he moved to America. Film of Bruce shot in Oakland shows him performing the *sil lum tao*; his movements are disciplined, refined and precise. On his return visits to Hong Kong, Bruce would seek out Yip Man specifically to complete his learning of the wooden dummy form, which he also practised intensively.

As Dan Inosanto said earlier, Bruce would sometimes point himself in one direction and his students in another. Bruce never taught forms to any of his students; he preferred to teach people who had already been through formal training since they could then appreciate what he had to offer. Bruce believed that novices needed to learn forms but that, once a certain level of understanding was reached the martial artist could go outside fixed boundaries to where the true expression of the art is found.

A martial artist can't begin from no stance, no form or no technique, just as a musician cannot go straight to being a virtuoso. Each must learn the fundamentals and forms of music or fighting out of which he can progress, and which he can then use as a basis for improvisation and creativity. Only then can he start 'rejecting what is useless' by throwing away what doesn't work for him personally. But, here again, self-knowledge must enter the equation; not being able to perform a technique successfully doesn't automatically mean that the technique is useless!

It is clear that Bruce Lee began his martial artistry with *wing chun* and then went on to study other methods. Yet this was not so much a process of adding and accumulating techniques, but of *incorporating** them into simple principles.

Neither does to 'add what is specifically your own' mean adding personal embellishments to the art. For example, none of us now drives the way we originally learned in order to pass our driving test. Through experience we have all made our own personal modifications, so that we can now steer with one hand and operate the radio with the other instead of having to steer with both hands.

What does Bruce Lee mean by 'Man the creating individual is more important than any established style or system'? The important distinction here is between 'style' and 'individual style'. All boxers, for example, have the same basic style, but

* From the Latin *in corpore*, meaning 'within the body'.

Muhammad Ali did not fight like Joe Frazier; modern boxers fight differently from the early champions. In the same way, Western martial artists have a more powerful build while Asian martial artists are lighter and faster. In going beyond basic technical skills, the fighter attempts to get the best from his or her own particular attributes – temperament, speed, power, strategic awareness, and so on. Again, the key factor is in actually doing it so that it is not merely theoretical knowledge but understanding based on experience.

Anyone who attempts to define *jeet kune do* runs the risk of being like those in the fable of the blind men attempting to describe an elephant. One felt the tail and thought the elephant was like a snake; another felt its leg and thought it was like a tree, and so on. Human nature, being what it is, means that each person can relate only to what he or she already understands. Naturally a *wing chun* practitioner will see the foundation of Bruce's art as *wing chun*.

Before he met Bruce Lee, Jim Kelly had already applied the principles of *jeet kune do* through his individual approach to karate, resulting in a different understanding to that of most of its practitioners. Bruce recognized what Kelly had done and paid him the ultimate compliment by not choreographing Kelly's fights in *Enter the Dragon*, telling Kelly that he understood his own art and should do what he wanted.

Conversely, anyone approaching *jeet kune do* nowadays might be forgiven for thinking that it is a Filipino martial art; through Dan Inosanto it has become closely associated with his own preferred art of *kali*.

The real meaning of *jeet kune do*, after a sufficient level of technical ability has been reached, is as a means of self-discovery and self-expression. *Jeet kune do* does not apply to those of us who are learning the basic skill; it is a concept or philosophy that implies a level of mastery and, consequently, of self-mastery.

In this way, a *kali* practitioner, a *karateka*, or a *wing chun* exponent may also evolve out of the techniques and forms of his or her style without dispensing with technique or losing form. And if they choose to, they may then call their mastery *jeet kune do*, or body, mind and spirit, or whatever they please.

Bob Wall comments:

> Bruce challenged the foundations of the traditional martial arts by saying that the martial arts should be an extension of yourself. Before he came along, the Koreans thought that their style was the best, the Japanese thought that their style was the best. Bruce said that a punch in the mouth was a punch in the mouth.

As student Pete Jacobs put it when asked what Bruce Lee's favourite move was, 'Hitting you!'

'My truth is not your truth,' said Bruce Lee. What worked for Bruce didn't necessarily work for Jim Kelly or Dan Inosanto, nor for Joe Lewis.

'I never believed in that "power side forward" stuff,' says Lewis. Yet in declining to adopt Bruce Lee's recommended stance, Lewis is actually embracing *jeet kune do*'s core philosophy. From his work with Bruce, Joe Lewis absorbed what was useful and freed himself from the constraints of classical karate.

As a consequence, within his first year of training with Bruce Lee, Joe Lewis became unassailable in tournament competition. Ten of the greatest karate men of the day fought Lewis, and all ten were knocked out before the end of the second round. Joe Lewis was the most successful competition fighter among Bruce's students.

It was Bruce who suggested to Joe Lewis that he try using boxing techniques in karate; he also showed him the use of the 'angular attack', a principle found in *wing chun*. Further encouraged by Bruce to try out more realistic forms of combat, Lewis became one of the pioneers of the sport of full-contact karate in the early 1970s. In effect, Bruce was devising strategies and Lewis was testing them out in the ring.

The *tae kwon do* master Jhoon Rhee, who respected both Bruce's skills and his rebellious attitude, devised and introduced the Safe-T equipment that was first utilized in the World Professional Karate Championships in 1974. Bruce's training methods were made public through Lewis's competition appearances and Jhoon Rhee's protective equipment. In this way, Bruce Lee was at the root of the growth of martial arts into a competition sport in the West. In its infancy, modern American kickboxing was nothing less than applied *jeet kune do*.

Joe Lewis and his student Tom Tannenbaum (the producer of *Longstreet* who had become head of Universal TV) were instrumental in producing a 90-minute special out of the 1974 championships. This event established the sport of full-contact karate.

As Bruce Lee himself never fought in tournament competition, the question of how he would have fared is open to debate. Jim Kelly, for one, has suggested that many of the martial artists he did spar against have not revealed all that they know because they are protecting their own and each others' reputations. Richard Bustillo and a Los Angeles policeman were both present at a sparring session between Bruce and Chuck Norris in which the karate champion was left 'red-faced'.

Howard Williams adds that Bruce wasn't tempted to involve *jeet kune do* in tournament sport because he didn't hold with rules in combat, and that both Bruce's methods and attitude would have led to disqualification.

Yet Bruce's influence continued to be felt in the ring. In his June 1982 interview for *Playboy*, boxing champion Sugar Ray Leonard said:

One of the guys who influenced me wasn't a boxer. I always loved the catlike reflexes and the artistry of Bruce Lee and I wanted to do in boxing what he was able to do in *karate* [sic]. I started watching his movies before he became really popular in *Enter the Dragon* and I patterned myself after a lot of his ways. Lee was an artist and like him I try to go beyond the fundamentals of my sport.

Bruce Lee always regretted that he came up with the expression *jeet kune do*, rightly anticipating that it would suffer the fate of being turned from a fluid concept into a fixed system. Given Bruce's feelings about classical martial arts, it is ironic that in 1981 the Kuosho Federation of the Republic of China made *jeet kune do* a legitimate martial art whose official hierarchy consists of 'elders' like Dan Inosanto and Taky Kimura and their 'descendants' such as Tim Tackett.

Although Taky Kimura still teaches a small private class in what he calls *jun fan gung fu*, it is obvious that Bruce's art has taken more than a few twists and turns since the day he told Taky, 'Get a nondescript little place and work out there; have a good time, develop strong friendships and a good philosophy.'

Bruce also knew that martial arts suffer the same fate as religions. There are already several versions of *jeet kune do*. There are those who teach the screen version of Bruce's fighting and call it *jeet kune do*. There are those teaching 'classic' *jeet kune do*, who list the ten pointers that distinguish the 'real' art. There are some who invent a hybrid style and teach whatever they like, then label it *jeet kune do*. Almost beyond belief are the so-called *jeet kune do* institutes that offer home-study correspondence courses, complete with diplomas, in street fighting!

Even Dan Inosanto has been accused of misleading people.

In recent years, Howard Williams has presented himself as a no-nonsense street fighter, explaining that he considers *jeet kune do* to be the 'original' art that Bruce taught in Oakland and adding that it cannot be mixed with other styles like *kali*. 'People think that they can mix up these things, but it's like oil and water: you can shake them up and they look like they've mixed, but if you leave them a while they begin to separate out.'

Jeet kune do instructor Richard Bustillo asks, 'But what does "original" mean? Is that original from Bruce's days in Hong Kong, Seattle, Oakland or Los Angeles? Anything that Bruce Lee might be teaching today would certainly have evolved to incorporate new energies.'

In teaching *jeet kune do* many of Bruce's descendants begin from points at which he himself arrived only after ten, twelve, or fifteen years of hard-won experience. None had the opportunity to study or practise the vital foundation which permitted his later growth. Bruce's *jeet kune do* was the blossom on a tree with very deep roots.

Bruce Lee continued to practise the *wing chun* forms long after he had left Hong Kong. It was only because the awareness they developed had become so *embodied* in him – so that he didn't merely know it but *was* it – that he could later use that body feel to be free enough to bend the rules.

It is pointless to make an empty imitation of Bruce Lee's freedom. One must first have practised clearly defined patterns. Creativity emerges from the limits of form – from having only seven colours, only twelve notes, or only two arms and two legs to work with. 'If there were people with four arms and four legs,' said Bruce, 'then there would be another way of fighting.' There would also be other forms of music!

To wander 'in a circle with no circumference' is not to be free but rather to be lost. Perhaps what Bruce Lee meant to say is that the (martial) artist must learn how to function in a small well-defined circle, until it may eventually be enlarged a little at a time until it *seemingly* has no edges.

'Keep blasting, pushing and flowing,' Bruce urged. But this kind of spirited flow has to be understood in its right relationship to form. For example, there are not a limitless number of ways to block a kick with one's hand; there are only a few ways to do this safely and effectively, and all are based on the laws of anatomy (human form) and physics (the flow of energy). One cannot expect simply to flow instinctively into the right move. The opposite is true; we have to practise the right move many, many times before we can flow into it.

We can only learn to do what we want to do by repeatedly doing it, by making all the required neuromuscular connections or, if you prefer, by opening the right energy channels. But the key to learning by repetition is never to allow it to become stale or mechanical but to practise with *awareness*. In this way, we never 'do' the forms or 'do' techniques, but *search* within them.

This process reveals the truth in its own time. Like the growth of a garden, it is not something that can be constructed but must unfold from the inside, from the ground of its own being. The body itself teaches you as it learns. This process allows continual refinement, and may also be likened to the sculptor who chips away at a block of stone to reveal the form within. In this way, any *inessential* emotional tension, physical stiffness or mental distraction may gradually be chipped away to reveal the master within.

In short, the truth unfolds from the inside, while what is unnecessary falls away.

Only this, and not empty imitation, leads to the development of economical and efficient movements and the speed and power that they bring. Practising with good form is the principal means for generating, and opening up, the channels for the internal energy of *ch'i*.

Bruce Lee explained the difference between 'having no form' and having 'no form'. Having no form (at all) means simply being slap-happy and incompetent. Having no (fixed) form means that one is not restricted by form but is able to use it without being tied to it. Combined with another useful habit, awareness of fighting range, all of these elements are then introduced into training. The pressure is gradually increased as the fighter attempts to hold form and not dissolve into useless human reaction. Only then can there be any possibility of the 'tools striking on their own' when faced with a serious attack. All of this is precisely what should happen in the practice of sticking hands.

The most valuable and, I believe, indispensable tool that Bruce Lee had for understanding the roots of combat came from his grounding in the practice of sticking hands, *chi sao*, which develops the awareness that allowed him to flow into spontaneous expression.

Bruce could say that he was 'no style, but all styles' because the reflexes that he'd acquired from sticking hands allowed him to automatically match any attack with the appropriate counter. In this way, his technique was the result of his opponent's technique. 'You don't know what I'm going to do,' Bruce would say. Neither did Bruce – until it had happened!

But just as Bruce did not teach his students any forms, he hadn't the time to spend years on the intensive one-to-one teaching of sticking hands. Yet the fact that Bruce Lee considered *chi sao* the cornerstone of his art is evident in the photographs showing him teaching it to Van Williams during a publicity shoot for *The Green Hornet*. Years later, in similar situations, he was also photographed doing the same thing with James Franciscus, and also with John Saxon on the set of *Enter the Dragon*.

The practice of *chi sao* serves to develop the 'contact reflex' and the experience of 'forward pressure' which, at their fullest expression, extend far beyond trapping range and even far beyond the physical realm to allow the instantaneous understanding of the energy and intention of the opponent while eliciting the automatic response to solve any problem being set by him. However, it should also be made clear that this *wing chun*-based exercise is only truly effective when allied to the strategic use of footwork. Bruce Lee discovered this, just as Derek Jones did, though each of them solved the problem in his own particular way.

Nowadays, the practice of sticking hands is almost universally misunderstood. Most people realize only a fraction of its potential by practising fragments of it as set moves often involving wrong positions. Properly understood, sticking hands is a continuously flowing exercise that primarily allows one to hold form and search within the interplay of energy.

Practised hour after hour and day after day as the basis of sparring, *chi sao* is performed as a kind of moving meditation that fuses with the practice of the form and techniques. This is the core which allows an organic understanding of the roots of combat, and which also allows the martial artist to transcend all styles.

In music, as in dancing and fighting, there is a continual flow of movement. Bruce Lee was aware of the relationship and would spend many hours listening to Indian music on headphones because he wanted to absorb its improvised melodies and fluid rhythmic patterns.

In my own experience, learning a martial art has parallels with learning to play music. The musical group with which I play has attempted to bring together rock, pop, country, soul, blues and reggae while retaining a recognizable style. Yet in order to be able to cross those musical boundaries freely, I had first spent many years rooting my technique in fundamental skills such as rhythm and timing (and playing the right notes!) by copying simple riffs from my favourite R & B records. Bruce Lee rooted his skills in *wing chun* before he integrated fencing, boxing, kickboxing, wrestling and ju jitsu.

Even if at times it looked as though Bruce Lee was teaching music that only he could play, what he hoped to do was teach people enough for them to be able to improvise, rather than merely play set pieces.

Yet whether a musician leans towards playing jazz, classical, or country music, the same forms – scales, chord structures, harmony and dissonance – apply to all. Having said that, one only has to listen to the attempts of the majority of classically trained musicians to improvise 'feel' music, like rock or blues, to realize the disadvantages of a purely formal training. So one must also begin with a certain amount of freedom. One musician may excel in one form of expression, another may take a different road; if they both have talent and work on it, both will get to where they want to go.

Playing music, like practising a martial art, may serve many purposes: to make money, to show off, to get laid, to terrify or to heal. It can be used by the narcissistic personality for its own ends; or it can be a vehicle for spirit and for truth.

In this way, awareness may combine with intention to form the basis not only of martial arts mastery but of the mastery of any form of art or means of expression. And it may also be the key to all forms of enlightenment – whether called philosophical insight, spiritual revelation, liberation or mastery.

32

MASTERY

AT THE HEART of his teaching Bruce Lee was not promoting a martial art; rather he was hoping to instill in his students a real sense of understanding. But understanding cannot be given, it has to be discovered at the heart of each individual. The real help that Bruce Lee offers is the inspiration to self-help.

Knowledge and understanding are not the same thing. Knowledge is built on the experience of the past; understanding is built on the experience of the present. Anyone who simply identifies with Bruce Lee or a system called *jeet kune do* has become trapped. But to be inspired to experience and understand for oneself what Bruce Lee understood is exactly what he intended.

Jesus Christ, another teacher whose insights have inspired dogmatic and fundamentalist followings, expressed the same truth when he said, 'Follow me and you will lose yourself; but follow yourself, and you will find both yourself, and me.' Organized dogmatic religion betrays its original visionary. And any martial artist who clings to his teacher's words denies his own possibility of understanding.

Bruce Lee intended *jeet kune do* to reflect the nature of the

Tao itself, to be a vehicle that could be used but not conveyed by words, grasped by the mind or fixed as a system.

Bruce often told the story of the Zen monk who uses a boat to cross a river and, having done so, builds a fire with it. Many of Bruce's followers have chosen to preserve the boat; some wish to sail back to the past on it, or fit it with a motor, and so on. The essence of Bruce's story is to allow something that has served a useful purpose to change its form and serve a more fitting purpose.

It is interesting to consider here what exactly is meant by the expression 'survival of the fittest'. The phrase was not invented by Charles Darwin, as many think, but was first used by Herbert Spencer in his 1867 book, *Principles of Biology*. Spencer used the word 'fittest' in the sense of most fitting or most suitable. In modern (mis)use it is taken to mean most strong, in the sense of people fighting for survival or exercising strength to prevail over the weak. 'Most Fitting' really refers to appropriateness and adaptability, and the ability to adapt to one's environment. The one who can best adapt to changing circumstances is the one who will survive, and is not necessarily the strongest.

Bruce Lee intended to illustrate this in the opening scene he had in mind for *Game of Death*, in which a branch of a strong but rigid tree snaps and breaks off under the weight of snow, while the pliable willow tree bends and allows the snow to slide off its branches and so survives unharmed. This image recalls that the very word 'Shaolin' means young tree – one that can bend and sway, and so prevail.

The real question that is beginning to emerge from the philosophy of *jeet kune do* is the nature of the relationship between form and freedom expressed as the ability to adapt to life. What is form? And what is freedom? And how does maintaining good form relate to being free? How does it all apply, not only to practising a martial art but to any other art, and especially to my life as a human being?

Maintaining form refers to many things. These will certainly include the efficient execution of a technique, economy of movement and an awareness of the flow of energy that includes both the mind and emotions – while involved in all the changing circumstances of life.

Having physical form means finding the most efficient and graceful way of using the natural flow of energy. This involves aligning with gravity both in stillness and in movement, and having no unnecessary tension while moving the body as a whole unit – centred, grounded and upright – so that every part coordinates in well-timed action and response.

Mental form means letting go of all idle speculation, worry, doubt and so on at the moment it arises, then redirecting one's attention either to a useful process of active thinking or to awareness of the physical form.

Emotional form means choosing to feel positive even without evident cause or reason so that this becomes a cause in itself. Being positive entails real effort.

There is ample evidence in this book that these were the deepest principles by which Bruce Lee sought to live his life. He sometimes failed but often he succeeded.

We are offered the same choice. At every moment, at every breath, *now*, one can lose awareness of form and then justify this loss and allow it to continue, or one can regain it. We may drift or barge our way through life, imagining we are free without even the vaguest prospect of stumbling accidentally on the true experience. But if we seek to maintain awareness of form *intentionally*, then, in that moment, we *are* free.

Freedom is not a thing that can be anticipated any more than I can satisfy today's hunger by thinking of a meal I might eat tomorrow. The freedom offered by self-awareness is either present, or it is not. We do not work to gain freedom; we simply *are* free.

When attention is present, then the mind is free of distraction. When the emotions are free of fears – not *without* fears, but not so bound up in them – then they can flow as more pure motivating energy. When the body is more relaxed and free of tension then it is sensitive to the energy of others and open enough to allow the energy of Spirit to flow freely into form.

Bruce Lee had his first taste of this possibility when as a teenager he took Yip Man's advice to stop trying so hard and went walking for a while by the water of Hong Kong's harbour. As he leaned over and punched his own reflected image, the water parted and splashed away. A second later it flowed back around his fingers and, as it settled again, perfectly formed itself around the shape of his hand.

Years later, in the *Longstreet* episode that he helped Stirling Silliphant write, Lee attempts to invoke the same insight in Longstreet when he tells him to be like water: 'When you pour water into a cup, it becomes the cup. When you pour water into a teapot it becomes the teapot.'

What is there that is more 'fitting' than water? Yet without the form to hold it, the free-flowing and adaptable nature of water is useless. A river without banks is simply a flood, but when channelled it has incredible force, enough to power an electrical generator. When the mind is attentive enough to direct the form of the body in both an efficient and a sensitive way, then in the same way this allows the entry of entirely new energy.

Bruce Lee knew that at the highest level of any art, the impulse to act comes from Spirit. As Lee shows the young monk in the opening sequences of *Enter the Dragon*, in the beginning it is necessary to acquire both a skilful technique and the correct psychological approach. The ambitious personal 'I' of the ego prevents the very success it desires. But when it is transcended, success comes, not as the result of mere will power and striving, but through the intervention of what might be called a super-natural force.

The missing dialogue from *Enter the Dragon* is a revealing exchange between Lee and the head monk showing the level of skill which Lee has attained. On the way to this *state of being*, Lee has first established a level of ability through practis-ing physical skills allied to intense alertness and perseverance. Mastery, in the real sense, only begins when the martial artist has dealt with the aggressive desires and fear of failure that obstruct his way. When 'it' hits by itself, it is because the small 'I' of the personal ego no longer interferes. The master has surrendered to another force, allowing the energy of the 'universal I' (what Lee calls 'it' and what Derek Jones calls 'Spirit') to act through him or her.

Bira Almeida, a master of the Brazilian art of *capoeira*, recalls his own experience:

> After I reached the limits of my physical skills I went into a depression. I had such good skills and a strong attitude that I could not easily find challenging opponents. I had no motivation and little possibility of improvement.

He then went three years without training, until he realized that he had missed something, and returned to training as a means of exploring the very roots of his being:

> Then I didn't care any more about strength, speed or any other physical skill. I simply began trying to read my opponent's mind. At the same time, I began to write and study music as an extension of this art. There eventually came a transformation to a further level,

where the opponent now has to do what your own mind orders him to do.

Such control has no other purpose than to help your opponent, even your enemy, to evolve and reach universal harmony. There is a rhythm to life and the universe. In doing a martial art you play to find it, to attune to it. As long as you tune to this rhythm you cannot fight a false fight. This rhythm is filled with life's imbalances, but it transforms them.

Angry people want to fight to injure and kill. The martial arts do not deny this teaching, but the true inner art turns this anger and alienation back on itself so that the challenge inherent in simply being alive is recognized in the artist himself.

Many people are unable to see a martial art as a means of spiritual unfoldment or inner work. In the West, we tend to think of winners and losers, with no other possibilities. In a fight, in martial arts training, the process of confrontation is absorbed by the participants so that each learns something. Neither the winner nor the loser will live for ever in a permanent form. In a fight, as in life, both engage in a process of learning and change. The opponent is not the enemy, he is just 'I' in another form.

At the moment you are fighting, your opponent becomes yourself. You confront your fears, your strengths and weaknesses, your life itself. I have been involved in thousands of fights, so I know what it is to feel this kind of thing inside. You know you must win, but to win is to win with yourself.

A martial art is like a mirror in which you look at yourself before you wash your face in the morning. You see yourself simply, the way that you are.*

* Adapted from Bira Almeida, *Capoeira: A Brazilian Art Form* (Berkeley: North Atlantic Books, 1982. Second Edition, revised and expanded, 1986).

33

COMPLETING THE CIRCLE

THE STORY OF creation, whether told by Taoist philosophers or by present-day scientists, is in essence the same story, differing only in its cultural perspectives.

In the Taoist concept, the creation of the universe occurs by a few simple principles and steps. In the beginning is the void – the *wu ch'i* – the unknown. Out of the void are created the two basic forms or processes of energy, *yin* and *yang*. The combining and interaction of *yin* and *yang* produces *ch'i* – energy or vibrations – and ultimately everything in existence.

The interplay of *yin* and *yang* is a way of ordering and understanding anything that can be conceived: left and right, hard and soft, birth and death. Within any situation there may be an overall quality of *yin* or *yang*, but it can be further subdivided into all its complexities until there are 'ten thousand' divisions and comparisons. The binary arithmetic of computer language (by which all information is conveyed in combinations of 0 and 1) is an example of combining the two to produce the many.

In the view of modern physics, the universe was created out of the void by the Big Bang. (Although in reality there was no before the Big Bang of creation since time itself is created along with Creation!) In the first milliseconds of creation, antimatter (*yin*) collides with matter (*yang*) to form light. Light forms the various energies of sound, colour and substance as some vibrations slow down and some speed up.

Scientist Jack Sarfatti pictures the universe as a kind of quantum foam in which objects and forces – everything in existence – are like the ripples on the surface of a great sea. This is *ch'i*, pulsating at different frequencies, which forms the substance of the universe: energy that interacts to form organic matter, stars, planets, animals, rocks, plants and all aspects of the human being: our physical bodies and their various processes, and our feelings, thoughts and spiritual insights.

What the Chinese call 'the flow of *ch'i*' (what physicists might call the 'universal energy flux' or the 'quantum field') has no beginning and no end. Though it continually manifests as different forms in time and space it remains basically unchanged, eternal and immutable. To truly experience every aspect of this flow would also be to know that ultimately everything has the same source of arising and the same destiny, beyond time, where there is no before or after, only an eternal now. Between the beginning and the return to the beginning, there appear all the interactions of life.

Bruce Lee depicted this process in a simple graphic way in the emblem of his school. The first rank was a blank circle, the original state of freedom and potential. The further ranks were represented by *yin/yang* emblems of various colours, signifying all aspects of life. The highest grade was again the blank circle: the return to the Source.

Despite appearances, all the various forms and activities of life are really one continuous flow of energy. Knowing this, Bruce often dismissed questions about the nature of *yin* and *yang*, not dismissing the concept itself but simply trying to point out that in reality all apparent opposites arise out of one unified force. This force, which expresses itself in an unending flux of form and movement, is the process sometimes known as 'the *Univ*erse.'

Einstein's conception of space is much the same as the Buddhist teaching on *shunyata*, the void. It used to be thought that space was a nothing, a vacuum. But Einstein said that space is alive, a field of possibilities from which 'every thing' or 'any thing' might come into existence. Matter is nothing more than a local condensation of energy in space. There is, then, no basic difference between matter and space or, in the Buddhist view, between form and the void.

Zen master Genpo Merzel Sensei has the following to say about it:

> The void is no mere emptiness but is real, free and existing. It is the source from which all things arise and return. It cannot be seen, touched or known yet it exists and is freely used. It has no shape, size, colour or form, and yet all that we see, hear, feel and touch is 'it'.
>
> It is beyond intellectual knowing and cannot be grasped by the ordinary mind. When we suddenly awake to the realization that there is no barrier, and never has been, one realizes that one is all things – mountains, rivers, grasses, trees, sun, moon, stars, universe are all oneself. There is no longer any division or barrier between myself and others, no longer any feeling of alienation or fear – there is nothing apart from oneself and therefore nothing to fear. Realizing this results in true compassion. Other people and things are not seen as apart from oneself but, on the contrary, as one's own body.*

Bodhidharma, the legendary founder of *kung fu*, devised a series of exercises for the monks of Shaolin, explaining,

---

* Quoted in David Scott and Tony Doubleday, *Zen* (Shaftesbury, England: Element Books, 1992).

'Although the way of the Buddha is preached for the soul, the body and the soul are inseparable. For this reason, I shall give you a method by which you can develop your energy enough to attain to the essence of the Buddha.'

Fighting, like any other art, is at its highest level an activity of Spirit in the body. At first the martial artist trains to be able to sense and experience his body as a whole unit; then to be able to sense and feel his opponent's energy as his own. When the years of training and encouraging the relaxed body to move as required are complete – and when the focusing of intent and emotional content has unified the body, mind and emotions – this then allows the intervention of a higher energy. Now, any action, large or small, has power. Even in punching, the punch itself punches and the energy of the universe is already there!

At the highest level the martial artist tastes and experiences the oneness of all energy, the unity of life. To begin to touch this energy and to be touched by it is to realize that ulti-mately I and my opponent, myself and my shadow, me and my father, are one. To know this state is to have neither allies nor enemies. To know this state is to know of no separation between life and death.

We can now perhaps understand how Bruce Lee had mastered his art to the degree that he could say, 'Nobody wins a fight.'

What did he mean by this? Simply that because everything arises and returns to the same source, any victory is for this One, even before any combat takes place.

In this way, at the highest level the martial artist develops a 'body feel' for everything in existence. Bruce Lee knew that at the highest expression of his art the impulse to action comes from Spirit.

In the end, I do not know whether it is through a greater awareness of my form and my surroundings that I have aligned myself with Spirit; or whether my efforts have been noticed by the greater awareness of Spirit and I have been chosen as a suitable vessel. The true martial artist is fearless because he knows that even if his body perishes he embodies a Spirit that will not die.

In the beginning is *wu ch'i* – the void – the unknown.

In Chinese, the word *wu* means martial. The word *ch'i* means breath, energy, or spirit. It needs no additional leap of reason or intuition to see that the very ground of Being, *wu ch'i*, also carries the meaning fighting spirit – not merely in the sense of being combative but in the sense of being vital and *interactive*.

All the same, a paradox is revealed. The discovery of the Way and harmony with the Tao is identical with the embodiment of fighting spirit.

PART FOUR

BRUCE LEE IN THE NEW MILLENNIUM

34

INTRODUCTION

SINCE WRITING THE original edition of *Fighting Spirit*
I've come to see Bruce Lee as both less, and more. On further
consideration, there's no doubt that Bruce Lee was both a
complex and a flawed man. And yet, in a strange way, he still
offers us a lot more than any mere icon.

Recently every one of Bruce's handwritten notes on philosophy, his diet sheets, exercise regimes (and probably his
shopping lists) have been published – annotated with all the
care and attention that you'd expect from a devotee. Some of
these notes are taken pretty much direct from their original
sources in Zen, Taoism and Western philosophy. As many of
Bruce's own notes are difficult to understand unless you
already have some background in what he's talking about, it's
unlikely that the layman, or anyone coming to them 'cold',
will gain a lot from them. And – it has to be said – all of this
meticulous cataloguing borders on the 'fossilization' that
Bruce always counselled against.

There has been, and probably always will be, a steady trickle of
'new' material on Bruce, but not much of it will shed further

light. Things move on. Bruce Lee would have undoubtedly moved one. He even told us what he intended to do, and he usually achieved what he intended. But first, there are one or two questions that just never seem to go away.

35
RETURN TO THE END

SINCE THE PUBLICATION of the original version of *Fighting Spirit*, the question I am still most asked about Bruce Lee is, 'But how did he really die?'

The coroner's official verdict after the inquest into the cause of death was that it had been due to 'a cerebral oedema, caused by a hypersensitivity to one or more of the ingredients in a single analgesic tablet'. But now the two men best able to answer the question feel that enough time has elapsed for them to say a little more, it's possible to settle the matter.

Bruce Lee's former doctor Don Langford states it plainly: 'He was the fittest man I've ever seen. Analgesic did not kill Bruce Lee. In my opinion, the cause of Bruce Lee's death is pretty obvious. He started believing his own hype. He didn't think there was anyone who knew what was best for him, except himself. The factors that caused his collapse in May are the same as caused his death in July. Bruce was affected by one or more of the alkaloids in cannabis. The official verdict wasn't so much a whitewash or a cover-up as an attempt to produce a verdict that was more socially acceptable.'

Dr Peter Wu, the neurosurgeon who actually saved Bruce's

life after the May collapse, echoes Don Langford's opinions: 'Bruce Lee was convinced that he was invincible, immortal. He could have died in May; he was in a very critical condition. It was sheer luck that there was someone there to help him. A lot of Nepalese hashish was taken from his stomach. Not wanting to damage his health by smoking cannabis, Bruce chose instead to eat it. Unfortunately, this overloads the body with the active ingredients of hashish far quicker than they can be processed. We gave him a good talking-to before discharging him from the hospital and told him not to eat the stuff again. But his very low percentage of body fat, along with the stress he was under, made him more vulnerable to the drug and dramatically intensified its effects. Since he'd already had such a bad reaction to it, we told him that if there was a next time, the consequences might be even more severe. But I knew he wasn't listening.'

After being introduced to cannabis by Steve McQueen, Bruce started taking it in Los Angeles; both Joe Lewis and James Coburn witnessed this. Bob Wall says that Bruce was using it while filming *Enter the Dragon*, and kept a jar of brownies on his desk, which he ate while they were talking between takes.

Bruce had started using cannabis to try and alleviate the stress he was under, but as a result he also started suffering from sleeplessness, headaches and memory loss. He would frequently tell people stories that he'd already told them more than once, or repeatedly show photographs that he carried.

Between early 1971, when Bruce was still living in Los Angeles, and May 1973, the time of his collapse, his weight fell from 145 to 122 pounds. Coupled with his punishing exercise regime and workload, the overall effect was that Bruce's body fat content fell to a seemingly impossible figure of less than one per cent. On some photo stills from *Enter the Dragon*, it's actually possible to see individual clusters of muscle fibres, particularly in his shoulders.

Ann Clouse (the wife of *Enter the Dragon* director, Robert Clouse) says that during the making of the film Bruce told her that he would be dead before his next birthday and admitted that he wondered just how much more he could push his body. So, did Elvis die because he was too fat, and Bruce Lee because he was too fit?

It's almost as if Bruce Lee trained and dedicated himself for twenty years to become the ultimate screen hero for just one movie. *Enter the Dragon* took Bruce from $7,500 a film straight to $2 million, and to the verge of fulfilling the seemingly impossible affirmation he'd written all those years before by becoming the first genuinely international Chinese star to make $10 million in ten years. But while his finger was pointing to the moon and heavenly glory on the set, off-set he was wearing a full-length mink coat and enough aftershave to attract a swarm of tsetse flies. He was also carrying an illegal handgun every time he left the house in Kowloon Tong.

How could he have possibly carried on anyway? How could he continue to write films, choreograph them, direct them, star in them, train as intensively and consistently as he needed to, eat the right food, travel to meetings, endorse products, appear in ads, promote movies, do interviews, spend time with his family? Something would have to give and it did. His last afternoon on earth was spent unconscious on the bed of his mistress. The fittest man in the world, the man whose every muscle was as hard as warm marble, had a weak spot.

In the final analysis, we always return to the same question. How could Bruce Lee have ever reconciled his ambitions – and the demands being made on him as the latest, greatest star in the world – with the incredible disciplines and regimes that took him there in the first place? The two worlds were always going to be impossible to reconcile.

36

THE ULTIMATE FIGHT OF ALL TIME

THE OTHER QUESTION that I am asked most about Bruce Lee is, 'But could he actually fight?' And, more times than I can count, people from outside the martial arts have asked, 'But how would he compare with a real fighter like Muhammad Ali?'

Discussing these questions over the years, I've become more and more fascinated by what would actually have happened if the two had met, in what would surely have been billed as The Ultimate Fight of All Time.

In 1966, the American public got its first glimpse of Bruce Lee in action when he co-starred in the short-lived TV series *The Green Hornet*. In a review of the first episode, one critic commented, 'Those who watch him would bet on Lee to render Cassius Clay senseless, if they were put into a room and told that anything goes.'

Cassius Clay was of course the 8–1 underdog who'd beaten Sonny Liston two years previously to become boxing's world heavyweight champion. Clay later embraced the Islamic faith, changed his name to Muhammad Ali, and went on to become the most outstanding boxer of the modern era, and probably the greatest of all time.

By the time Bruce Lee shot to international movie stardom in 1973, he was recognized as the supreme screen fighter. Like Ali in boxing, as a martial artist Bruce Lee was the fastest, most exciting and most innovative of his day, and perhaps of all time. And in the early 1970s, theirs were two of the most famous faces in the world. They still are.

So what *would* have happened if the two men had actually fought at the height of their powers? Would Bruce Lee's speed and mobility have overcome Ali's tremendous advantages in weight, height, and reach? What experience did each have of the other's way of fighting? Let's begin at the beginning.

BACKGROUND

Bruce Lee and Muhammad Ali were born only two years apart (in 1940 and 1942) and right from the start both were natural fighters. By the age of twelve, Ali was devoting all of his energies to boxing, maturing rapidly, and already showing the unique abilities that would make him a great champion. An amateur boxing official, Chuck Bodak, recalled: 'You'd have had to be blind not to see how good this kid was. I thought he must be from outer space because I'd never seen anyone like him in my life.' The young Ali fought 108 amateur bouts, going on to win six Golden Gloves tournaments and two national AAU titles by the time he was eighteen, and on his way to the Olympics.

At the age of thirteen, Bruce Lee had the same obsessive dedication to practice and the same natural gifts that Ali was blessed with. Although he came from a relatively well-off showbiz home, being Chinese in the colonial Hong Kong of the 1950s was probably not very different from being black in

Louisville, Kentucky. Telling his parents that he wanted to 'protect himself from bullies' Bruce persuaded them to let him start learning *wing chun*.

'You never had to ask Bruce twice about a fight,' said his younger brother, Robert. But one of Bruce's teachers tried to divert this instinct into boxing for his college in the Hong Kong Inter-Schools Championships. His natural abilities saw him through all the qualifying rounds, where he scored three first round KOs. But now he had to face the three-times champion, a British schoolboy named Gary Elms, in the final.

Although it was the first time that Bruce Lee had ever put on boxing gloves to fight, it wasn't the first time that he'd ever fought against boxers and used the strategy of evading their punches and kicking their lower legs. But the Inter-Schools Final was fought under strict Marquess of Queensberry rules – and in the first round Bruce was soon in trouble, reeling against the ropes and pinned in a corner. But in the following round he began using *wing chun* blocks against Elms's attacks, neutralizing everything that was being thrown at him, before countering with a flurry of centreline punches. Suddenly, there was a new champion.

Soon after Bruce's arrival in Seattle to work as a waiter in Ruby Chow's restaurant, he started an informal *kung fu* class in the parking lot behind the restaurant. Immediately, he found it necessary to make major changes to the way he was used to fighting, in order to contend with Western opponents who weighed twice as much as he did. His biggest change was to adopt a leading stance with one side of the body forward, like a boxer or fencer. But because Bruce had one leg slightly longer than the other, rather than using the conventional left lead stance, he found it more efficient to adopt the stance of a southpaw. To help him adapt to this new approach, he studied many boxers in action, but particularly Muhammad Ali. He set up a film projector so that he could study and copy Ali's movements, viewing the picture in a mirror so that Ali's stance was reversed to show the right side leading. 'I'm getting to know how he moves and thinks,' Bruce told one of his friends. When asked how he thought he would fare against Ali, Bruce looked down at his hands, and replied, 'Look at my hand! That's a little Chinese hand. He'd kill me!'

Would Bruce Lee have been 'killed' by Ali, a man who weighed nearly twice as much as him? Although Ali was far bigger, let's first take into consideration the enormous internal energy that the martial artist can generate.

POWER

In 1964, Muhammad Ali was world boxing champion, while Bruce Lee's reputation had yet to be established. But in the July of that year, at Ed Parker's International Karate Tournament in Long Beach, Bruce gave a demonstration of what was then the unknown art of *kung fu*. The crowd in the arena was restless from a long day in the stifling heat and people were none too impressed when Bruce first appeared. But any dissent was silenced the moment he demonstrated the amount of power he could generate by harnessing his internal energy.

Bruce loosely extended his arm lightly against a volunteer's chest. Then without any drawing back of his fist, he simply locked out his arm the last inch, exploding his fist into the man's chest and sending him sprawling backwards several yards. Happily for Bruce Lee this had been filmed and it was this film that eventually found its way to the TV producer who offered him the role of Kato in *The Green Hornet*.

At the same time as he was making inroads into TV and movie work, Bruce was attracting a number of showbiz celebrities as students. James Coburn used to work out with Bruce in his garden. One day, Coburn showed Bruce a new heavy bag he'd bought on which to practise kicking and punching at full power; it weighed over one hundred pounds and was suspended by a heavy steel chain from an angle iron. Bruce took a look at the bag and offered to 'soften it up' a bit. He did a running sidekick and hit the bag, ripping it from the chain and sending it sailing into the middle of the garden where it fell, split open with its seams ripped.

When Stirling Silliphant contrived to include a fight scene in a film he had written (a love story called *A Walk in the Spring Rain*) the best he could do was to appoint Lee as the fight choreographer because, unfortunately, the story was set in Tennessee, where there were not too many Chinese. On the set, by a swimming pool, the writer introduced Bruce to the two redneck stuntmen who were to perform the fight scene. When they saw the man who was supposed to show them how to fight they said, 'Shit!' The writer suggested that Bruce show them what he could do. 'Sure,' they replied. 'No problem,' said Bruce. Before he'd realized what was happening, the first stuntman was sailing through the air to land in the middle of the pool, while his buddy only just missed hitting the far edge.

Muhammad Ali had his own taste of the power that can be generated by a martial artist. In October 1973, during a visit to Singapore, the champion was the guest of honour at a lunch organized by Cathay Pacific Airlines. At this event was Wong Yau Kay, a thirty-year old who had begun practising *wing chun* as a child to overcome ill health, and who had been invited to give a demonstration of the power that can be produced through meditative breathing techniques. Wong allowed Ali to strike his throat several times, full force, with a karate-style chop. Wong suffered no injury and Ali added his own applause to that of the spectators and expressed the view that *kung fu* was 'a profound art'.

HEIGHT AND REACH

If, as the evidence suggests, Bruce Lee could call on enough power, then how would he have dealt with Ali's vastly superior height and reach? The nearest we can come to answering that question lies in some film that Bruce shot in 1972 for *Game of Death*, which featured another of Bruce's celebrity pupils, the seven-foot-tall basketball ace, Kareem Abdul Jabbar.

While it's true that this was a scripted fight where there could be only one outcome, the resulting footage shows a strangely elegant David and Goliath confrontation. It reveals that Bruce Lee had both the manoeuvrability to penetrate a big man's defence along with the flexibility and leaping power to land kicks to the head. Remember, during rehearsals Bruce succeeded in landing kicks to Jabbar's head 300 times.

SPEED

Bob Surkein, an AAU referee and judge during Ali's schoolboy years, once commented, 'God had given this kid reflexes like no one had ever seen. I said to myself, "It can't be." But after watching him in the ring many times, I knew this kid had it.' Ali was undoubtedly the fastest heavyweight of all time. We can only marvel at the devastating combinations of punches that he could string together, like the deadly barrage that finished off Ron Lyle during his title defence in 1975. Ali was losing on points until he suddenly turned on the style. The resulting onslaught caused even Ali to gesture to the referee to end the punishment.

During the time that Bruce Lee was living in Seattle, he would hang out at the Imperial Bowl making spare cash by betting that nobody could beat his reflexes. His usual trick was to ask his opponent to hold a dime in the palm of his hand, saying that he would snatch it away before they could shut it. Bruce would move suddenly and the opponent would snap his hand shut, smiling when he felt the dime still in his grip. Bruce would pretend disappointment, then ask his opponent to show him the dime. In its place, there would be a nickel!

What is perhaps more relevant is that Bruce was equally fast with his feet. He would place his foot on the chest of a student and ask him to hold his hands about an inch either side of the foot. Then Bruce would withdraw his foot and stand in front of the student, telling him that he was going to kick him in exactly the same spot as he had just placed his foot without being caught. No one ever managed to catch his foot.

Further proof of Bruce Lee's speed is there for anyone to see in the footage shot at the Fox Studios during the screen test for *The Green Hornet*. Bruce demonstrates a series of combination strikes against a reluctant and terrified volunteer, as the air pops around him. In most of Bruce Lee's later filmed fight scenes the cameras had to be adjusted to film at thirty-two frames per second instead of their normal rate of twenty-four because his movements were so fast that some of them wouldn't register in a single frame of film. The resulting footage shows that Bruce was capable of landing as many as eight separate strikes in one second. Although, for a heavyweight, Ali was supernaturally fast, Bruce Lee would certainly have beaten him on speed.

STRATEGY

Bruce Lee first met the heavyweight karate champion Joe Lewis in 1967, on a promotional tour of martial arts tournaments, appearing as Kato. Some time later, Lewis began training with

Bruce Lee when he realized that many of Bruce's innovations could be applied to tournament karate.

'He emphasized footwork to me, and the importance of using distance and mobility against an opponent,' says Joe Lewis. 'We used to analyze strategies on old boxing films. We studied the way Ali punched and moved, and the way that he could control people even while backing up. And then I would go out in a karate tournament and prove whether it worked there, too.'

An account of Lewis's win at the US National Karate Championships in 1968, which came about as a result of his training with Bruce Lee, describes Lewis as a fighter reborn. His usual surly disposition had been put to one side and he displayed an agility that had never been seen before, one that made the runners-up seem like faint shadows against his new abilities. When Lewis was awarded the crown he humbly thanked his teacher, Bruce Lee, giving him the credit for his improvement, something that Lewis had never done before. Within a year of beginning training with Bruce, Joe Lewis had become unbeatable in tournament competition; he was even dubbed the 'Muhammad Ali of karate'.

Kareem Abdul Jabbar comments, 'Bruce said that he wanted to train Ali how to kick. He said that if he could do that, then Ali would be like someone from another planet.'

'Bruce was in awe of Ali until the day he died,' adds Lewis. 'He idolized Ali, his footwork, his speed, his elusiveness; he believed Ali was the best there was.' In Bruce Lee's fight with Chuck Norris in *Way of the Dragon* (the best fight scene Bruce put on film) he overwhelms Norris with a cluster of punches too quick to count. This is taken directly from Ali's fight with Cleveland Williams, even from the same camera angles. Bruce would play the Williams fight again and again on his movie projector.

Before Chuck Norris took the part, Bruce had originally

offered Joe Lewis the role of his adversary in *Way of the Dragon*. But Lewis had declined, claiming that Bruce wanted to use him as a punchbag. Lewis said that, in a real fight, the power of the stronger heavier martial artist would prevail over the faster lighter man. 'You can't believe how hard these big guys hit,' says Lewis, echoing Bruce Lee's own opinion of what would happen if someone like Muhammad Ali were ever to land a blow on him. 'If they hit a little guy like Bruce, it could literally kill him.'

Ali was as brilliant a tactician as he was a technician, able to get the edge on the toughest of opponents through his ability to manipulate them psychologically. For example, at a crucial stage in his 1972 title defence against Bob Foster, for the first time in his career Ali was cut. Foster landed another good shot. Ali stumbled and staggered, hurt. Seconds later he was dancing, then staggering again, then dancing, to show Foster that he had only been faking. This flattened Foster's moment-ary elation so completely that, soon after, Ali took the fight.

In his clash with Ken Norton, Ali fought flat-footed and heavy through the opening rounds then, suddenly, he was up on his toes and dancing as if it were a one-round sparring session, and just as suddenly, Ali had won.

But the most awesome demonstration of Ali's mental strength came in the legendary fight with George Foreman, the 'Rumble in the Jungle', which was the subject of the award-winning documentary film *When We Were Kings*. Ali was genuinely afraid of his much stronger opponent, but prevailed through his tactics of getting the crowd on his side then goading Foremen until he'd punched himself out.

One evening Bruce Lee was at a dinner where one of the other guests was Senator John Tunney, the son of the former heavyweight champion Gene Tunney. Bruce amazed the sen-ator by being able to describe all his father's fights in detail and added that he had books and films on him in his library. Senator Tunney then asked Bruce if he thought he could have beaten his father. Bruce replied, 'If I sat still and your father hit me, then forget it! The question is: Could he have ever got close to me?' Bruce then said that while the boxer had only two weapons, he had four: his fists and his feet. Bruce might well have added that he also had his knees, elbows and fingers available as weapons.

The question now is would Bruce Lee have been allowed to use his feet? Would Ali have fought bare-knuckled? Would they have fought in a ring, or would they have been locked in a room and told anything goes?

RULES

At the age of fifteen, Howard Williams trained with Bruce Lee when he was living and teaching in Oakland. Williams says that Lee wasn't tempted to involve himself in tournament fighting because he didn't hold with rules in combat, adding, 'Anyone who fought using the methods he was advocating would have been disqualified.'

In our Ultimate Fight of All Time any rules, or lack of rules, would immediately favour one fighter or the other. Ali could inflict far greater damage if he fought bare-knuckled. Having to wear gloves would leave Bruce Lee unable to use his *bil jee* strikes or sticking hands skills.

In his first title defence against the Canadian, George Chuvalo, a contemptuous Ali allowed his opponent a dozen free shots at his ribs, defying Chuvalo to hurt him. So while it might appear that Bruce Lee's punching power would be made ineffective through having to wear gloves, there just isn't any way of calculating this. My own teacher, Derek Jones (who stood five feet ten inches and weighed 155 pounds), fought in street fights for prize money in his younger days. In one of these fights he landed a punch that not only split his glove but broke his opponent's ribs into the bargain.

Problems over rules arose when Ali did actually fight a martial artist, the Japanese professional wrestler Kanji 'Antonio' Inoke, in Tokyo, on 25 June 1976, for what was billed as 'The Martial Arts Championship of the World'.

Joe Lewis claims that, in the run up to this contest with Inoke, he visited one of Ali's training sessions and challenged him, claiming that a boxer is vulnerable to an attack at ground level by a skilled martial artist. After a lot of messing around and faking, accompanied by irritating questions from the spectators, Ali finally backed off and invited Lewis to go for it. Lewis faked an explosive jab at Ali's head and then dropped for his legs, using a fireman's takedown to slap Ali down hard and fast on the canvas. Ali was flat on his back with Lewis on top of him but reached out and grabbed the bottom rope of the boxing ring, saying that boxing rules state that when a boxer touches the bottom rope, his opponent must stand back and let him up. Lewis says the Ali camp suppressed all photos of this incident. He adds, 'Ali showed me just how slick he was. I knew then that he was going to play the whole Inoke fight up against the ropes, and he did.'

In the days prior to the contest Ali did his best to hype up public interest, calling Inoke 'the Pelican' because of his protruding jaw, and predicting a knockout with a newly developed 'acupunch'. Ali maintained it was the biggest single-sport event in the history of the world and, in public at least, appeared to take it seriously saying, 'I can't let my fans down; I can't lose to that fat-bellied old wrestler.' But few people were convinced by this talk. Many thought the whole affair degrading, both for Ali personally and for sport in general. Ali responded on CBS TV's *Face the Nation*: 'People want to know what a boxer would do with a wrestler. What's going to happen if Ali's arm gets twisted? What will happen if he kicks Ali? I'm betting that I can hit him before he can grab me. With my dancing and moving, I can't see him getting close enough to hit me without me hitting him. The man is a wrestler; he's not used to taking hard shots to the head. The minute I go upside his head, it's over.'

The reality turned out to be somewhat different. According to boxing promoter, Bob Arum, the fight was to be as rehearsed and phoney as any wrestling match. The script called for Ali to beat up Inoke for several rounds, even to the extent that he would be pouring blood. Inoke suggested that, if the blood flow was not profuse enough, he might help things along with a hidden capsule. At this point Ali was to appeal to the referee to stop the fight. Then, in the middle of Ali's humane appeal, the Japanese would jump him from behind and pin him.

But after arriving in Japan, Ali became more and more disturbed about his part in this sham and refused to go along with it. Suddenly it looked as if a real fight might be on the cards. Now nobody knew what to do, particularly what rules to use. In the end the fight was set for fifteen three-minute rounds in which Ali was to box and Inoke was to wrestle, on the assumption that either Inoke would get KO'd or Ali would be pinned.

'It was awful,' said Bob Arum. 'The Japanese guy was so terrified of Ali that he came out and lay on his ass the whole fight, kicking to keep Ali away from him. At that point any moron knew it wasn't fixed, because a fixed fight couldn't have been that awful. It was the nightmare to end all nightmares.'

The result of the embarrassing affair was declared a draw. In fifteen rounds, Ali had thrown just six punches, while Inoke had spent the whole time crab walking around the ring, kicking at Ali's legs. The motivating force for this encounter had undoubtedly been the $6 million that Ali had been guaranteed, although 'financial irregularities' and broken contracts meant that Ali ended up with just over $2 million, while his opponent, who had been guaranteed $2 million, ended up with very little.

But the consequences of the fight went beyond boredom and rip-offs. Ali's legs, particularly his leading left leg, had been kicked dozens of times and appeared badly bruised and swollen. In fact, the blood vessels were so seriously ruptured that his leg had to be drained of almost a quart of blood, and when Ali returned home to the US he had to be hospitalized for blood clots and muscle damage.

Accounts of similar contests show that it is usually the boxer who comes off worse. In the earliest account of a martial artist fighting a champion boxer one of the first heavyweight champions, the great John L. Sullivan, took a terrible kicking from a French *savate* practitioner.

In the 1950s, a contest was staged at the University of Illinois between the boxers and wrestlers in eight weight divisions. A bout was regarded as won if the boxer achieved a solid blow to a vital area or if the wrestler achieved a fall. Of the eight bouts, the wrestlers won seven, while the one boxer who did win was also a wrestler. However, the result would surely have been a lot different if the boxers had been *kick*boxers.

One of Bruce Lee's colleagues on *The Green Hornet* was the wrestler and stuntman Gene LaBell. The two became great friends, and it was LaBell who taught Bruce most of the grappling skills that he incorporated into his art.

In 1962, LaBell had held the World Professional Wrestling Championship – but only for twelve seconds. He would have held it longer had it not been for a ring fracas in which he 'accidentally' kicked the Texas Wrestling Commissioner in the head. LaBell had studied virtually every form of fighting around at the time and, in 1963, accepted a public challenge to appear as a judo-karate practitioner against a boxer. LaBell's opponent for this bout, held in Salt Lake City, was the world-rated light-heavyweight Milo Savage. LaBell picked up a few thousand dollars when he left the boxer unconscious in the second round.

Chuck Norris reckons that Gene LaBell is the toughest man alive. In his seventies, he is still in demand as an instructor. Norris says that LaBell has 'stretched' most of the world's best martial artists including Norris himself, Joe Lewis, and 'pretty much anybody else he wanted to'. On the set of *The Green Hornet*, LaBell used to pick up Bruce Lee and sling him over his shoulder.

REALITY CHECK

Muhammad Ali's record as a boxing champion is without equal and beyond reproach. As a screen fighter Bruce Lee is without equal. But Bruce Lee's actual experience of fighting 'for real' needs closer examination. How did he fare when he *did* fight for real?

It hardly needs pointing out again that Bruce Lee's screen fighting, and the fighting method he actually advocated, were two entirely different things. The spinning and flying movie style is impressive, but when he fought for real there were no fancy moves and no animal cries or bird shrieks, only direct efficient strikes with no facial expression except a fierce and unflinching gaze.

In between takes on the set of *Enter the Dragon*, Bruce was continually challenged by extras who claimed that he was a phoney. While Bruce would never actually initiate a fight, if the kid kept insisting or insulting him, hoping for his moment of glory, then Bruce would do just as much as was needed to convince his opponent that he was on a hiding to nothing.

During this period, newspaper ads in the Hong Kong press were actually offering rewards, in the form of movie contracts, to any challenger who could topple Bruce Lee. One aspiring hero succeeded in actually getting over the wall and into the Lee home in Cumberland Road, where he confronted Bruce with, 'So, just how good are you?' The trespasser soon found out; he was sidekicked in the abdomen and then thrown off the property. Bruce later admitted that he'd kicked him harder than he'd ever kicked anyone in his life. 'I gave it all to him,' he said. And recall that while filming *Enter the Dragon* he sidekicked Bob Wall so hard that the guy behind Wall, who caught him, suffered a broken arm.

Bruce Lee's critics have made much of the fact that he never fought in competition and chose instead to have people like Joe Lewis and Chuck Norris as his unofficial representatives. One of these critics is Joe Lewis himself. Lewis was voted by his fellow martial artist competitors 'Fighter of the Century' and did himself succeed, in 1976, in getting Ali to the floor and tying him up pretty quickly, and so his comments deserve a hearing.

'Angelo Dundee [Ali's trainer] never fought,' says Lewis, 'but he understood the science of fighting. And Robert De Niro looks good in *Raging Bull* – he throws some good-looking punches. I must've heard Bruce say a thousand times, "You can't swim without getting in the water, Joe," but here's a guy who never competed. We never really saw him "get in the water".' While acknowledging that Bruce Lee had phenomenal attributes – amazing speed, power, strength and reflexes – Lewis has also said that he tried to get Bruce Lee to spar with him on numerous occasions, but he never would. 'But what he did is he *thought* about fighting. You want to understand what makes Bruce Lee tick; it's pretty simple, it's vanity.'

Other martial artists who knew or met Bruce feel differently. Jim Kelly, one of Bruce's co-stars in *Enter the Dragon*, was asked who he considered to be the greatest tournament fighter, and replied, 'I would dearly love to say Bruce Lee, but I can't, because he never fought in competition. But I've heard tales about "name" martial artists that he sparred against, and there are people who don't tell everything they know about his ability. There's a code of silence, people protecting their friends, and their own reputations and egos. It's not that they were no good; it's just that Bruce was incredible. I would stake my life on Bruce doing extremely well in competition. In fact, I doubt there was anyone in the world who could have beaten him.'

Ernest Lieb, a fifth dan karate black belt who won forty-two tournaments, didn't consider himself a match for Bruce Lee. Another top karate man, Ken Knudson, said that when Bruce sidekicked him, he felt as if his eyeballs had been left where he'd been standing. Fred Wren, one of the top ten karate practitioners in America when Bruce was around, says that he never met anyone with more fighting knowledge *and ability* than Bruce. Louis Delgardo, who once beat Chuck Norris for the Grand Championship, maintains that Bruce Lee baffled him completely, adding, 'I was completely in awe when I fought with him.'

Though some have considered Bruce Lee a middle-class tough rather than a hard-core fighter, Dan Inosanto did see Bruce fight in the streets of Hong Kong. 'We're talking street fights,' he says. 'I've seen him in what I don't even call fights. I've seen guys who wanted to break his bones, or whatever. But they could never do it, so it turned into a lesson. They found out that he could just, literally, play.' Inosanto adds a telling comment: 'A match in the ring is not a fight. To this day you can get an outstanding boxer and he will lose out on the street. But get him in the ring and it's within his confines.'

Muhammad Ali himself once said that, in a real street fight, he wouldn't give much for his chances.

THE VERDICT

Let's try and put everything in perspective. First of all, there's no doubt whatever that Bruce Lee would have made short work of all those who have tried to step into his shoes; he would have hung Jean-Claude van Damme and Steven Seagal out to dry. Yet it is also true that Bruce Lee remained untested as a competition fighter and, it has to be said, it appears that he preferred it that way.

In the end, it's probably true that if Muhammad Ali and Bruce Lee had been locked in a room together and told anything goes, then it would have been Bruce Lee who walked out first. But while it is fascinating to debate the outcome of such a fight, neither Lee nor Ali could ever be regarded as a loser. Both are winners. Ali was not only the greatest boxer of his era but arguably the greatest boxer of all time and one of the greatest men of the modern era, who has shown even greater courage outside the boxing ring than he has inside it. Both Bruce Lee and Muhammad Ali are men of good heart and generous spirit who continue to be regarded with the affection and respect they deserve. Bruce Lee raised the self-esteem of millions of Chinese just as Ali did for millions of African-Americans, yet they have inspired people all over the world.

Bruce Lee once said that fighting styles are merely parts disconnected from a unitary whole which, like dogmatic and uninspired religions, limit the way to genuine understanding and keep men apart rather than uniting them. Had it not been for his sudden and untimely death at the age of thirty-two, Bruce Lee might have followed Muhammad Ali into public life as a benign and venerated figure whose fighting spirit continues to be expressed in his commitment to the brotherhood of humankind.

37

IN SEARCH OF THE
WARRIOR SPIRIT

THERE HAVE ALWAYS been tales told of those who lived heroic lives, with special knowledge, powers or skills not available in ordinary experience. The accounts of these heroes and their journeys are told to show us our own untapped potentials. There is a long tradition of the warrior archetype, reaching as far back as Arjuna in the sacred Indian epic, the *Bhagavad Gita*. In Greek myths, the same archetype is found in Homer's *Odyssey*. In northern European culture, there is King Arthur and his Knights of the Round Table. The Japanese samurai are heirs to the same mythic tradition, as are the *shambala* warriors of Tibet.

In modern times, many of the old myths have been re-invented, in the film *Star Wars*, for example. One or two more recent examples also deserve a mention.

Ang Lee's film, *Crouching Tiger, Hidden Dragon* deserved all the accolades it received. It's a film that harks back to the old style of martial arts film-making that Bruce Lee would have watched as a boy – where characters can leap twenty or thirty feet in the air and run along the treetops. It's a film with a magical quality to it, despite the fact that even with all its sophisticated digital image enhancement you can still 'see the wires'.

In *The Matrix* (1999), the hero has his martial arts skills 'downloaded' directly into his nervous system. It's an impressive movie, although it owes everything to the brilliance of its special effects rather than the martial arts skills of the actors.

But there still isn't a film in which the warrior myth is portrayed more sublimely than in Bruce Lee's movies. What comes closest is something I believe Bruce would like to regard as his true legacy.

In recent years, monks from the Shaolin temple have toured the West with a stage show that has also been made into a video. It is a simply and beautifully presented show relating the history of the temple and demonstrating their incredible skills. As a schoolboy, I would rush home to watch David Carradine fight weekly (weakly) as a Shaolin monk in *Kung Fu*. I would never have believed that one day the real thing would come and visit me.

This is all due to the interest that Bruce created. And Bruce Lee is also the reason that in the past thirty years no film-maker has been able to get away with ham-fisted slugging matches in a fight scene. Even *Buffy the Vampire Slayer* could give Kwai Chang Caine a good beating!

When Bruce Lee arrived in the US, there were a mere 500 martial arts schools. Now there are probably a hundred times that number. But as a martial arts innovator Bruce Lee has fared less well. None of his direct students has ever really shown anything like enough insight or ability to keep his teaching alive, and *jeet kune do* is rapidly going the way of all religions.

In alluding to what he also calls the 'geek *kune do*' fraternity, Davis Miller writes, 'In music certainly, there *can* be life. But there's death in music, too. That plaintive stuff you hear as fat-ass congregations of white folks sing sorrowfully, obligingly, of Christ bringing them alive. Maybe Jesus has something going.

But Christ, how can any sane person take anyone's followers seriously?'

The true warrior is neither a mere fighter, nor a paid soldier. For the warrior, the mastery of a fighting art isn't concerned just with defeating an opponent, but with mastering the self, and with a path of personal and spiritual development.

The concept of warriorship as a spiritual path became widely known through the writings of Carlos Castaneda, a UCLA anthropology student who wrote of his initiation and experiences under the guidance of the Yaqui Indian 'sorcerer', Don Juan Matus. In this teaching, the warrior is not a man or woman who goes to war, but someone who seeks spiritual insight, knowledge and power through a wholehearted life and 'impeccable' actions.

It doesn't matter whether the events in Castaneda's writings or the events related in tales such as the adventures of King Arthur's knights actually happened, they are still true! Myths don't aim to relate facts; they deal with experiences of powerful energies that can only be related through metaphors or descriptive analogies.

In this way, for example, a guiding spirit may be an 'angel' if you are Christian, a 'power animal' if you are a shaman, or an 'ally' if you are a sorcerer. It's even perfectly possible for a Western agnostic, following the disciplines of a Chinese martial art, to see visions of a Hindu deity – once the appropriate stage is reached. Some people explain spirits as archetypal energies; others prefer to say that spirits arise from these energies. But it's the same riddle as that of the chicken and the egg – they are one and the same thing.

Our common biological inheritance is said to account for the similarity of our myths – as veiled explanations of the truth – throughout the world. But it says little for modern culture that the word 'myth' has come to have the same meaning as 'lie', or is used to downgrade or trivialize a belief. Yet, all too often, it seems that all the modern world has to offer people with any energy and aspiration is the pursuit of status and possessions, or the invitation to 'have a good time'. A great void is felt by many who, while they can't actually identify what it is that they need or recognize what it is that they have been cut off from, are certain that there must be more to life. In other people, unfocused energy simply erupts into violence and excess. It's not surprising that those same cities that depersonalize people and prevent them from living in healthy tribes find themselves overrun by 'warrior' gangs. It's not surprising that these warriors try as best they can to create their own rites of passage by having temporary truces to attend showings of *Enter the Dragon* with all the reverence of a congregation attending midnight mass.

The warrior has also become a familiar figure in business. Warriorship has attractive overtones for those who have no real conception of what it entails. Nowadays, it's not uncommon to see the principles of the samurai translated into business strategies for the Western boardroom. Warriorship has encouraged many business people to pursue greed and manipulation in a new disguise.

True warriorship arises from an inner source that doesn't recognize any hierarchy except the single valid one: a hierarchy based on degrees of self-understanding free from any consider-ations of gender, race, nationality or status. And even though the warrior archetype is continually evoked by those recruiting for the armed forces, the true warrior spirit is a long way removed from the activities of the paid soldier – or from the half-robot, half-caveman action heroes of Hollywood. The real warrior spirit is surfacing in men and women who are meeting the challenge of finding 'new' holistic ways of perceiving and acting in the world. On retiring from his post at the US Army College, Lieutenant Colonel Jim Channon proposed the founding of a new corps of warriors – the First Earth Battalion – whose allegiance would go beyond duty, honour and country in order to serve the needs of all people and the planet itself.

> 'The oneness of all life is a truth that can be realized only when the false notions of a separate self, apart from the whole, are forever annihilated . . . Whoever realizes this [void] is filled with life and power and the love of all things.'

This is one of the aphorisms that Bruce Lee took from the *Sourcebook of Chinese Philosophy* and included in his personal notes, eventually published as *The Tao of Jeet Kune Do.*

After his collapse in May 1973, Bruce Lee told his brother Peter that he planned to live to be a hundred, and told Chuck Norris, 'When I'm thirty-five, I'll stop working and spend the next ten years living quietly with my family and will see nobody. Then I'll come out again and see what I can do for my society.' He'd made a drawing of himself as a cartoon hero – not unlike an image from a modern *manga* comic – but he'd also pictured himself as a wise old man like a classical Taoist priest.

George Tan says, 'The common view of Bruce is that he was a sort of Taoist; he used the word *tao* over and over again. But in reality he was more of a Confucian. The basic precept of Taoism is that you accept things as they are, and the world as it is. Taoists don't try and push the river. But Confucians manipulate the world. Bruce Lee was someone who had somewhere to get to, and he had to get there quick. And he wasn't about to let anyone stop him. Bruce was a Confucian in Taoist clothing.

In the 1970s, ideas of self-help were still quite new, but in the decades since Bruce Lee's death, the robust 'go for it' ethos has become the stuff of sport equipment ads and corporate seminars. The idea that we can reinvent ourselves instantly and become whatever we want is now the new faith.

In a letter to a girlfriend, Bruce Lee declared his intention of achieving 'impossible' goals before adding, 'People will say that I'm too conscious of success.' But Bruce also quoted the late Dr Charles Steinmetz, who was once asked which branch of science would make the most progress in the next twenty-five years; the doctor had replied 'spiritual realization'.

Earlier, I went some way towards answering the two questions most often asked about Bruce Lee. *My* question is: Would Bruce have ever made that leap from action hero to wise man? Stirling Silliphant, for one, believes that, 'If he'd lived, I think Bruce would have become a genuinely great man.' Would Bruce Lee have stuck to his intentions, survived fame and fortune, and gone on to live out the fullest potential of the Dragon? Because it is the Dragon who knows that the nature of Spirit, and the spirit of Nature are one and the same thing.

While studying philosophy at the University of Washington, Bruce Lee wrote notes entitled, 'The Relationship of the Organism to its Environment'. In these notes he describes how our limited fixed sense of self is like the armour of a turtle's shell. Further on, he describes how a living organism consists of thousands and thousands of processes that go on beyond its personal boundaries – like our need to touch, get in contact and stretch our limits.

What Bruce Lee is talking about here is that there's really no such thing as independence. For example, the paper of this page is made from a tree. A tree only grows through sunlight and rain – you don't have to be a mystic to be able to see the sun and the clouds in it. There have been hundreds of people involved in bringing this idea to you: the lumberjack who cut down the tree, the publishers, printers, distributors and so on. If you look even deeper, you'll see the food that gave everyone the energy to work, and so forth – all so that you could read these words, now. If we take this process to its ultimate conclusion, we see that *everything* is connected and always related.

The way I think of my 'self' is usually only symbolic. I can choose to limit my self to where my skin ends or I can extend it to my career, my ambitions, my family, my country, my race, and so on. My self is a concept that expands or contracts at any given moment. But my *felt* self – the dynamic experience of my body in life and the life in my body – knows, feels and senses that, even if I'm living in England, I'm not immune to nuclear reactors exploding in the Ukraine. Or, living in America, I'm not unaffected by the destruction of rainforests half a world away.

The soil is my skin and the forests are my lungs. I can't be independent as long as I eat and breathe. And if I were dead, my material remains would be absorbed back into the earth – while traces of my spirit would still affect living people.

Of course Bruce Lee had big personal ambitions; he had ambivalent goals, too. And he had more than the occasional ulterior motive. He was human, and the warrior gods put him through almost epic ordeals. Perhaps it is Bruce Lee's fate that the unrealized possibilities will forever be the footnotes to Bruce Lee the icon. The 'what if?' questions will remain forever.

But if the ultimate outcome of Bruce Lee's labours is that in continuing to ask the questions that try and help us to understand him a little better, we come to understand ourselves a little better – and realize our shared humanity – then those labours were not in vain.

DEDICATION

IN LATE 1991 I was working in Los Angeles. Also there was martial artist Derek Jones, with whom I had been training in London for some years. Derek was in the United States to pursue an ambition to break into films.

Derek Jones began martial arts training after being inspired by Bruce Lee. As a teenager he left his native Wales, came to London and sought out Victor Kan, one of Bruce's fellow students from Hong Kong. It wasn't long before Derek's natural talent found him, as the Chinese say, 'standing on the shoulders of the master', or in Victor's case, knocking him on his back. In order to further advance his abilities, Derek then sought out William Cheung.

Derek always said that he had understood more about fighting by watching Bruce Lee than through any other method. Like Bruce Lee, Derek Jones later went on to establish his own fighting art, Body, Mind and Spirit, based on a core of traditional *wing chun* elevated to his own level of understanding of body mechanics, energy flow and fighting strategy. Derek's depth of insight and abilities were second to none. Quite simply, he knew what he was talking about and backed his words with actions time and again.

Once I suggested to Derek that Bruce Lee realized all his ambitions except one: to live in peace and contentment.

'He found his peace by dying,' Derek replied. A little while later, he added, 'He knew he was going to die, you know.'

At the end of Derek's two-week visit to the States, I drove him to the airport and helped him to the check-in desk with his luggage. We were too early for the flight. 'There's no point in both of us hanging about,' he laughed. We embraced and said, 'So long.'

That was the last time I saw my friend and teacher. A few days later I received a phone call from his wife, Julie. That evening, Derek had died instantly after his motorcycle had been hit by a car. He was thirty-four. I shared the sadness of his family and my fellow students.

Sadly, the unsurpassed insight and skills of Derek Jones will not now be witnessed by the wider audience they deserve. All those who knew Derek Jones remember him as a bright and positive spirit, an inspirational teacher, and a very good friend.

I dedicate this book to Master Derek Jones
with respect, gratitude and love.

And let us also wish Bruce Lee well in the knowledge that just as he brought a powerful spirit to life he now has a powerful life in Spirit because, in truth, there is no separation between the two.

Appendix I

Bruce Lee: Films and Publications

Childhood Films (1940–58)

Bruce Lee's first screen appearance was at the age of three months. Used more as a stage prop than anything else, he was carried on by his father in a Chinese picture called *Golden Gate Girl* made in San Francisco.

His first professional role was at the age of six in the Hong Kong-made film, *The Birth of Mankind* (1946).

When he was six, Bruce also played his first role under the name Lee Siu Lung (Lee Little Dragon), appearing with his father in *My Son, Ah Cheun*. Bruce had the more important role, co-starring with top Cantonese film comic Chow Shui.

Young Bruce made several other films, playing street urchins and orphans both in tragedies like his first films and in comedies like *It's Father's Fault*. Later he played juvenile delinquents and rebels in films such as *The Thunderstorm*, which imitated the *Blackboard Jungle*-style films being made in the United States.

Altogether Bruce Lee appeared in twenty films as a child actor, the best known being *The Orphan*, a film about Hong Kong street gangs made when he was eighteen, and in which he had his only leading role.

It is certain that there would be no interest in any of these films today were it not for Bruce Lee's presence in them.

The Green Hornet (1966–7)

The TV series had various writers and directors, mainly Jerry Thomas and Norman Foster. For detailed plot synopses, cast and writers' and directors' credits for all *Green Hornet* episodes, see Edward Gross's *Bruce Lee: Fists of Fury* (Las Vegas, NV: Pioneer Books, 1990).

Executive producer: William Dozier, Greenaway Productions, for Twentieth Century-Fox TV.

Produced by Richard Bluel and Stanley Sheptner.

Starring: Van Williams (Britt Reid/The Green Hornet), and Bruce Lee (Kato).

Characters originated by George W. Trendle.

Music by Al Hirt.

Twenty-six weekly episodes aired by ABC-TV, from 9 September 1966 to 14 July 1967; Fridays 7.30 to 8.00 p.m.

Two further 'crossover' episodes were made to launch the second *Batman* series, plus the characters made a guest appearance on *The Milton Berle Show*.

The Green Hornet (1974)

This Twentieth Century-Fox production is a full-length film put together from three of *The Green Hornet* TV episodes: 'The Praying Mantis', 'The Hunters and the Hunted' and 'Invasion from Outer Space', augmented by additional fight scenes from other episodes.

Marlowe (1969)

MGM
Directed by Paul Bogart.
Written by Stirling Silliphant.
Based on Raymond Chandler's novel *The Little Sister*.

Starring: James Garner (Philip Marlowe), Bruce Lee (Winslow Wong) and Rita Moreno.

Running time: 95 minutes.

Re-released in 1974 with Bruce Lee in top billing.

Private eye Philip Marlowe is hired by a nervous girl to find her missing brother. A confused story is made even more obscure by quirky directing, resulting in a film that is tiresome rather than amusing.

BIT PARTS (1968–9 SEASON)

Blondie This TV sitcom adapted from the newspaper cartoon strip was aired by both the NBC and CBS networks between January 1957 and January 1959. Bruce Lee had a walk-on part.

Ironside This TV series starred Raymond Burr as a wheelchair-bound investigator and was a spin-off from his hit *Perry Mason* series. The show was aired by NBC between September 1967 and January 1975. Bruce Lee had a cameo appearance in one episode, playing a martial arts instructor.

Here Come The Brides Bruce Lee had a small, non-speaking role in the episode 'Marriage, Chinese Style' from this series produced by Paul Carver for ABC/Columbia TV, aired between September 1968 and September 1970.

FIGHT ARRANGING

A Walk in the Spring Rain (1969)

Columbia Pictures
Directed by Guy Green.
Written by Stirling Silliphant, adapted from the novel by Rachel Maddox.

Running time: 98 minutes.

Starring Ingrid Bergman and Anthony Quinn, the story is a middle-age romance. A college lecturer's wife on holiday in the mountains falls in love with a local man. Bruce Lee was hired to direct the fight scene that Silliphant contrived to fit into the story. The film met with an indifferent response.

The Wrecking Crew (1969)

Columbia Pictures
Directed by Philip Carlson.
Written by William McGivern, from the novel by Donald Hamilton.
Running time: 104 minutes.
Special agent Matt Helm recovers stolen gold bullion in a campy spy spoof with both flashy and fleshy production values. Bruce Lee was hired as the fight arranger; the film starred Dean Martin, Sharon Tate and Elke Sommer.

Longstreet (1971)

Produced by Tom Tannenbaum for Paramount TV.
Aired weekly by ABC-TV, 9 September 1971 to 10 August 1972, on Thursdays between 9.00 and 10.00 p.m.
Starring: James Franciscus (Mike Longstreet) and Bruce Lee (Lee).
Bruce starred in the two-part opening episode 'Way of the Intercepting Fist', written by Stirling Silliphant, and had small parts in three further episodes: 'Spell Legacy of Death', 'Wednesday's Child', and 'I See, Said the Blind Man'.

The Big Boss (1971)

US title: *Fists of Fury* (see note pp. 367–8).

Written and directed by Lo Wei (Bruce Lee did much on-the-spot rewriting).

Produced by Raymond Chow for Golden Harvest.

Starring: Bruce Lee (Cheng), Maria Yi (Mei Lin), James Tien (Chen) and Han Ying Chieh (Mi, the Boss).

Fight arranger: Han Ying Chieh (Bruce Lee did much on-the-spot fight arranging).

Filmed on location in Pak Chong, Thailand.

Running time: 97 minutes; UK version censored.

This film established Bruce Lee as a supreme martial arts star.

Fist of Fury (1971)

US title: *The Chinese Connection* (see note pp. 367–8).

Written and directed by Lo Wei.

Produced by Raymond Chow for Golden Harvest.

Starring: Bruce Lee (Chen Chen), Nora Miao (Yuan Li Ehr), James Tien (Fan Chun Hsia), Bob Baker (Russian) and Lo Wei (detective).

Filmed at Golden Harvest Studios and on location in Hong Kong.

Running time: 103 minutes; *nunchaku* scenes censored in UK version.

After this film's release, Bruce Lee became a Chinese national hero.

Way of the Dragon (1972)

US title: *Return of the Dragon* (see note p. 367).

Written and directed by Bruce Lee.

Produced by Bruce Lee and Raymond Chow for Concord Productions.

Starring: Bruce Lee (Tang Lung/China Dragon), Chuck Norris (Colt/Kuda), Nora Miao (Chen Ching Hua) and Bob Wall (Robert).

Cinematography: Nashinoto Tadashi.

Filmed on location in Rome and at Golden Harvest Studios in Hong Kong.

Running time: 90 minutes; UK version heavily censored.

Made as a light comedy, this film features Bruce Lee's best fight scene.

Game of Death (1972; not completed)

Written and directed by Bruce Lee.

To be produced by Bruce Lee and Raymond Chow for Concord Productions.

Starring: Bruce Lee, Chi Hon Joi, Dan Inosanto and Kareem Abdul Jabbar. Further starring roles were intended for George Lazenby and Betty Ting Pei.

Filmed at Golden Harvest Studios, Hong Kong.

Bruce Lee had twenty-eight minutes of film in the can at the time of his death.

Enter the Dragon (1973)

Directed by Robert Clouse.

Written by Michael Allin.

Produced by Paul Heller and Fred Weintraub (Sequoia) and Bruce Lee and Raymond Chow (Concord) for Warner Brothers.

Starring: Bruce Lee (Lee), John Saxon (Roper), Jim Kelly (Williams), Ahna Capri (Tania), Bob Wall (Oharra), Shih Kien (Han), Angela Mao (Su Lin), Yeung Sze (Bolo), Betty Chung

(Mei Ling), Geoffrey Weeks (Braithwaite) and Peter Archer (Parsons).

Cinematography: Gilbert Hubbs.

Editing: Kurt Hirshler and George Waters.

Music: Lalo Schiffrin.

Filmed on location in Hong Kong.

Running time: 98 minutes; UK version censored.

This is the classic film of the martial arts genre.

Note on US Film Releases and Title Changes

Enter the Dragon (1973) was Bruce Lee's fifth film, but the first to go on general release in the United States.

His fourth film, *Game of Death* (1972), was incomplete at the time of his death and was finished and released posthumously.

As Bruce Lee's third film, *Way of the Dragon* (1972), was released in the United States after the success of *Enter the Dragon*, it is known there as *Return of the Dragon*.

Bruce Lee's first two films were muddled in transit to the US. *The Big Boss* (1971) was to be retitled *The Chinese Connection* for America. *Fist of Fury* (1971) was mistitled *Fists of Fury*. Further confusion was caused when the films were placed in the wrong cans in transit. As a consequence, Bruce Lee's first film, *The Big Boss*, is known in the US as *Fists of Fury*, while his second film, *Fist of Fury*, is known as *The Chinese Connection*.

Game of Death (completed 1978)

Directed by Robert Clouse.

Produced by Raymond Chow for Golden Harvest.

Additional footage shot featuring: Hugh O'Brien, Bob Wall.

Music by John Barry.

Opening titles by John Christopher Strong.

Bruce Lee's *nunchaku* duel with Dan Inosanto is censored in UK version.

Bruce Lee's twenty minutes of brilliance is padded out with exploitative dross.

Game of Death II (1982; a.k.a. *Tower of Death*)

Ng See Yuen's attempt to rework Bruce Lee's twenty minutes of film for Golden Harvest is no worse than the first version.

BOOKS AND PUBLICATIONS

Chinese Gung Fu: The Philosophical Art of Self Defense (1963)

A small manual written by Bruce, with photographs taken in the parking lot of Ruby Chow's restaurant illustrating the *wing chun/jun fan* techniques he was using at the time.

Wing Chun Kung Fu (1972)

A small book dealing with the basic principles of *wing chun* compiled while Bruce was working with James Lee in Oakland. The book shows James demonstrating the first *wing chun* form, the *sil lum tao*. Bruce passed the book on to James as he believed that he had moved too far away from *wing chun*, and because James was seriously ill. Bruce is credited as 'technical editor'.

The Tao of Jeet Kune Do (1975)

Not written for publication as such, the book that eventually emerged was drawn from notes made for Bruce's own personal study while he was laid up with his back injury in 1970. It discusses various fighting systems such as *kung fu*, boxing, wrestling and fencing. Much of the material was taken from other books on fencing and from the *US Army Boxing Manual*. Also included are philosophical aphorisms taken from various sources such as *The Sourcebook of Chinese Philosophy*, D. T. Suzuki's *Commentaries on Zen*, and the teachings of Krishnamurti.

Although Bruce had no intention of publishing these notes, fearing that they would be exploited, they were edited by Gilbert Johnson and published in 1975 on the initiative of Linda Lee.

Bruce Lee's Fighting Method, Vols. 1–4 (1977)

These four volumes (1. *Self Defense Techniques*, 2. *Basic Training*, 3. *Skill in Techniques*, and 4. *Advanced Techniques*) show Bruce Lee's system evolving and feature photographs of him working with Dan Inosanto.

Bruce Lee also wrote several articles for various newspapers including the *Hong Kong Standard*, and for martial arts magazines. One such article, 'Liberate Yourself from Classical Karate' was written in 1971 for *Black Belt* magazine, and is reprinted in *The Legendary Bruce Lee* (1986).

Appendix II

Wing Chun –
and Beyond

IN RECENT YEARS a controversy has arisen within the *wing chun* world.

William Cheung claims that Yip Man practised and taught two very different versions of *wing chun*. Two generations before Yip Man learned the art, its grand master Leung Jan, while teaching his two sons, was spied on by his neighbour, Chan Wah Shun. At the times when he was being observed, grandmaster Leung Jan deliberately modified what he taught. Although he decided eventually to take his neighbour as a pupil, Leung Jan continued to teach him a less effective version, fearing that the bigger and stronger Chan would claim mastership after Leung's death. These fears proved to be well founded; after Leung and one of his sons had died, Chan drove the remaining son away and assumed mastership of the *wing chun* lineage.

Thirteen-year-old Yip Man trained with Chan for four years before moving to Hong Kong to study at college. There he met an eccentric old man with a formidable reputation for *kung fu*. Yip Man challenged this man and was defeated. The old man was Leung's surviving son, who then told Yip Man about the two different versions of *wing chun*, and went on to teach him the authentic, or traditional method.

Yip Man returned home and spent many years working as a police inspector until he fled to Hong Kong during the communist revolution. When he was fifty-six, he revealed himself as the authentic master of *wing chun* and began teaching. In 1953, William Cheung joined the school and brought along the pupil who was to become *wing chun*'s most famous exponent, Bruce Lee.

William Cheung has always asserted that Yip Man taught the modified version of *wing chun* to his students and the traditional version only to him. Although Bruce was a pupil of Yip Man's school, the bulk of his teaching came from his two senior students, Wong Sheun Leung and William Cheung. Cheung had been sworn to an oath not to reveal the authentic system to anyone during Yip Man's lifetime, and so he taught Bruce the modified form but continued to drop hints about the lack of effectiveness of some of the techniques.

The principal differences between the two forms of *wing chun* are in the body posture, arm positions and footwork. The modified exponent leans back with his toes turned in and shuffles forward – all with the idea of maintaining a stable base with which to meet any opposing force. The traditional practitioner has a more upright and evenly balanced stance; he uses footwork to achieve the optimum position from which to attack and defend – both to 'bridge the gap' to enter into fighting range, and to sidestep and retreat from danger.

My own teacher Derek Jones studied both the modified system with Victor Kan and the traditional system with William Cheung. Whether or not Derek took William Cheung's assertions at face value is another matter, but he was in no doubt as to which was the more effective system. He told his students, 'The modified system lacks footwork, entry techniques and advanced strategy. It is very limited.'

Bruce Lee's teenage friend and fellow student, Hawkins Cheung (William's nephew), teaches what he calls classic *wing chun* at his school in Culver City, Los Angeles. 'Modified, traditional – it's all bullshit,' says Hawkins. 'That's just William making mischief.'

Hawkins implies that William completely invented this historical divergence in the art simply to promote his own version of it. If this is true, then William Cheung should take credit for making it more effective. As Bruce Lee, William Cheung and Derek Jones evolved as martial artists, each adapted *wing chun* in his individual way. Whether all this is William Cheung's mischief, Bruce Lee's genius or Derek Jones's common sense doesn't really matter. It simply serves to prove that if something is true in one place, then it is usually true in another.

SOURCES AND READING LIST

WORKS CITED

Almeida, Bira, *Capoeira: A Brazilian Art Form* (Berkeley CA: North Atlantic Books, 1982). Second edition, revised and expanded, 1986.

Beasley, Jerry, *In Search of the Ultimate Martial Art* (Boulder, CO: Paladin Press, 1989)

Carradine, David, *The Spirit of Shaolin* (Boston MA: Charles E. Tuttle, 1991)

Cheung, William, *Wing Chun Bil Jee* (Burbank CA: Unique Publications, 1983)

Chow, David, and Spangler, Richard, *Kung Fu – History, Philosophy, Technique* (Burbank CA: Unique Publications, 1982)

Clouse, Robert, *The Making of Enter the Dragon* (Burbank CA: Unique Publications, 1987)
– *Bruce Lee: The Biography* (Burbank CA: Unique Publications, 1988)

Dennis, Felix, and Atyeo, Don, *Bruce Lee: King of Kung Fu* (London: Wildwood House, 1974)

Hyams, Joe, *Zen in the Martial Arts* (Los Angeles: J. P. Tarcher Inc, 1979)

Inosanto, Dan, and Sutton, Alan, *Jeet Kune Do: The Art and Philosophy of Bruce Lee* (Los Angeles: Know Now Publishing, 1980)

Palmer, Doug, 'A Summer in Hong Kong' (Unpublished manuscript)

Scott, David, and Doubleday, Tony, *Zen* (Shaftesbury, Dorset: Element Books, 1992)

PERIODICALS AND NEWSPAPERS CITED

Bruce Lee: His Life in Pictures (Burbank CA: CFW Enterprises, 1988)

Bruce Lee: The Untold Story (Burbank CA: Unique Publications, 1986)

Combat (Walsall, England: Martial Arts Publications)

    Glover, Jesse, 'The Art of Bruce Lee', October 1991.

    Logan, Bey, Interview with Kwan Tak Hing, August 1987.

Fighting Arts (Liverpool, England: Ronin Publishing)

    Noble, Graham. Interview with Dan Inosanto: 'Bruce Lee: The Real Story', n.d.

KOA Yearbook (London: Paul H. Crompton)

    Crompton, Paul. 'William Cheung: The Best Fighter and No Apology', 1985.

Inside Kung Fu (Burbank CA: CFW Enterprises)

    'Bruce Lee Returns in *The Game of Death*', September 1979.

    Cater, Dave, 'Jason Lee: The Part He Couldn't Refuse', December 1992.

    Corcoran, John, interview with Tom Tannenbaum, January 1980.

    – Interview with Joe Hyams, April 1980.

    Cheung, Hawkins. 'Bruce Lee Discovers Jeet Kune Do', December 1991.

    – 'Bruce Lee's Hong Kong Years', November 1991.

    – 'Cleaning Up Bruce's Classical Mess', February 1992.

    – 'Wing Chun: Bruce Lee's Mother Art', January 1992.

Interview with Grace Lee: 'The One Who Knew Bruce Best', September 1979.

Painter, Dr John, 'Will the Real Yin and Yang Please Stand Up?', December 1991.

Peters, Jennifer, 'Brandon Lee: Trying to Fill Some Mighty Big Shoes', November 1992.

Poteet, Jerry, 'Single Direct Attack: Jeet Kune Do's One Punch K.O.', November 1991.

Kung Fu Monthly 1–76, 1975–82 (London: H. Bunch Associates, Ltd)

'Bruce Lee's Game of Death'

'Bruce Lee in Action'

'The Power of Bruce Lee'

'The Second Sensational Bruce Lee Scrapbook'

'The Secret Art of Bruce Lee'

'The Unbeatable Bruce Lee'

'Who Killed Bruce Lee?'

Kung Fu Monthly

Special Issue 100, 1992 (London: H. Bunch Associates, Ltd)

Martial Arts Illustrated (Huddersfield, England: Martial Arts, Ltd)

Bruce Lee Supplement, Vol. 1, March 1992.

Johnston, Will, 'Brandon Bruce Lee: A Life Worth Remembering', June 1993.

Kent, Chris, 'Bruce Lee Gets His Due', July 1993.

Logan, Bey, interview: 'A Guy Named Joe: Part Two', June 1991.

– Interview: 'A Guy Named Joe: Part Three', January 1992.

– Interview with Richard Bustillo: Part One, November 1992.

– Interview with Taky Kimura, January 1992.

Martial Arts Legends (Burbank CA: CFW Enterprises)

Corcoran, John, 'One on One with Stirling Silliphant', January 1993.

Imamura, Richard, 'Daniel Lee: The Harmonious Jeet Kune Do/Tai Chi Synthesis', July 1991.
– 'Ed Parker: The First Twenty Years', July 1991.
Maslak, Paul, 'The Fine Art of the Fight Scene', January 1993.
– (with Don Wilson) 'The William Cheung Story: Bruce Lee in the Early Years', January 1993.
Shivel, Rick, and Corcoran, John, 'Elvis Presley: The Man and the Martial Artist', July 1991.
Tan, Rick, 'Who is Shek Kin?', July 1991.
Martial Arts Masters (Burbank CA: CFW Enterprises)
Montaigue, Erle, interview: 'Dan Inosanto: on Life After Bruce Lee', 1992.
Martial Arts Movies (Burbank CA: CFW Enterprises)
'Dragon: The Life Story of Bruce Lee', 1992.
Rhodes, Scott, '25 All-time Great Movie Fights', 1992.
People Magazine, Brandon Lee feature, Vol. 38, 10, 1992 (New York: Time, Inc)
Playboy Magazine, Sugar Ray Leonard interview, June 1982.

The author gratefully acknowledges permission to quote copyrighted material from the sources listed above.

In particular, the author extends his thanks to Jerry Beasley and Paladin Press for permission to quote from conversations with Dan Inosanto, Tim Tackett and Larry Hartsell. Thank you to Bey Logan for *carte blanche* to delve into his comprehensive series of interviews with Joe Lewis for *Martial Arts Illustrated*. Thanks also to Curtis Wong for permission to quote from *Inside Kung Fu* and from various Unique Publications. Special thanks are also due to Doug Palmer for allowing extensive use of his personal notes.

Not all quotations in the text of this book are verbatim. However care has been taken to retain their essential meaning and changes have only been made to maintain continuity.

ADDITIONAL READING

Block, Alex Ben, *The Legend of Bruce Lee* (St Albans, Hertford-shire, England: Mayflower Books, 1974)

Bly, Robert, *Iron John* (New York: Addison Wesley, 1990)

Chao, K. T., and Weakland, J. E., *Secret Techniques of Wing Chun Kung Fu* (London: Paul H. Crompton, 1976)

Confirmation Committee of the VTAA, *Genealogy of the Ving Tsun Family* (Kowloon: Hong Kong Ving Tsun Athletic Association, 1990)

DeMile, James W., *Bruce Lee's One-Inch and Three-Inch Power Punch* (Kirkland WA: Tao of Wing Chun Do Publications, 1975)

Deng, Ming Dao, *Scholar Warrior* (San Francisco: Harper-Collins, 1990)

Draeger, Donn, and Smith, Robert, *The Fighting Arts of Asia* (New York: Berkeley Medallion, 1974)

Durckheim, Karfried Graf, *Hara: The Vital Centre of Man* (London: George Allen and Unwin, 1962)

Fields, Rick, *The Code of the Warrior* (New York: Harper Perennial, 1991)

Gross, Edward, *Bruce Lee: Fists of Fury* (Las Vegas NV: Pioneer Books, 1990)

Hartsell, Larry, *Jeet Kune Do* (Burbank CA: Unique Publications, 1987)

Hartsell, Larry, and Tackett, Tim, *Jeet Kune Do, Volume 2* (Burbank CA: Unique Publications, 1987)

Heller, Stuart, *The Dance of Becoming* (Berkeley CA: North Atlantic Books, 1991)

Inosanto, Dan, *Absorb What Is Useful* (Los Angeles: Know Now Publishing, 1985)

– *Jeet Kune Do Guidebook, Volume 1* (Burbank CA: Unique Publications, 1987)

– *Jeet Kune Do Kickboxing* (Los Angeles: Know Now Publishing, 1986)

Kent, Chris, and Tackett, Tim, *The Jun Fan/Jeet Kune Do Textbook* (Los Angeles: Know Now Publishing, 1988)

Krishnamurti, Jiddu, *Freedom from the Known* (New York: Harper and Row, 1969)

Lee, Bruce, *Chinese Gung Fu: The Philosophical Art of Self Defense* (Burbank CA: Ohara Publications, 1963)

– *The Tao of Jeet Kune Do* (Santa Clarita CA: Ohara Publications, 1975)

Lee, Bruce, and Uyehara, Mito, *Bruce Lee's Fighting Method, Volumes 1–4* (Burbank CA: Ohara Publications, 1977)

Lee, James Yimm, *Wing Chun Kung Fu* (Bruce Lee, technical editor) (Burbank CA: Ohara Publications, 1972)

Lee, Linda, *Bruce Lee: The Man Only I Knew* (New York: Warner Paperbacks, 1975)

– *The Life and Tragic Death of Bruce Lee* (London: Star Books, 1975)

Lee, Linda, and Bleecker, Tom, *The Bruce Lee Story* (Burbank CA: Ohara Publications, 1989)

Lewis, Peter, *Martial Arts* (Leicester, England: Magna Books, 1987)

Meyers, Richard, Harlib, Amy, Palmer, Bill and Palmer, Karen, *Martial Arts Movies* (Secaucus NJ: Citadel Press, 1985)

Millman, Dan, *The Warrior Athlete* (Wallpole NH: Stillpoint, 1979)

Mintz, Marilyn, *The Martial Arts Movie* (Boston MA: Charles E. Tuttle, 1983)

Needham, Joseph, *Science and Civilization in China* (Cambridge MA: Cambridge University Press, 1954)

Ralston, Peter, *Cheng Hsin: The Principles of Effortless Power* (Berkeley CA: North Atlantic Books, 1989)

Roote, Mike, *Enter the Dragon*, from the original screenplay by Michael Allin (London: Tandem Books, 1973)

Salzman, Mark, *Iron and Silk* (London: Hamish Hamilton, 1987)

Stewart, Lucretia, 'Postcards from China's Edge' (London: *The Independent on Sunday*, 15 December 1991)

Thomas, Bruce, *The Body of Time* (London: Arkana, 1991)

Van Hise, James, *Video Superheroes* (Las Vegas NV: Pioneer Books, 1991)

Vaughn, Jack, and Lee, Mike *The Legendary Bruce Lee* (Burbank CA: Ohara Publications, 1986)

Wall, Bob, *Who's Who in the Martial Arts* (Los Angeles: R. A. Wall Investments, 1985)

Wing, R. L., *The I Ching Workbook* (New York: Doubleday, 1979)

– *The Tao of Power* (Wellingborough, England: Aquarian Press, 1986)

PERIODICALS AND NEWSPAPERS

Bruce Lee: King of Kung Fu, 1–8. (Stanmore, Middlesex, England: Poster Magazine Publishing Co)

Exciting Cinema, Kung Fu Special Issue, 1974 (Pennine Magazines)

Farewell to the Dragon (Philadelphia: The Cinema Attic, 1974)

Fighters' Monthly, Vol. 1, 1 (London: Fighters' Publications)

Films and Filming, 229 (London: Hansom Books, 1973)

Great Dragon Magazine, 3.

The Hollywood Reporter, 7 May 1993. Alex Ben Block article on *Dragon* film. (Los Angeles: H. R. Industries Inc.)

JKD Magazine, 1–12, 1976–8. (Hong Kong: Bruce Lee Jeet-Kune-Do Club)

'Bruce Lee: Combats'
'Bruce Lee: His Privacy and Anecdotes'
'Bruce Lee: His Unknowns in Martial Arts Learning'
'Bruce Lee Memorial Monthly No. 1'
'Bruce Lee's Nunchaku in Action'
'Bruce Lee Revenges . . .'
'Bruce Lee: The Fighting Spirit'
'Bruce Lee: The Immortal Dragon'
'Bruce Lee: The Secret of JKD and Kung Fu'
'Reminiscence of Bruce Lee'
'Studies on Jeet Kune Do'
Karate Illustrated, June 1977 and February 1979.
KO Magazine, June 1984.
Kung Fu Supplies Co. 1978–9 (Hong Kong)
    Bruce Lee: Farewell My Friend
    Bruce Lee in *The Game of Death* [sic]
Kung Fu Magazine Publishing Co. 1983–4 (Hong Kong)
    Bruce Lee: His Eternities
    Bruce Lee's Nunchaku Method
Ochs, Phil, 'Requiem for a Dragon Departed', *Time Out*,
    February 15–21, 1974 (London: Time Out Publications)
Official Karate, July 1970.
Penthouse, Albert Goldman feature on Bruce Lee, Jan/Feb
    1983 (New York: Penthouse International Ltd)
Popster, 23 and 26 (London: Planet News)
    'Was Bruce Lee Killed By a Secret Death Touch?'
    'What is Kung Fu?'
Real Kung Fu, Victor Kan interview, Vol. 2, 6, 1977 (Hong
    Kong: Comray Publications)

INDEX